MOVING PEOPLE TO DELIVER SERVICES

MOVING PEOPLE TO DELIVER SERVICES

Aaditya Mattoo and Antonia Carzaniga,
Editors

**A copublication of the World Bank
and Oxford University Press**

Library of Congress Cataloging-in-Publication Data has been applied for.

Cover photo: Ken Reid/Getty Images

CONTENTS

Figures

Tables

FOREWORD

The General Agreement on Trade in Services (GATS) is one of the historical achievements of the Uruguay Round. The agreement seeks to create a more liberal, transparent, and predictable policy environment for one of the most dynamic areas of international trade. The GATS recognizes that in many cases openness will be accomplished only gradually and that successful liberalization must be conducted within a conducive regulatory environment. Since the establishment of the WTO in 1995, the process of progressive liberalization of services has continued with considerable success. Governments and policymakers around the world have become increasingly aware of the benefits that services liberalization could bring to their economies, and are eager to use the multilateral forum to promote and consolidate the process.

One area has, however, reaped only limited benefits from this climate of openness: the supply of services through the "temporary movement of individual service suppliers" (mode 4). The Uruguay Round negotiations on mode 4 served primarily to facilitate exploratory business visits and the movement of high-level personnel within multinational corporations. Developing countries were disappointed by the limited commitments in their area of comparative advantage and are now seeking greater openness. At the same time, many multinational firms would like to see more scope for international movement of their personnel. This shared interest has created a sense of optimism about mode 4 negotiations in the current round of GATS negotiations. The key question is whether and how this coincidence of interest can be harnessed to deliver greater openness.

Conditions in many developed economies—ranging from aging populations to shortages of skilled labor—suggest that this may be a propitious time to put labor mobility squarely on the negotiating agenda. At the same time there is concern about the possible social disruption and security consequences in host countries and the brain drain from poor countries. Yet there is limited awareness of how the GATS mechanism can be used to foster liberalization in this area of services trade without undermining national political and social objectives.

The papers in this volume were first presented at a conference April 11–12, 2002 organized collaboratively by the World Bank and the World Trade Organization. The main purpose was to provide a comprehensive economic and legal analysis of the key issues. The conference brought together, for the first time, economists, regulators, negotiators, and private sector stakeholders, to illuminate the WTO negotiations and enhance public understanding of mode 4. In the longer term, the conceptual and empirical research papers generated by the workshop should stimulate further research work on this important, yet underexplored, area of policy. A more immediate result, I believe, will be informed participation in, and thus an impetus to, the mode 4 negotiations that are a critical part of the Doha Development Agenda.

Dr. Supachai Panitchpakdi
Director-General
World Trade Organization

ACKNOWLEDGMENTS

The editors would like to thank Richard Self and B. K. Zutshi for guidance on every aspect of this project, and Bernard Hoekman and Abdul-Hamid Mamdouh for extremely valuable advice and support. The comments of Simon Evenett, Carsten Fink, Patrick Low, Julia Nielson, and Pierre Sauve helped significantly to improve this volume.

The generous financial support of the U.K. government's Department for International Development made the background research possible. The staff of the WTO's Trade in Services Division, particularly Rhian Wood, helped organize the conference with incomparable efficiency and grace. Finally, thanks are due to Susan Graham for being a superb production editor, to Santiago Pombo-Bejarano for his wise guidance on the publication process, and to Bennet Akpa and Nora Ridolfi for managing the printing of the book.

1

INTRODUCTION AND OVERVIEW

*Aaditya Mattoo**

Today, the World Trade Organization (WTO) is dealing with an issue that lies at the interface of two major world challenges: trade liberalization and international migration. Greater freedom for the "temporary movement of individual service suppliers" is being negotiated under the General Agreement on Trade in Services (GATS). Negotiations on this so-called fourth mode of supplying services (mode 4) first took place during the Uruguay Round of trade talks held from 1986 to 1993, but they were not particularly successful—in fact, they served primarily to facilitate exploratory business visits and the movement of high-level personnel within multinational corporations.[1] Developing countries, in particular, were disappointed by the dearth of commitments in their area of comparative advantage—that is, the movement of workers unrelated to a commercial presence abroad (foreign direct investment or FDI)—and they are now pushing for greater openness. At the same time, many multinational firms would like to see more scope for international movement of their personnel. This shared interest has created an unusual, though still guarded, sense of optimism about mode 4 negotiations in the current round of GATS negotiations.

Indeed, there is good reason to believe that reduced barriers to the temporary movement of service providers will produce substantial global benefits. Significant gains already are being realized, for example, in the software industry—some 60 percent of India's burgeoning exports are provided through the movement of software engineers to the site of the consumer. And with greater liberalization of barriers to the movement of people, many more developing countries could

*Aaditya Mattoo is lead economist of the International Trade Group at the World Bank.

"export" at least the significant labor component of services such as construction, distribution, environmental services, and transport. Furthermore, a major benefit of the fact that such movement is temporary is the presumption that both the host country and the home country would gain. For exporting countries the financial and knowledge benefits would be greatest if service suppliers return home after a certain period abroad, and for importing countries the temporary movement would create fewer domestic problems than immigration.

These gains remain notional, however, because today many different barriers constrain the movement of people. The most obvious are explicit prohibitions or tight visa quotas on foreign service providers. Then there are various forms of economic needs tests—for example, requirements that employers take steps to recruit and retain sufficient national workers before they can employ foreigners. Compounding the problem are the many formalities (e.g., obtaining a visa), alongside which the red tape related to FDI seems trivial. Finally, the entry of foreigners is impeded by a host country's refusal to recognize professional qualifications, by burdensome licensing requirements, and by the imposition of discriminatory standards.

Progress in eliminating these barriers is critical not just to realizing the potential gains from mode 4 trade, but also to achieving successful whole services negotiations. The main driver of liberalizing outcomes in the WTO has always been the exchange of market opening concessions. Developing countries must see room for enhanced access in their area of comparative advantage in order to engage fully in the services negotiations. Otherwise, there is a danger that the GATS will remain a harvester of autonomous liberalization in services rather than act as a catalyst for further liberalization.

Conditions in many industrial economies—ranging from aging populations to shortages of skilled labor—suggest that this may be a propitious time to put labor mobility prominently on the negotiating agenda. Yet there is limited awareness of how the GATS mechanism can be used to foster liberalization in this area of the services trade. In addition, many governments are uncertain about the full economic consequences of opening mode 4. Importing countries are concerned about its social and political implications and face resistance from domestic workers in service industries; exporting countries are concerned about issues such as the "brain drain."

As a first step in improving understanding of the implications of mode 4 liberalization, this volume brings together contributions from service providers, regulators (e.g., from ministries of labor and justice), researchers, and trade negotiators that provide different perspectives on one central question: How is such liberalization best accomplished, but in a way that benefits both home and host countries? The result, it is hoped, will be more informed participation in, and thus an impetus to, the WTO mode 4 negotiations. In the longer term, it is hoped that the conceptual and empirical research papers presented will stimulate further research on this important, yet underexplored, area of policy. The rest of this chapter summarizes 10 main conclusions that emerged from the contributions.

1. GATS Mode 4: Ambitious in Scope but Unclear in Definition

In Chapter 3 Richard J. Self and B. K. Zutshi, two architects of the GATS, provide a historical and negotiating context for the original agreement. They point out that the GATS definition of trade in services emerged from a grand North-South bargain: when industrial countries sought the inclusion of investment in services, developing countries insisted on a symmetrical treatment of all factor movements—that is, parity between capital and labor. This parity led in turn to the modal approach to the definition of trade in services and the emergence of "commercial presence" and "presence of natural persons" as, respectively, modes 3 and 4 of supplying services.

The movement of a person from one country to another for economic reasons has at least three dimensions: length of stay, level of skills, and nature of the contract. Each dimension allows for significant variation. An individual can move for a single day or migrate permanently, possess no professional skills or be the master of a particular field, move as an independent professional or be transferred from headquarters to a local branch. The legal and economic implications of each type of movement are different.

What precisely is covered by mode 4? In Chapter 2 Antonia Carzaniga shows that the answer is to be found in the Annex on Movement of Natural Persons Supplying Services under the Agreement. Two categories of measures are covered: those affecting "service suppliers of a Member" of the GATS (i.e., self-employed suppliers who obtain their remuneration directly from customers) and those affecting the natural persons of a Member who are "employed by a service supplier of a Member, in respect of the supply of a service." The annex also states that the GATS does not apply to measures affecting persons seeking access to the labor market of a member country or to measures regarding citizenship, residence, or employment on a permanent basis.

Therefore nothing in the GATS limits the scope of natural persons to particular levels of skill, but the agreement is less clear on other dimensions. It has become customary to speak of the GATS as covering the *temporary* movement of service suppliers. But how long is temporary? The agreement draws no clear lines beyond the exclusion of permanent migration, and this issue is left to the discretion of individual countries. Thus Japan allows foreign business travelers to stay for a maximum of 90 days, but certain categories of intracorporate transferees can stay as long as five years. Such flexibility is an advantage of not creating a definitional straightjacket. But the seemingly open-ended notion of temporary may render more difficult a credible distinction between mode 4 and migration—which could have provided significant political reassurance.

It also is not completely clear what types of contracts are covered. It appears that measures affecting an Egyptian accountant's ability to sell his services abroad, either as an independent consultant or as an employee of an accounting firm, would be covered by the GATS. But do natural persons "employed by a service supplier of a Member" include foreigners employed only by foreign firms or also those employed by host country firms (e.g., an Egyptian accountant employed by a U.S. firm in the United States)? Insofar as foreigners seeking employment with host country firms can be deemed to be accessing the labor market of a country, they would seem to fall outside the scope of the GATS. It has been suggested that this is a sensible delineation and that to argue otherwise would provoke opposition and the prospects of even more limited liberalization. On the other hand, the exclusion could create economic distortions; a service delivered by a foreign worker under an employment contract to a local provider may be treated differently from the same service provided by the same person acting as an unattached service provider, say under a consulting contract. Such a distinction would channel into one form of service delivery transactions that ideally should take another form (Winters and others 2002). More important, including employment-based delivery would greatly enlarge the set of transactions to which GATS liberalization could apply, with correspondingly larger economic gains. As Self and Zutshi note, recruitment from foreign sources is widespread on a bilateral basis and in the context of regional agreements, and so a case can be made for harvesting and promoting such openness by including it in the GATS definition of mode 4.

2. GATS Mode 4 Trade: Already Important in Several Service Sectors

How large is mode 4 trade? The evidence presented by L. Alan Winters in Chapter 4, Vaibhav V. Parikh for India in Chapter 8, Josephine J. Francisco for the Philippines in Chapter 10, Enos A. Brown for Jamaica in Chapter 11, and Pierre E. Page for Switzerland in Chapter 13 suggests that it is already quite significant.

During the period 1995–2001, between 81,000 and 93,000 Filipinos were hired each year to work abroad as service providers, other than seamen. As much as a quarter of the world's seamen population is Filipino. If other groups of workers who also are likely to be working as service providers are included, then the number of Filipino service providers could range from 127,000 to 198,000. Reflecting this large presence abroad, remittances from outside the country were as much as 8.42 percent of the gross national product (GNP) of the Philippines in 1999, a threefold increase from 2.67 percent in 1990.

Systematic information on what the Filipinos abroad are doing and where they are is scarce. In the mid-1990s the number of short-term service providers was estimated at 60,000, intracorporate transferees at 40,000, and long-term skilled migrants abroad at 100,000. Nearly half of the overseas Filipino workers were in Asia. Many were domestic workers in Hong Kong and Saudi Arabia and entertainers in Japan and Southeast Asia. More skilled professionals, such as information technology workers and accountants, gravitated toward the United States.

The movement of service-supplying personnel remains a crucial means of delivery for the Indian software industry (see Chapter 8). Even though the share of onshore services in Indian software exports has declined (in 1988 the percentage of onsite development was almost as high as 90 percent), about 60 percent of Indian exports are still supplied through the temporary movement of programmers to the client's site overseas. The dominance of onshore delivery stems from, among other things, a reduction in information asymmetries regarding the performance of programmers, the need for continual client-developer interaction, and demands by Indian programmers to be sent abroad, in part to improve their skills and to gain access to international markets.[2]

A strong impetus to movement is the large gap between potential needs and the domestic availability of certain skills in host countries. Page notes that Switzerland, and Europe more generally, are facing severe shortages of information technology (IT) personnel (see Chapter 13). Switzerland needs more than 10,000 IT specialists every year, but the Swiss Federal Institutes of Technology in Lausanne and Zurich and the engineering schools produce only some 600 graduates in informatics a year. The shortfalls in IT staff for Europe have been estimated at about 200,000. Page concludes that, in these circumstances, the temporary inflow of IT specialists is not only needed but welcome.

In general, there appears to be little doubt that despite the dramatic development in technologies for electronic delivery, mode 4 will remain important. In fact, as Winters notes in Chapter 4, as their populations age and their average levels of training and education rise, industrial countries will face an increasing scarcity, in particular, of less skilled labor. Given that there is really no substitute for human labor, at least in some occupations (e.g., the caring occupations, personal services, and the delivery of goods), the demand for mode 4 is likely to increase over time.

3. GATS Mode 4 Trade: Facing a Range of Stringent Barriers

Chapter 3 by Self and Zutshi, Chapter 8 by Parikh, and Chapter 10 by Francisco reveal the pervasive and multiple restrictions on mode 4 trade. The barriers fall into three broad categories. The first broad class of restrictions is **immigration issues**, particularly visa-related barriers. One general problem is that the temporary movement of service providers comes under the purview of immigration legislation and labor market policy rather than that of international trade. Almost everywhere, immigration regulations impose *quantitative restrictions* on the movement of natural persons with the aim of creating a protected labor market. Frequently, a *prior adequate search* in national markets is required, regardless of any differences in the quality of the foreign and national service providers. For example, even though an Indian software professional may possess better qualifications or work experience, if a local person can provide the services, that person must be given preference over the Indian. The widespread use of *economic needs tests* has emerged as one of the major barriers to the free movement of service providers. The discretionary and nontransparent nature of such tests certainly reduces the predictability of trading conditions. Then there are *wage parity requirements*. These mandate that a foreign service provider must be paid wages equal to those paid to domestic service providers. Although this requirement is intended to provide a nondiscriminatory environment, it tends to erode the cost advantage of hiring foreigners. Finally, the work permits issued by countries are of a *limited duration*. These permits are extendable or renewable, but the procedure for extending or renewing them is cumbersome, expensive, and stringent. In fact, a general problem is unpredictability and lack of transparency, as well as the cumbersome visa procedures.

Discriminatory treatment of foreign service providers is the second broad class of restrictions that impede mode 4 trade. Residency or citizenship requirements are frequently imposed as eligibility conditions, putting foreign providers at an immediate disadvantage. Then there is discrimination through social security contributions and taxes. For example, in the United States foreign service providers have to pay Social Security and other taxes for which they do not get adequate tax credits in their home country unless a treaty exists between the United States and the home country.[3] In some cases, the service provider also must continue to pay taxes in the home country. This double taxation tends to erode the cost advantage of working in the United States. Discrimination also takes the form of preferences in government procurements granted to domestic service providers over foreigners. The government approval required by foreign service providers to set up operations and to remit money to their home country can be burdensome as well.

Finally, **inadequate recognition** of qualifications, training, and experience has a significant impact on certain types of professionals seeking to provide their services abroad. As noted by Self and Zutshi in Chapter 3, certain services, such as those of IT service providers, are not regulated, and many that are regulated allow for trade through subcontracting (e.g., a U.S. consumer may be obliged to use a U.S. architect, but the U.S. architect may buy the services of a foreign architect).

In these areas, regulatory barriers are probably not major impediments. But undoubtedly in other regulated professions, ranging from doctors to lawyers, barriers exist. The difficulty here is in distinguishing between the legitimate denial of recognition and the denial that has a protectionist motive. This is precisely the subject of GATS negotiations on domestic regulation.

4. GATS Mode 4 Trade: The Potentially Huge Gains from Its Liberalization

How large are the stakes in mode 4 trade? Chapter 4 by Winters provides a preliminary response to this difficult question. To date, mode 4 has defeated attempts to fit it into a robust analytical model. At one extreme, it can be viewed as no different from cross-border services trade (mode 1), which, in turn, is often pronounced to be no different analytically from ordinary goods trade. At the other extreme, mode 4 has much in common with regular migration, in which workers relocate from one country to another. This is particularly true when the periods of stay are long or where a particular job in country B is filled by a continual flow of temporary workers from country A, each being replaced by another as his or her contract expires. Such a "revolving door" provision could be particularly relevant to agency-provided flows of middle-level professional workers such as nurses and teachers. Thus another issue related to mode 4 is the economics of factor mobility.

As Winters argues, the very heart of international trade, be it in goods or in factors, lies in exploiting differences. The larger the differences, the larger are the potential gains from opening up international trade. In the case of mode 4, potentially large returns would be feasible if medium and less skilled workers, who are relatively abundant in developing countries and for whom the proportionate gap in productivity between home and host countries is greatest, were allowed to move and provide their services in industrial countries. The existing empirical studies of factor mobility and the new estimates described in Chapter 4 agree that there are huge returns to even relatively small movements of labor. For example, it is estimated that an increase in industrial countries' quotas on the inward movements of both skilled and unskilled temporary workers equivalent to 3 percent of their work forces would generate an increase in world welfare of more than US$150 billion a year.[4] Both industrial and developing countries would share in these gains, and they would be largest if both high-skilled mobility and low-skilled mobility are permitted.

Although these estimates are broadly plausible, neither of the polar models—trade or migration—capture the full essence of mode 4 mobility. From the host country point of view, temporary presence does avert some of the social and political costs of permanent migration, but it entails other "turnover" costs for both employing firms and society (e.g., in terms of recurring investment in firm-specific technical and limited social integration). From the home country point of view, temporary migration under mode 4 averts the costs of a brain drain, implying a higher repatriation of incomes and skills, but it deprives migrants of opportunities for cumulative learning and saving, which could have significant long-term benefits for home countries.[5] More conceptual and empirical analysis of these issues would help in the development of suitable policies.

5. GATS Mode 4: Limited Commitments

That these gains remain largely unrealized is evident from the lack of depth in existing commitments to mode 4, as Carzaniga shows in Chapter 2. Most commitments pertain to business travelers and intracorporate transferees who must be managers, executives, or specialists. Such commitments are of limited interest to countries that are not significant foreign investors and whose comparative advantage lies in relatively unskilled, labor-intensive services. Moreover, commitments are often qualified by other restrictions: prior employment, numerical quotas, economic needs tests, and residency requirements. It is widely acknowledged that WTO Members' mode 4 commitments do not generally reflect actual entry conditions for natural persons, because Members have bound less than the access granted in practice.

No significant differences exist between the commitments scheduled by industrial and developing countries; both groups seem to have been equally hesitant in undertaking liberal commitments for mode 4. But countries that acceded to the WTO after 1995 have been more willing to make commitments for "contract suppliers" (i.e., employees of a foreign enterprise that has concluded a contract to supply a service in a country but does not have a commercial presence in that market).

6. Existing National Regimes: More Open and Less Narrowly Defined than the GATS

Temporary flows of labor between countries have taken place for a long time. In Chapter 6 Julia Nielson and Olivier Cattaneo focus on the actual conditions for temporary entry at the national level, based on case studies of the United States and Australia. The chapter presents a preliminary attempt to map mode 4 against existing migration categories for temporary entry. However, even in the context of highly detailed, state-of-the-art migration systems, problems, highlighted in the chapter, have arisen in identifying the precise regimes relevant to mode 4. For example, although temporary and permanent entrants are separated, no distinction is made in migration categories between service and nonservice activities.

Nor is it always possible to judge whether the activities covered by some visa categories are truly commercial (i.e., that they would constitute trade for GATS purposes), while other categories include persons both consuming (mode 2) and supplying (mode 4) services.

Notwithstanding these difficulties, the chapter notes that the actual U.S. and Australian systems for temporary entry are broader, more detailed, and more flexible than their respective GATS commitments. Actual trade under mode 4—and numbers of temporary entrants—is also much greater than the commitments would suggest. Temporary entry is increasing for both countries, but is directed toward those with high level of skills or education. Special facilitation or entry schemes are offered to nationals of certain countries, including on the basis of regional trade agreements. Both countries require sponsored workers to be paid the same rates as nationals and to benefit from the same working conditions, and both use a range of measures to limit any possible negative impact on nationals.

Information on country regimes also is provided for Canada by Paul Henry (Chapter 14), for Germany by Torsten Christen (Chapter 15), for the United States by Howard R. Dobson (Chapter 16), and for South Africa by Ivan Lambinon and Mario G. R. Oriani-Ambrosini (Chapter 17). South Africa's regime is in a state of transition, but the regimes in Canada and Germany are in some ways similar to those described earlier. Like those in the United States, Canada's immigration laws and regulations treat permanent and temporary residency differently, with separate rules for each. Notably, Canada's mode 4 commitments contain no labor market tests or work permits for general business visitors and no labor market tests for three categories of intracorporate transferees and nine categories of independent professionals. Dobson confirms that the temporary admission categories contained in U.S. law are used in a general manner that does not specify services activities, and that many activities undertaken by foreigners may involve production of both goods and services.

Christen notes that in Germany the admission of third-country (non-European Union) nationals has been restricted since 1973. But in the future a more flexible approach will be taken, especially toward the admittance of highly qualified employees. An example of this approach is the scheme implemented in 2000 for the admission of up to 20,000 IT experts. Furthermore, Germany allows entry of "contractual service providers," a category for which there is no counterpart in the United States. The length of the service contract must not exceed three months, and the services permitted include those such as home country legal advice and accounting and tax advice.

Winters and others (2002) found that several European countries have programs for less skilled, short-term foreign workers—for example, seasonal workers in agriculture, tourism, and the hotel trade; project workers in construction; and various other employment-specified workers. Several reasons are suggested for why these programs have not been included in the GATS commitments. One is that these schemes are often implemented on a bilateral basis (e.g., with Eastern and Central European and North African countries) to mitigate immigration pressures and therefore would not necessarily comply with the nondiscriminatory obligation of the GATS. The other reason is that a GATS binding may deprive the host countries of the flexibility with which the schemes are currently implemented. These issues are examined further in the final section.

7. Regional Agreements: Much Achieved on Labor Mobility, Some Relevant to the GATS

In Chapter 5 Nielson examines the coverage and treatment of movement of natural persons in a range of regional trade agreements (RTAs), and then compares this coverage and treatment with that in GATS mode 4. In all, Nielson examines 20 RTAs, covering both industrial and developing countries and encompassing a range of approaches to labor mobility. For Nielson, RTAs basically assume two forms: free labor mobility (or close to it) or provision of mobility for some categories of persons related to trade. Within each of these forms the agreements generally contain similar provisions, with differences arguably reflecting the depth and extent of commitments rather than fundamentally different approaches. The symbiotic relationship between the GATS and RTAs is highlighted—some RTAs were the model for the GATS, while others, in turn, use the GATS framework, sometimes simply by reference. RTAs similarly serve as models for each other.

RTAs also are grouped according to the extent of liberalization offered and whether the extent represents a "GATS-plus" treatment. GATS-plus observations are made by determining whether the agreements include elements not covered by the general GATS provisions, rather than by attempting to compare them with the specific commitments of individual WTO Members. Such GATS-plus elements can include, for example, access to the labor market or special visas or access for certain groups, including those beyond service suppliers.

Generally, agreements among countries enjoying geographic proximity and similar levels of development (e.g., the European Union [EU], the European Free Trade Association [EFTA], the European Economic Area [EEA], Trans-Tasman Travel Arrangement) have a more liberal approach to labor mobility as compared with agreements among geographically distant members of differing levels of development (e.g., the Asia Pacific Economic Cooperation forum [APEC], U.S.-Jordan Free Trade Agreement). An interesting example of a liberalizing North-South accord is the North American Free Trade Agreement (NAFTA), which provides for more open and flexible movement of business persons and professionals between member countries than does the GATS. NAFTA sets forth no conditions—such as labor certification tests or prior approval procedures—and, with one exception, no numerical quotas.[6] NAFTA also encourages the mutual recognition of accreditation, licensing, and certification requirements for professionals.

In Chapter 11 Brown draws lessons from initiatives within the Caribbean Community (CARICOM) to facilitate the movement of service providers, particularly lessons related to the role of standards. One reason existing measures cover only professional occupations is the perceived absence of a mechanism to recognize through a formal methodology the knowledge, skills, and attributes of all CARICOM nationals. Brown emphasizes the need for nations to document and publish the standards required for employment in all occupational areas. He argues that occupational certification is an approach preferable to that of professional qualifications, because it opens up the possibility of including semiskilled and skilled workers in nonprofessional areas. The approach recognizes both on-the-job experience and the academic qualification, and has proved to be a useful vehicle through which Jamaican agricultural, hospitality, home care, and health care workers can be nationally certified and declared eligible to offer their services in foreign markets. In fact, Jamaica has a bilateral farm worker program with the United States and Canada, a hospitality worker program with the United States, and a schoolteacher work program with the United States and Britain.

That regional initiatives may limit the scope for multilateral commitments emerges from Chapter 15 by Christen. Germany has concluded several bilateral agreements with several Central and Eastern European countries related to guest workers, border commuters, and contractual workers. Christen notes that, given the large migration expected from Eastern Europe, it is important to Germany that any future GATS rules do not apply to measures affecting natural persons seeking access to the employment market.

8. Mode 4 Liberalization: The Subject of Legitimate Political Concerns—But Which Can Be Addressed

As Winters points out in Chapter 4, unlike with the mass migration of less skilled workers, fears about cultural identity, problems of assimilation, and the drain on the public purse are not really relevant to mode 4. Host country concerns, other than the purely xenophobic, pertain to national security, the difficulty in enforcing temporariness, and the impact on the labor market. Indeed, they pertain primarily to the loss of skilled resources—a weaker version of the concern about the brain drain associated with migration.

Any attempt to facilitate individual mobility must confront today's increased concerns about national security. Meaningful liberalization of mode 4 requires that security clearance be quick and reliable. The challenge politically is to separate the security arguments from labor market or service export considerations. As Winters and others (2002) note, even national security has a finite price in terms of civil liberty and economic well-being. Economic efficiency does not require one to neglect security considerations, but to ensure that if tradeoffs are made between security and income at one rate in one area—say, the maintenance of armed forces—then tradeoffs should be made at the same rate in another area—say, the exclusion of foreigners from national territory.

Immigration authorities often report abuse of their visa systems by individuals purportedly traveling for tourist or business reasons, but whose real purpose is to gain permanent residence. In Chapter 3 Self and Zutshi acknowledge that this has become a sensitive political issue in some countries, and that there is support for measures that have the intent or effect of making it more difficult for people to obtain a visa for temporary entry. Yet many of these measures are overtly discriminatory and have the effect of denying market access to legitimate services suppliers. Furthermore, despite the considerable flexibility in the GATS annex about enforcement of measures that address abuse of the visa system, authorities remain concerned that bound commitments in country schedules will undermine their ability to administer temporary entry measures.

Clearly, the political difficulties would be alleviated, though not eliminated, if it could be ensured that movement will be temporary, not permanent. A key challenge is to devise a precommitment mechanism in this respect. The enforcement difficulties are evidently less with intracorporate transferees—the local juridical presence can be penalized—than with independent service providers. One proposal to deal with this problem is contained in the draft model schedule presented by Mark Hatcher in Chapter 7 and discussed later in this chapter.

The second major concern, after national security, is fears about job instability and wage and salary erosion. On social equity grounds, there is a particularly strong concern about the impact of mode 4 liberalization on local less skilled workers. In Chapter 4 Winters acknowledges that the adjustment stresses that mode 4 liberalization could engender could be both large and concentrated on a vulnerable section of society. He argues that, in the short run, sensitivity about the timing and extent of liberalization may contain the pressures and that existing compensatory schemes could cope with those that actually arise. In the longer run, when deeper liberalization has been achieved, more active redistribution will be required to try to ensure that fewer nationals of industrial countries are actually in the sectors competing with foreign workers. This effort will require education and training as well as giving thought to asset distribution. However, these difficulties are neither more nor less serious than those posed for less skilled workers by imports of labor-intensive goods from developing countries—a problem overcome by policies to ease adjustment among local less skilled workers in industrial countries. Applied with the same sensitivity and the same sorts of policies as trade policy reform in goods has received in the past, the temporary movement of less skilled workers between countries would offer the chance to reap large gains from trade.

In Chapter 12 Mike Waghorne emphasizes a slightly different set of issues relevant to ensuring that workers, domestic and foreign, do not suffer adverse consequences. He suggests, first of all, that some of the uncertainties inflicted on both domestic workers and foreign service providers might be reduced if governments, business, and unions collaboratively develop sectoral employment and industry plans. He also highlights the need for governments to ratify and respect workers' rights, including those of foreign workers covered by the GATS. These rights must include the right to belong to a trade union and to use grievance procedures. For health and education services, it is essential that governments, employers, and recruitment agencies commit themselves to commonly accepted ethical recruitment policies, such as those developed by the International Council of Nurses. In general, the issue is not so much that temporary employment could become permanent, but that the movement of workers could be used to undermine wages and working conditions.

A key concern in developing countries is the possible loss of skills through movement abroad, as Suwit Wibulpolprasert reports from the Thai perspective in Chapter 9 and Brown describes from the point of view of Jamaica in Chapter 11. Local hospitality interests in Jamaica have seen their permanent trained employees leave to work temporarily in more developed markets abroad. In principle, this short-term negative impact could be addressed through Jamaica's well-developed infrastructure for training hospitality workers. However, this solution would require generally predictable growth in overseas demand.

Under the schoolteacher work program with the United States and Britain, Jamaican teachers were recruited to meet shortages in inner-city schools in New York City and London. As a result of the direct recruitment drive, conducted without the involvement of the Jamaican government, more than 500 teachers left Jamaican classrooms in 2001 to take up temporary assignments in the host countries. The loss of approximately 3 percent of the Jamaican teacher work force, many of whom were the more experienced and qualified teachers, was a large shock to the Jamaican school system. The country does not have a competitive infrastructure for training teachers, a process that takes more than four years. It was against this backdrop that the Jamaican government intervened and is now seeking to control the outflow of teachers.

In Chapter 9 Wibulpolprasert describes how in the 1960s more than a third of Thailand's new medical graduates, all of whom had received hugely subsidized educations, left that country for the United States, never to return. The Thai government then implemented a range of policies to deal with the phenomenon, including those calling for compulsory public work for a certain period of time, an increased supply of graduates, as well as greater opportunities for specialization and higher salaries. Chapter 9 also demonstrates that the external brain drain was perhaps a less serious problem than the internal brain drain. In the period of rapid economic growth from the late 1980s to the mid-1990s, the doctor density in Bangkok was more than 10 times greater than that in rural areas. Although there was a 300 percent oversupply of private hospital beds, more than 20 rural district hospitals were functioning without a single full-time medical doctor. Ironically, the economic crisis of the late 1990s contributed to a reversal of the internal brain drain.

Wibulpolprasert argues that external and internal brain drains can occur independently of any bilateral or multilateral trade agreements, and that they have much more to do with the structure of economic incentives. Nevertheless, commitments under the GATS may reduce each country's freedom to regulate the degree of openness of its market in line with domestic needs. In any case, the extent of brain drains, both external and internal, is not affected by mode 4 alone. For example, the promotion of health tourism though GATS mode 2 could contribute to an internal brain drain, and Thai investment in private hospitals in other developing countries could take Thai doctors abroad. Therefore, an integrated strategy is needed to promote universal access to health services.

9. Economic and Political Changes since the Uruguay Round: Justifying Expectations of a More Liberalizing Outcome on Mode 4

In Chapter 3 Self and Zutshi describe how during most of the Uruguay Round mode 4 issues were framed—at least rhetorically—as differences between industrial and developing countries. The debate polarized countries unnecessarily and provoked a more defensive posture by both sides. Industrial countries feared that they would be pressed to make politically unsustainable concessions at lower skill levels, and developing countries that placed a premium on this issue did nothing to assuage these fears.

At the same time during the Uruguay Round, few stakeholders pressed their interests upon their own governments as well as on others, with some notable exceptions. The Indian National Association of Software and Service Companies (NASSCOM) actively and effectively devoted time and resources to persuading countries to make commitments affecting software engineers. In the United States a powerful and diverse lobby used the GATS negotiations to generate a U.S. binding of the H1B visa provision covering the temporary employment of highly skilled foreign workers in U.S. firms.

Since the Uruguay Round, many countries have undertaken a more comprehensive assessment of their needs in the area of temporary entry and stay. Indeed, today more stakeholders are active in both industrial and developing countries. In an increasingly globalized world, firms need to be able to deploy personnel for short periods to meet specific project and contract requirements in different countries, often with tight deadlines. But they are frustrated by visa procedures that can delay entry of personnel by months. To remedy these problems, the U.S. Coalition of Services Industries and the European Services Forum have both endorsed improved mode 4 commitments by all countries to expedite the movement of professional-level personnel. Self and Zutshi believe that the emergence of mode 4 as a strategic component of efforts to provide services in a large number of countries contrasts sharply with the environment in the Uruguay Round.

A question that has not been fully explored is how the demands created by aging populations and shortages of skilled workers in industrial countries will play out against the greater security concerns in a post–September 11 world. In any case, there does seem to be a coincidence of interest in the movement of skilled workers among industrial countries and a set of more advanced developing countries. The greater challenge is to draw in other developing countries by venturing down the skill ladder without sinking into the realm of political infeasibility.

10. The GATS: Making It a More Effective Instrument of Mode 4 Liberalization

Evidently, mode 4 trade faces a large number of impediments, ranging from explicit prohibitions to nontransparent and cumbersome procedures. Greater openness cannot be thrust upon governments. The question is then: Can governments develop certain instruments that facilitate an exchange of access commitments and define an acceptable set of multilateral rules that lead to more transparent and less burdensome policy?

Most of the chapters in this volume provide useful suggestions on how the GATS can be used and improved. The most detailed proposals are contained in Chapter 3 by Self and Zutshi and Chapter 7 by Hatcher. Their suggestions build on two types of precedents in the GATS negotiations: the maritime model schedule and the telecommunications reference paper. At the risk of some oversimplification, one could think of the former as a framework for commitments to market access (through the elimination of quotas and discriminatory measures) and the latter as a set of principles on domestic regulations that have an impact on trade.

Both can be more or less flexible tools that set common negotiating objectives. Participants may assume levels of obligations that are different from those in the model schedule or reference paper, but each participant then bears the burden of demonstrating why it cannot bind according to the standard. Such an approach encourages greater uniformity of scheduling (but does not impose it) and, by providing a common focal point, may create a better climate for negotiations than the more traditional request and offer method. However, negotiating through a model schedule or reference paper cannot succeed unless the proposal strikes an appropriate balance between ambition and realism.

Chapters 3 and 6 make fairly similar proposals. They envisage commitments essentially for natural persons with professional skills on short-term, intracorporate visits (category 1) and short-term visits to fulfill contracts (category 2). Short term is defined in each case as a stay of less than a year. The main idea is to create for these two classes of movement a GATS visa or permit in order to separate procedures that affect temporary and permanent entry and therefore streamline those for temporary entry.[7] This idea has been elaborated before, both in the negotiating proposal by the government of India and in the model schedule approach endorsed by the service industry bodies of the United States and the European Union. The idea of a special permit is also central to the regime proposed for South Africa, described in Chapter 17 by Lambinon and Oriani-Ambrosini.

The Hatcher proposal described in Chapter 7 allows different conditions to be imposed on the two categories, presumably to address their differing implications for enforcement and the labor market. Wage parity or labor certification requirements, as well as economic needs tests, would not apply for category 1, but could apply to category 2 if the value of the contract is less than EUR50,000 (US$44,000). The applicant company of a category 2 permit holder would be required to post a bond of EUR250,000 ($220,000) with the local embassy of the GATS country to which its employee is seeking access.[8]

The second part of the proposal encompasses certain obligations designed to improve the transparency of regulatory procedures. It is argued that existing GATS transparency rules, which simply require publication or public availability of measures, are not adequate. Some additional elements might be included in a "best practices" set of commitments by all Members, regardless of the level of market access and national treatment obligations they have assumed. Members would be required to make available, in a consolidated text, all measures that pertain to the temporary admission of natural persons; provide information on the materials or evidence required of an applicant seeking temporary admission into their territories; and grant approval of applications for temporary admission within a defined period of time. Interested parties would be given a reasonable period of time to comment on any measures that a Member proposes to introduce to govern the temporary entry and stay of natural persons. Finally, Members would assume obligations to make any economic needs tests employed more transparent and predictable, including by establishing and making available the conditions for granting temporary entry and by providing the quantitative or qualitative criteria used to make determinations.[9]

At the same time, several regulators, including Henry (Chapter 14) and Christen (Chapter 15), point to the need for greater transparency in GATS rules and commitments. At ports of entry opaque commitments can lead to implementation burdens for immigration officers and business people. Henry and Christen also argue for the harmonization of the definitions of the various mode 4 categories. In this context, Self and Zutshi suggest that an adapted version of the International Labour Organisation's International Standard Classification of Occupations (ISCO-88) could serve as a basis for negotiations and scheduling of commitments.

The proposed GATS visa for skilled professionals raises two types of concerns. First, the choice of the category of skilled professionals is politically convenient, but is it sufficiently ambitious? As Winters demonstrates in Chapter 4, the largest global benefits will arise precisely from the greater movement of unskilled workers. And as Brown argues in Chapter 11, unless the movement of unskilled and semiskilled workers is given parity of consideration along with the movement of persons with professional qualifications, many developing countries will be deprived of an opportunity to participate in the global provision of services.

The second concern, raised by Henry in Chapter 14, is the practical effects of the temporary entry provisions negotiated in international trade agreements. The special rules on temporary entry created by these agreements can, ironically, result in a burden for both immigration officers and business people. For example, some business people, instead of sailing smoothly through a port of entry, may be pulled out of the queue and directed to a secondary inspection area where immigration officers must interview them to ensure they comply with the special rules of trade agreements. Henry favors improved rules that are generally applicable.

In fact, the descriptions of the (temporary) immigration regimes reveal that most do not treat mode 4 as a distinct category, raising a concern about how any future liberalization can be made compatible with Members' migration regimes (Chapters 6, 14–17). The private sector too seems to regard the GATS category as a somewhat artificial construct (Chapter 8). For example, an Indian software engineer working for Credit Suisse in the United States falls within the scope of the GATS, whereas working for American Express in the United States may not, and working for General Motors does not. Would it, therefore, make sense to take a horizontal view of mode 4 to cover temporary movement regardless of whether the natural person is involved in services or goods production? If the WTO does extend its domain to investment in goods, should a symmetrical treatment of factors of production imply a wider view of mode 4?

And one final issue must be confronted: Could the GATS insistence on nondiscrimination and binding commitments actually inhibit liberalization in an area in which there is a greater willingness to liberalize on a regional, preferential, and cyclical basis (Chapter 5)? The tension between bilateral or regional agreements and the most-favored-nation (MFN) principle is evident, and it has affected virtually all service sectors.[10] To an extent, this tension is accommodated for mode 4 by flexibly applying the MFN principle to measures such as visa requirements. However, as with discriminatory regional trading arrangements, currently favored suppliers may be reluctant to support MFN liberalization if they believe that they have more to lose than to gain.

The constraining effect of international binding commitments is noted by Henry, who states that there is a preference in Canada for the general provisions of Canada's current immigration regime and the policymaking flexibility it allows. The general provisions are preferred because they can be used to respond to changes in the domestic labor market or economy, and because they allow for temporary and managed policy responses.

Even though there is a preference for policy flexibility, Henry notes that there is a willingness to make legally binding horizontal commitments on mode 4 in exchange for specific benefits. Devising such negotiating tradeoffs across sectors and modes will in fact be central not only to progress on mode 4 but also to the success of the whole services negotiations. Moreover, Brown's suggestion about safeguards may represent a possible compromise between GATS commitments and policy flexibility. Nations could be allowed to take temporary actions to shield the labor force of both home and host countries from rapid, uncontrolled outward or inward movement of service workers. Yet it will not be easy to develop rules that permit safeguard action but prevent its protectionist abuse—an issue that WTO Members have been grappling with for several years in the negotiations on emergency safeguards in services.

Despite these qualifications, chapters in this volume provide useful suggestions on the conduct of mode 4 negotiations. They include negotiating market access and national treatment commitments from a common template that is sufficiently flexible for parties with differing interests and varying levels of ambition; developing a set of agreed-on regulatory principles that would improve the transparency of procedures granting temporary entry to service providers; reaching an agreement on the skill levels of workers affected by the temporary entry negotiations, as part of the negotiating process itself; and enhancing collaboration between trade, immigration, and labor policy communities, and between officials from developing and industrial countries.

Notes

1. Mode 1 is "cross-border supply," which is analogous to trade in goods; mode 2 is "consumption abroad" (e.g., tourism or study abroad); and mode 3 is "commercial presence" (e.g., the supply of a service through a subsidiary or branch in another country).

2. As Parikh points out, often a strong complementarity exists between modes. For example, even to take advantage of open trading conditions under mode 1 usually requires some movement under mode 4.

3. For example, Desai, Kapur, and McHale (2001) estimate that the U.S. government collects as much as $22.5 billion a year in the form of payroll taxes from H1B visa holders of Indian origin alone.

4. All dollar amounts are U.S. dollars.

5. A recent survey conducted for the Public Policy Institute of California of more than 1,500 first-generation Indian and Chinese migrants in Silicon Valley found that 74 percent of Indian migrants and 53 percent of Chinese migrants said they hoped to start a business back home. Furthermore, based on the finding that many members of this group frequently return home on business, the investigators argue that "brain circulation" is a more appropriate way of describing what is happening to these groups than "brain drain" (*Economist*, November 2, 2002).

6. The exception is the quota imposed on Mexican professionals seeking entry to the United States (5,500 a year), which is to be phased out 10 years after the signing of the agreement—that is, in 2004.

7. The GATS permit would be issued without unreasonable delay (no more than three weeks), and if the GATS permit is denied, the applicant would have an opportunity to appeal the decision. Fraudulent use of the GATS permit could lead to its suspension for a period of time, not to exceed one year.

8. Alternatively, the enforcement of exit in German subcontracting schemes may offer a useful example (Winters and others 2002). First, such schemes involve the rigorous investigation of sites where temporary workers are likely to be employed to locate transgressors. Second, they place an enforcement responsibility on local companies that benefit from cheaper foreign services and the overseas subcontracting firm. Finally, at least in the beginning, part of the payment of foreigner service providers was withheld until the workers returned home.

9. Chanda (2002) discusses this approach in detail.

10. But note the possibility of MFN exceptions and integration agreements (including for the labor market alone).

References

Chanda, Rupa. 2002. "Movement of Natural Persons and the GATS Major Trade Policy Impediments." In Bernard Hoekman, Aaditya Mattoo, and Philip English, eds., *Development, Trade and the WTO*. Washington, D.C.: World Bank.

Desai, Mihir A., Devesh Kapur, and John McHale. 2001. "Sharing the Spoils: Taxing International Human Flows." Weatherhead Center for International Affairs Working Paper 02-06. Harvard University, Cambridge, Mass.

Winters, L. Alan, Terrie L. Walmsley, Zhen Kun Wang, and Roman Grynberg. 2002. "Negotiating the Liberalisation of the Temporary Movement of Natural Persons." Economics Discussion Paper 87. University of Sussex, Brighton.

2

THE GATS, MODE 4, AND PATTERN OF COMMITMENTS

Antonia Carzaniga[*]

Member countries of the World Trade Organization (WTO) have committed themselves to the progressive liberalization of trade in services. The new round of services negotiations launched on January 1, 2000, is expected to promote further market liberalization, or at least the legal binding of liberalization already achieved autonomously. It may therefore advance or consolidate developments that have been under way for years in many countries.

Basic Structure of the GATS

The General Agreement on Trade in Services (GATS) allows member countries to assume legally binding commitments on their use or renunciation of trade-related measures in individual service sectors. These commitments are laid down in country schedules, one for each Member. There is, however, wide scope to adjust schedules to domestic policy objectives and constraints. For example, the GATS does not prescribe the number, level, or sectoral pattern of a country's commitments and does not compel Members, even in sectors they include in schedules, to offer conditions that are more liberal than the prevailing trading conditions. A large majority of schedules have been confined to confirming the status quo or to guaranteeing only some form of minimum trading rights below present levels.

Reflecting the need in many service sectors for direct physical interaction between supplier and consumer, the range of transactions covered by the GATS is particularly broad. The agreement not only embraces the traditional concept of cross-border trade in the form of country A importing services from abroad

---

[*]Antonia Carzaniga is economic affairs officer of the World Trade Organization Secretariat.

(mode 1), but also extends to the residents of country A consuming services in foreign markets (mode 2), foreign suppliers establishing a commercial presence in country A (mode 3), and people (designated legally as "natural persons") moving temporarily into country A for the purpose of providing a service (mode 4).

For any sector included in its services schedule, a Member must specify the commitments it is prepared to undertake on market access and national treatment. The granting of market access implies that the Member will refrain from operating any of six types of restrictions, mostly quota-related barriers, enumerated in Article XVI of the GATS. Article XVII defines national treatment as the absence of any measure that modifies the conditions of competition to the detriment of foreign services or service suppliers. Departures from market access and national treatment are not prohibited per se, but they must be listed in the schedule as limitations. Limitations applying to all scheduled sectors may be inscribed in a horizontal section to avoid repetition. The GATS is therefore based on a "hybrid" approach: it combines a positive listing of sectors with a negative listing of restrictions.

Because market access and national treatment each apply to the four modes of supply, trading conditions are defined in the form of eight entries per sector. These conditions may vary within a spectrum whose opposing ends are guaranteed market access and national treatment without limitations (full commitments) and the denial of any such guarantees (no bindings). Although the relevant entry would be "none" for full guaranteed market access and national treatment, the absence of commitments would be indicated as "unbound."

The nonscheduling of a sector or a noncommitment on a particular mode does not imply that the relevant policies are beyond all GATS disciplines. Some basic obligations—first and foremost, the most-favored-nation (MFN) principle—apply regardless of such circumstances. The MFN obligation prohibits any form of discrimination between trading partners on grounds of nationality. Thus, although a WTO Member may prohibit all trade in a noncommitted sector or mode, it must, as a rule, apply this prohibition on an MFN basis—that is, to all its trading partners. Exceptions are the preferences granted among participants in economic integration agreements. In addition, exemptions from MFN treatment could have been sought, for a period not exceeding 10 years in principle, at the date of entry into force of the GATS or, for new WTO Members, at the date of accession.

Mode 4

The presence of natural persons, otherwise referred to as mode 4, is one of the four possible ways of trading a service under the GATS. Mode 4 is defined in Article I.2(d), as entailing "the supply of a service . . . by a service supplier of one Member, through presence of natural persons of a Member in the territory of any other Member." The Annex on Movement of Natural Persons Supplying Services under the Agreement specifies that two categories of measures are covered: those affecting natural persons who are "service suppliers of a Member" (i.e., self-employed suppliers who obtain their remuneration directly from customers), and those affecting natural persons of a Member who are "employed by a service supplier of a Member, in respect of the supply of a service." These natural persons can either be employed in their home country and be present in the host market to supply a service or be employed by a service supplier in the host country.

The annex clarifies that the GATS does not apply to measures affecting individuals seeking access to the employment market of a Member, nor to measures on citizenship, residence, or employment on a permanent basis. The GATS does not specify a time frame for what constitutes "temporary" movement; rather, this movement is defined negatively, through the explicit exclusion of permanent presence. A cursory look at Members' schedules shows that the maximum length of stay permitted under mode 4 varies with the underlying purpose. Thus business visitors are generally allowed to stay up to 90 days, whereas intracorporate transferees, another frequently scheduled category, tend to be limited to stays of between two and five years. The annex does provide for the possibility of scheduling commitments, and therefore access conditions, by "categories of natural persons," thereby introducing an additional element of flexibility.

The annex also clarifies that, regardless of their obligations under the agreement, Members are free to regulate the entry and stay of people in their territory, including through measures necessary to protect the integrity of, and ensure the orderly movement of natural persons across, their borders. However, the measures may not be "applied in such a manner as to nullify or impair the benefits accruing to any Member under the terms of a specific commitment." The application of visa requirements only to the natural persons of certain Members, but not of others, is not regarded as nullifying or impairing such benefits.

Pattern of Mode 4 Commitments

The Uruguay Round negotiations were concluded in December 1993. However, negotiations on basic telecommunications, financial services, and maritime transport services, as well as on the movement of natural persons, were extended beyond the end of the Uruguay Round because of widespread dissatisfaction with the level of liberalization achieved in these areas. Negotiations on mode 4, which were extended until June 30, 1995, produced no major breakthrough. Only Australia, Canada, the European Union (EU), India, Norway, and Switzerland improved on the commitments made in the Uruguay Round, and these improvements were annexed to the Third Protocol to the GATS. The improvements mainly concerned access opportunities for additional categories of service suppliers (usually independent foreign professionals in various business sectors) or extension of their permitted duration of stay.

A cursory look at Members' current GATS schedules reveals that levels of commitments vary strongly across modes of supply. Within a given sector, trade conditions for mode 4 tend to be significantly more restrictive than conditions for other modes. No industrial country has scheduled a "none" entry for its mode 4 commitments, and only 1 percent of market access commitments undertaken by developing countries are fully liberal. By contrast, one out of two entries for mode 2 are full commitments.[1] The shallow level of commitments for mode 4 is to a certain extent also reflected in the pattern of horizontal limitations, which apply across all sectors: there are five times as many such limitations scheduled for mode 4 than for mode 2. This shallow level reflects, in turn, the basic approach used by many Members to scheduling mode 4 entries. In contrast with other modes, the negative list approach to scheduling limitations has been turned upside down: schedules start with a general "unbound," which is then qualified by liberalization commitments, mostly limited to specified types of persons (e.g., managers), movements (e.g., intracorporate), and stays (e.g., up to four years).

Commitments are often exclusively governed by what is inscribed in the horizontal part of the schedule, so that identical access conditions apply to all scheduled sectors. Commitments are usually based on functional or hierarchical criteria, related either to the type of person involved (e.g., executive, manager, specialist) or to the purpose of his or her movement (e.g., to establish business contacts, negotiate sales, set up a commercial presence). Besides, no generally agreed-upon definitions or precise descriptions exist of the types of natural persons to whom access is granted, which can detract from the predictability of entry conditions.

Many schedules have established links across modes of supply. Members' schedules are mostly biased in favor of intracorporate transferees, and thus the economic value of such commitments is dependent on access conditions for mode 3. Such commitments are of limited interest to Members, which, given their level of economic development, are not significant foreign investors. Schedules also are more open for highly skilled labor, and here developing countries tend to be net importers, because their comparative advantage lies in relatively unskilled, labor-intensive services. It also is widely acknowledged that Members' mode 4 commitments do not generally reflect actual entry conditions for natural persons, because Members have bound less than the access granted in practice.

An overview of Members' horizontal commitments as of April 2002 reveals that the majority of the entries scheduled—almost 280 out of a total 400—pertain to executives, managers, and specialists. Of these, about 170 entries explicitly

**TABLE 2.1   Types of Natural Persons Supplying Services
(Horizontal Commitments), April 2002**

		Number of Entries	Number of Aggregate Entries	Percent of Aggregate Entries
Intracorporate transferees	Executives	56	168	42
	Managers	55		
	Specialists	56		
	Others	1		
Executives		24	110	28
Managers		42		
Specialists		44		
Business visitors	Commercial presence	41	93	23
	Sale negotiations	52		
Contract suppliers		12	12	3
Other		17	17	4
Total[a]		400	400	100

a. Total number of entries by those WTO Members that have included commitments on mode 4 in the horizontal section of their schedules.

Source: WTO Secretariat.

relate to intracorporate transferees, whose economic value is thus determined by commitments on mode 3 (see Table 2.1). An additional feature is the schedules' general bias in favor of qualified labor; only 17 percent of all horizontal entries may cover low-skilled persons as well ("business sellers" and "other").

No significant differences exist between the commitments scheduled by industrial and developing countries; both groups seem to have been equally hesitant in undertaking very liberal commitments for mode 4. Access conditions scheduled by countries that acceded to the WTO after 1995, the date of its entry into force, also are almost identical to the ones scheduled by Uruguay Round participants. This situation contrasts with those for the three other modes of supply, where recently acceded Members have generally undertaken deeper commitments—that is, subject to fewer limitations. The only detectable difference for mode 4 is the relatively higher number of commitments scheduled by recent WTO Members for "contract suppliers"—that is, employees of a foreign enterprise that has concluded a contract to supply services in a country but does not have a commercial presence in that market.

The periods for which entry may be permitted have not always been indicated. This situation is surprising, because one might expect that, in the absence of a definition of "temporary" in the GATS annex, Members would be more precise in their schedules.[2] Where time limits have been specified, the relevant periods are shorter for business visitors than for executives, managers, and specialists.

The focus of existing commitments on employed persons also is reflected in Members' frequent use of employment links as an entry criterion: "preemployment," usually of one year, is one of the most recurrent restrictions scheduled. Numerical quotas and economic needs tests rank next in frequency of limitations. Although most of the quotas relate to the total staff of a company, some Members also have reserved the right to operate quotas based on parameters such as senior staff or wages. Significant administrative discretion is produced by the frequent scheduling of economic needs tests without indication of the criteria on which they operate; with such entries, the relevant government agency grants access to foreign natural persons provided that—not further specified—economic-related conditions are met.

Measures denying national treatment include residency requirements and noneligibility of foreigners under subsidy schemes. Members also have scheduled horizontal limitations on the right to own real estate, which are likely to impinge in particular on activities requiring stays of significant duration. Requirements to train local staff also appear in schedules. But these were added only by developing country Members, mainly those in Latin America and Africa.

Notes

1. Calculated on a sample of 37 sectors deemed representative for various services areas (WTO 1999).
2. The revised guidelines for the scheduling of commitments adopted by the Council for Trade in Services March 23, 2001, state that "in the absence of a reference to a specific duration for the temporary stay of a foreign service supplier, it could be understood that no binding is being undertaken in respect of the duration of that stay. . . . Commitments should include the duration of temporary stay of natural persons for the purpose of supplying a service. In any event a Member's regulatory measures would still be subject to the general requirement, in paragraph 4 of the Annex on the Movement of Natural Persons, that they do not nullify or impair the benefits accruing to any other Member under the terms of a specific commitment" (WTO 2001).

References

WTO (World Trade Organization). 1999. *Structure of Commitments for Modes 1, 2 and 3.* Document S/C/W/99, March 2. Geneva.
———. 2001. "Trade in Services—Guidelines for the Scheduling of Specific Commitments under the GATS—Adopted by the Council for Trade in Services on 23 March 2001." Document S/L/92, March 28 <*www.wto.org*>.

3

MODE 4: NEGOTIATING CHALLENGES AND OPPORTUNITIES

*Richard J. Self and B. K. Zutshi**

In the post–World War II period, services in the member countries of the Organisation for Economic Co-operation and Development (OECD) grew dramatically. This growth was driven largely by advances in information technology (IT) and telecommunications. Before these technological developments, services were considered largely nontradable because they could not be stored and because they had to be simultaneously produced and consumed. But computerized storage of data and remote delivery of services by modern means of communications helped to increase the tradability of services dramatically, which, in turn, fostered bilateral trade in many service sectors. Because industrial countries were the major suppliers of services, pressures grew within them to seek changes in the regulatory environment to further improve opportunities for the exchange of services on a cross-border basis.

Inclusion of "trade in services" as an issue for negotiations in the Punta del Este Ministerial Declaration that launched the Uruguay Round negotiations in September 1986 was preceded by a long and controversial debate on the tradability of services and thus on its relevance as a subject for multilateral trade negotiations. This debate included the issue of applying trade rules to investment in services, because regulations and the marketplace required establishment in the host country as a condition for doing business. Investment had never been recognized as "trade" under the General Agreement on Tariffs and Trade (GATT), which contributed to the difficult debate on tradability. The debate continued well into the Uruguay Round and was colored by sharply differing perceptions between the industrial

---

*Richard J. Self is senior international advisor, Akin, Gump, Strauss, Hauer and Feld. B. K. Zutshi is former ambassador of India to the World Trade Organization.

and developing countries about the possible impact of multilateral rules and disciplines in services trade on their economic and developmental interests, even though the nature of such rules and disciplines was unclear. The possible application of the GATT paradigm for goods raised not only doubts about its appropriateness for the services sector, but also great fears and anxieties among the developing countries about its implications for their development aspirations, given the significance of the sector in economic terms and its strategic role in development. Reluctant participants in the beginning, toward the end of the Uruguay Round the developing countries became enthusiastic supporters of a multilateral regime of rules in services trade, even more so than the *demandeurs*, whose earlier expectations of generating trade liberalization were not being realized. This change in the attitude of the developing countries had as much to do with the emerging structure of the framework agreement as with the autonomous liberalization undertaken by them in their quest for greater integration into an increasingly interdependent global economy—a quest greatly fostered by technological developments in computing and telecommunications.

A major achievement of the Uruguay Round multilateral trade negotiations was bringing services into the multilateral trading system through the General Agreement on Trade in Services (GATS) and securing through extended negotiations the initial commitments made under the agreement. However, the actual commitment to liberalizing trade in various sectors was modest, with the exception of telecommunications services and, to a lesser extent, financial services. The present commitments, except in these two sectors, indicate a standstill, or even a rollback in some cases—that is, the then-applicable regimes were more liberal than those bound under the agreement. If Members take into account autonomous liberalization since the conclusion of the extended negotiations, the gap between the applicable and the bound regimes has widened further, particularly for developing countries. Even by these modest standards of liberalization, little was achieved toward the temporary entry of natural persons (known as mode 4 under the GATS framework). Commitments for the movement of persons were mostly for movement associated with the establishment of a commercial presence (known as mode 3 under GATS) and confined to intracorporate transferees at senior levels and highly skilled professionals and specialists. In addition, commitments were subject to conditions and qualifications such as various kinds of needs tests and wage parity requirements, which further reduced their value in providing effective market access.

The Uruguay Round commitments failed to address the procedural requirements for granting visas and work permits, which remained unchanged and subject to the considerable discretionary powers exercised by the issuing authorities, resulting in further erosion in access opportunities. As for professional services, many observers believe strongly that the recognition of qualifications and verification of professional competence, without which no effective access is possible, have left much to be desired in implementation. By contrast, others suggest that, in practical terms, the absence of mutual recognition agreements and harmonized rules does not act as a constraint to the temporary movement of most licensed professional services, because professionals provide their services as a "consultant," leaving it to a locally licensed associate to meet the legal requirements of authenticating, by signature, such things as audit reports and architectural plans. On that basis, it is argued that recognition and harmonization of qualifications are less relevant to providing services through mode 4. This argument also holds that, in a negotiating environment, it would be difficult, if not impossible, to improve temporary entry regimes and to harmonize professional qualifications. This argument should be explored further.

Issues that have a bearing on equity (contributions without benefits), and possibly on the conditions of competition (raising costs) such as social security payments, were left unresolved, because participants differed over the ability to manage such complex issues through negotiations over temporary entry and stay under mode 4. The present negotiations provide an opportunity to address all of the issues, substantive and procedural, that appear to stand in the way of effective market access under mode 4.

Fortunately, it is now a propitious time to do so in view of the revolutionary developments in computing and IT, the demand-supply imbalance in skilled manpower among groups of countries, and the demographic changes globally, resulting in age profile changes—all of which have resulted in labor shortages in industrial country markets. As evidence of these shortages, Germany, France, and the United Kingdom recently changed their immigration policies and regulations to attract foreign workers. The United States also has enhanced the H1B visa quota ceiling (these visas cover the temporary employment of highly skilled foreign workers in U.S. firms).

Developing countries, by contrast, have abundant labor, some in the skilled and professional categories. The movement of natural persons between industrial and developing countries will, therefore, meet mutual needs and provide mutual benefits. The opportunity provided by the ongoing services negotiations in the World Trade Organization (WTO) must be exploited to promote liberalization in temporary movement of natural persons under the GATS to the mutual benefit of industrial and developing countries. Realization of this objective could start by involving all stakeholders in a discourse on the issue, especially labor representatives, immigration authorities, the services industry, academicians, trade policy experts, and negotiators. This discourse has to start with a better understanding and appreciation of the GATS provisions on the movement of natural persons, on the one hand, and demystification of the immigration laws and regulations related to temporary movement, on the other. The joint WTO–World Bank symposium that produced this collection of articles has perhaps served as the first in a series of such initiatives.

One of the principal objectives of this discourse between stakeholders should be to allay fears that industrial country labor markets will be inundated by cheap labor from developing countries; this is a sensitive issue in some developing countries as well. Indeed, the developing countries do not appear to be interested in the migration of their skilled manpower, because that is not in the interest of their long-term growth and development. A related area of concern is the possibility that those workers seeking temporary entry in industrial countries under the GATS will abuse the system by using it as a vehicle for permanent entry. Home and host country cooperation in enforcement may be one way of addressing this concern.

The rest of this chapter is organized as follows. The first section describes the scope and coverage of mode 4 and includes a brief history of the negotiations that established the definition of trade in services and the emergence of mode 4, as well as an interpretation of the legal provisions of the GATS relevant to mode 4. That description is followed by an examination of the present-day mode 4 commitments and their brief negotiating history, an analysis of commitments by the major industrial countries, and an assessment of the political and regulatory dynamics leading to mode 4 commitments to date. The next section describes the issues and challenges in the current negotiations on mode 4, starting with an analysis of the negotiating mandate and a comparison of the current negotiating environment surrounding mode 4 liberalization with that of the Uruguay Round. This section also takes a look at the issues related to the classification of natural persons as service providers and the approaches to liberalization negotiations, as well as the barriers to and challenges in effective market access through and under mode 4. Finally, it addresses how temporary entry of service providers under the GATS might be facilitated. The section closes with an examination of related GATS disciplines having a bearing on effective market access under this mode. The final section provides conclusions and some recommendations.

Mode 4: Scope and Coverage

Defining Trade in Services and the Emergence of Mode 4

An important step toward defining trade in services was taken in December 1988 at the midterm review ministerial meeting in Montreal. Ministers directed that "work on definition should proceed on the basis that the multilateral framework may include trade in services involving cross-border movement of services, cross-border movement of consumers, and cross-border movement of factors of production where such movement is essential to supplies." This mandate conceded the principle of parity/symmetry in the treatment of capital and labor, a core demand of developing countries in any multilateral framework of rules for the services trade. For industrial countries, the language had its own significance, because it represented a breakthrough in gaining agreement to include investment in services. The definition also was to take into account (a) the cross-border movement of services and payment; (b) specificity of purpose; (c) discreteness of transactions; and (d) limited duration. Inclusion of these four elements, along with a caveat about "essentiality" in factor movement, was intended to balance the perceived interests of the industrial and developing countries.

The elements of specificity of purpose, discreteness of transactions, and limited duration, along with the essentiality caveat about factor movement, reflected developing countries' fears that the framework would become an investment agreement in services, as well as industrial countries' opposition to the inclusion of the uncircumscribed movement of labor in the services agreement. As described in the rest of this section, these elements inform not only the definition of trade in services, but also some important elements of the structure of the GATS itself, though not necessarily in the way and to the effect intended by participants at the time. The modal approach to the definition, if not embedded in these elements, was implied therein. Furthermore, it was inherent in the insistence on formal parity/symmetry in factor movement. In the immediate post–midterm review period, negotiations on the definition were put on the back burner so that delegations could achieve a better understanding and feel about the kind of regime appropriate for services before coming to grips with the issue.

The post–midterm review period examined the implications and applicability of the main GATT rules and principles for particular sectors. This exercise in the fall of 1989 helped negotiators to recognize the enormous challenges posed by the effort to address the diversity and complexity of different service sectors, subject to diverse regulatory regimes across sectors and countries, by means of a single set of framework rules. It was during this process that the idea of sectoral annexes that would identify and address sector-specific issues was raised, resulting in the appointment of eight sectoral working groups consisting of negotiators and sectoral experts. The group on labor mobility was asked to examine (a) the need for a specific annotation or an annex on labor mobility, and (b) the possible nature and content of such an annotation or annex. The group was unable to reach any consensus, however, on both the need for and the nature and contents of an annex on labor mobility.

The Negotiating Group on Services (GNS), composed of GNS negotiators and sectoral experts, was appointed in August 1990 to take stock of the work of the sectoral working groups and to finalize draft texts of whatever sectoral annexes or annotation was required. Although there was no consensus or even any clarity about the need for and contents of an annex on labor mobility, the work of the labor mobility group and informal consultations on definition had led to a consensus on the modal approach to the definition of trade in services.

Because the Annex on Movement of Natural Persons Supplying Services under the Agreement is a part of the definition of trade in services, the negotiating history of the annex is described here only briefly before continuing the analysis of the definition and scope of coverage under mode 4. The negotiations at the Brussels ministerial meeting in December 1990 on a possible annex on labor mobility addressed the following issues:

- Mobility as defined as the temporary movement of physical persons to perform particular services covered by previous access commitments
- Exclusion of individual job seekers, and thus their access to the employment market, from coverage by the agreement
- An illustrative list of natural persons performing particular services that cover broad categories of sectors but at undefined skill levels
- Market access commitments specifying the categories for the provision of a particular service to be negotiated in accordance with Article XVI of the framework, drawing on the illustrative list
- Application of national treatment to persons admitted under a market access concession on a modal basis
- Extension of flexibility to parties so that they are able to regulate the temporary entry and stay of natural persons to ensure, on the one hand, the integrity of and the orderly movement across borders and, on the other, the nonfrustration of benefits through the application of national laws, regulations, and administrative practices related to the temporary movement of physical persons
- Treatment to be accorded to the integration of labor markets.

All of these issues or elements, other than the illustrative list of natural persons performing particular services and the treatment of labor market integration, were subsequently incorporated in the annex on the movement of natural persons, which forms part of the GATS. At that stage in the negotiations there was still no clarity on the scope of application of the annex to the temporary movement of natural persons associated with commitments under mode 3. This issue was discussed during the post–Brussels negotiations. As noted earlier, the Brussels ministerial meeting was designed to conclude the Uruguay Round, but it failed to do so. However, the negotiations that continued in earnest during 1991 produced at the end of the year the "Draft Final Act" under the authority of the chairman of the Trade Negotiating Committee. The services components of this document, later to become the GATS, were, with some exceptions, kept largely intact at the conclusion of the Uruguay Round in 1993. The labor market integration issue was conceded at the end of the round and incorporated into Article V *bis*.

Negotiators were unable to settle on an illustrative list of natural persons performing services because of a lack of widespread support and enthusiasm and the perception that the task could not be accomplished within the time frame of the Uruguay Round negotiations. Although some industrial country delegations were in favor of drawing up an illustrative list of natural persons associated with mode 3 commitments, some developing countries, led by India, were looking for an illustrative list covering different levels of skills—not just highly skilled professionals and executives associated with mode 3. A remarkable degree of uniformity in classifying professionals and executives associated with mode 3 movement did emerge in the process of commitment negotiations, without a formal decision to that effect. Meanwhile, the idea of classifying natural persons to help promote liberalization under mode 4 and bring about a degree of certainty and uniformity in commitments has been revived in the current negotiations. (This issue is examined in more detail later in this chapter.)

Thus by the time of the Brussels ministerial meeting in December 1990, even though there were formal and tactical reservations about some elements of the definition of trade in services in Article I.2, and the precise content of a labor mobility annex, negotiators did in general agree on the modal approach to the definition of trade in services and possible coverage of issues under the labor mobility annex, except for the movement of natural persons associated with mode 3. In fact, not much thought had been given to the movement of natural persons associated with mode 3 from the perspective of the annex. The understanding was clear on the temporary nature of the movement; the exclusion of access to the employment market of a Member and to citizenship, residence, or employment on a permanent basis; and the need to extend considerable flexibility to Members in regulating the temporary entry of natural persons subject to the nonfrustration of specific commitments. The contentious issue of the scope of the temporary movement in terms of skill levels was settled by agreeing to leave it to specific commitments negotiations covering all categories of natural persons. The fact that it was understood that the movement of natural persons under the agreement was temporary, without any such qualification for investment under mode 3, implied a modification in the negotiating stance of developing countries on "limited duration" as an element of symmetry in factor movement (capital and labor).

In 1991 negotiators addressed the issue of mode 3 commitments. The issue also had come up in the negotiations on specific commitments in the financial services sector. It was clear that any discussion of the movement of natural persons associated with mode 3 would have to address the same set of concerns applicable to mode 4. It seemed, therefore, logical and necessary to include in the annex on the movement of natural persons measures affecting natural persons movements under both modes—that is, measures affecting natural persons who are supplying services to a Member and the natural persons of a Member who are employed by a service supplier of a Member to supply a service under the agreement.

Interpretation and Explanation of the Legal Provisions of the GATS Relevant to Mode 4

Article I.2(d) of the GATS defines mode 4 as "the supply of a service . . . by a service supplier of one Member, through the presence of natural persons of a Member in the territory of any other Member." In view of the scope of the annex on the movement of natural persons, which covers movement associated with mode 3, some commentators believe the definition of mode 4 has created an "important ambiguity at the very heart of the GATS" inasmuch as it seeks to distinguish between "service supply" and "employment" on the basis of the nature of engagement of a foreigner in a domestic firm whether as an employee or as a service supplier on a contract basis (Winters and others 2002). It also has been argued that because the annex covers natural persons "employed by a service supplier of a Member," such a definition could include foreigners employed by host country firms, but such employment was not covered by the disciplines of the GATS. Furthermore, as pointed out by Winters and others, "a service delivered by a foreign worker under employment contract to a local provider may be treated differently from precisely the same service provided by precisely the same person acting as an unattached service provider or under contract to a foreign company" (Winters and others 2002).

The issue of employment of foreigners by local firms apparently did not come up for detailed examination, because it was understood that access to the labor market was outside the scope of the coverage under the GATS. The negotiating history of this issue is less than clear, and the descriptive language that emerged for mode 4 is ambiguous on the treatment of a service supplied by a foreign person who is employed by an indigenous services company or firm. This particular issue of legal applicability did not arise, however, when the United States offered to bind its H1B visa provision, which would apply. It certainly can be argued that recruitment from foreign sources is a service. It also is true that the use of such services is widespread on a bilateral basis and in the context of regional agreements. Therefore, a sound case could be made in favor of multilateralization of such recruitment from foreign sources. Participants in the current negotiations should explore this avenue for further liberalization under mode 4.

Another issue on which commentators have faulted the annex on the movement of natural persons is the absence of a definition of temporary movement in terms of time period. Such a definition was debated extensively during the negotiations. It was believed that defining the period for the purpose of temporary movement would introduce rigidity into the framework agreement because different situations would call for different periods of stay. The commitment itself was viewed as permanent (unless renegotiated), and the movement of individuals under that commitment was time-limited, as specified in the schedule of commitments produced by the negotiations.

In the context of mode 4, one of the issues raised by some delegations was the treatment of stand-alone labor market integration agreements outside the economic integration arrangements covered under Article V. This issue was of particular concern to the Nordic countries and to India because of its integrated labor market with Nepal. The issue was addressed through Article V *bis*, which permits Members to enter into labor integration agreements. This provision may be redundant, however, because the annex on the movement of natural persons excludes access to labor markets, and labor market integration agreements are precisely meant to provide such access.

Article XXVIII of the GATS covers definitions. Definitions relevant to mode 4 are those for supply of the service (includes the production, distribution, marketing, sale, and delivery of a service—as comprehensive as it can get) and natural person of another Member (means a natural person with residence in the territory of that Member as a national or with the right to permanent residence).

Other Provisions Relevant to the Movement of Natural Persons under the GATS

The other provisions and general disciplines pertinent to the movement of natural persons include Article III on transparency, Article VI on domestic regulations, and Article VII on recognition. Article III on transparency requires Members to publish all relevant measures of general application that pertain to or affect operation of the agreement. Article VI obliges Members to ensure that in sectors where specific commitments are undertaken, requirements related to qualifications and procedures, technical standards, and licensing are based on objective and transparent criteria and do not in themselves constitute a restriction on the supply of the service. It also obliges Members to provide for objective and impartial reviews of administrative decisions affecting trade in services. Article VII on recognition gives Members discretion to recognize the education, experience, licensing, and certification of foreign service providers either in whole or in part, and either autonomously or by mutual agreement or by harmonization. It prohibits Members from using criteria or standards for authorization as a disguised restriction on trade. Some of these issues, particularly those pertinent to effective market access under mode 4, are discussed later in this chapter.

An Assessment of Specific Commitments Undertaken to Date under Mode 4

Uruguay Round Negotiations

As indicated earlier, the four modes of supply, including that covering the temporary entry of natural persons, were a well-established part of the draft framework for services when request and offer negotiations commenced in 1991. Although the Uruguay Round lasted seven years (1986–93), only the final two years of the round were devoted to the negotiation of specific commitments among the participants, a relatively short period in which to negotiate commitments in an area completely new to the GATT/WTO. Trade negotiators ordinarily calibrate their requests and offers on the basis of statistics, as part of the effort to obtain a theoretical balance of concessions among the parties. But for services this was not possible, because no reliable data were (and are) available on a sufficiently disaggregated basis to enable countries to assess the quality of their concessions. Similarly, participants had very little basis on which to assess the value of commitments by mode of supply because of lack of services trade and investment data.

Inevitably, this shortage of data led to disagreements among delegations. There was not a rough balance of commitments among the modes of supply, they argued, in particular between modes 3 and 4. Generally, participants paid greater attention to the third mode of supply (commercial presence). According to some developing countries, the greater concentration of commitments under mode 3 compared with mode 4 had resulted in asymmetries in the level of obligation participants were to assume. By the conclusion of the round in December 1993, there was a consensus that the participants had failed to capture market access and national treatment commitments in several sectors of critical importance to the negotiations, making it impossible to conclude the services portion of the Uruguay Round. Negotiations on basic telecommunications, financial services, and maritime services were extended 18 months in the hope that a package of improved commitments could be achieved in these sectors. India proposed successfully that the extended negotiations include those governing the temporary entry of natural persons.

The extended negotiations on mode 4 commitments were, on the whole, not successful. The issue of making legally binding commitments affecting temporary entry regimes remained a sensitive one for most countries (this problem is described in more detail later in this section), and the environment associated with the extended negotiations in specified areas did not lend itself to greater pressure on countries to consider improvements to their obligations in mode 4. Regulators responsible for considering new commitments (i.e., visa control authorities, labor certification personnel) generally remained hostile to incorporating additional obligations, in contrast to their counterparts in telecommunications and financial services. As a result, the negotiations produced very little progress beyond what was achieved in the Uruguay Round. Indeed, no more than a handful of countries showed a real interest in addressing this issue. Termination of the negotiations in July 1996 could be described as a low point in efforts to improve mode 4 commitments. Only eight participants made modest changes to their commitments in mode 4, most of which had been pulled from the table at the conclusion of the Uruguay Round to improve negotiating leverage in the extended negotiations.

Mode 4 Specific Commitments and Their Effect on Liberalization of Trade in Services

Nearly all countries made commitments under mode 4. In fact, a comparison of the number of commitments made in this mode compared with those made in the other three modes of supply reveals that mode 4 fared quite well. Moreover, nearly all commitments were made for all service sectors listed in country schedules—that is, they were entered horizontally in the "Headnotes to Schedules" section of the countries' "Specific Commitments." This development is largely attributable to the manner in which regulation is applied to temporary entry. Most countries apply temporary entry rules on the basis of skills, education, and other factors regardless of the sector involved. However, there are exceptions. In a few instances, rules governing temporary entry address a single service sector, such as the treatment of nurses under U.S. visa laws.

The horizontal commitments did not, however, capture the breadth of services sectors, particularly if one assesses the overall coverage of sectors entered in country schedules. An analysis by the OECD Secretariat concluded that industrial countries made mode 4 commitments in only 50 percent of service sectors and developing countries in only 11 percent of service sectors. Its analysis of sectors deemed particularly critical to mode 4 delivery—health, legal, and accountancy services—concluded that entries were limited and largely incomplete. Generally, mode 4 commitments were made in these sectors at least in 90 percent of entries, but most of these were limited to the senior manager, executive category, which captures a very small portion of service providers critical to these sectors. The analysis by the WTO Secretariat, which tabulated the number of entries, underscores these conclusions by worker category (WTO 1998a). Ninety-four percent of entries fell in the rarefied category of business visitors, senior executives, managers, and specialists with proprietary knowledge of company technology. Only 6 percent of entries fell in other categories of workers.

Generally, then, mode 4 commitments barely touched the level of activity taking place in the provision of services by persons traveling to other countries, as revealed in the WTO Secretariat computation. Most mode 4 entries had value only if Members had inscribed commitments under the commercial presence mode (mode 3), because the value of such an obligation depended on the ability of a service provider to establish a commercial presence in the host country market. Furthermore, these entries, while useful in their own right, were limited to the very top of the ladder of company hierarchy. The only other category covered by most countries (70 percent) was that of services salespersons—generally a less sensitive category because the person entering under this category is not allowed to perform a service in the host country. Activity is limited either to marketing a service or to laying the groundwork to establish an overseas affiliate office.

A survey of country entries in the mode 4 category reveals a remarkable consistency among country schedules in the extent of the obligations and the manner in which these obligations are inscribed. For example, virtually no distinction is made among the many entries covering the category of senior managers, executives, and specialists with proprietary company knowledge. These similarities reflect the common format under which negotiations were conducted on this mode. The relative harmony in the conditions and qualifications under the senior manager/executive/specialist category is partly associated with policies of reciprocity that immigration authorities have practiced for some time. Philosophical differences, to the extent they exist, are subordinated to matching what other countries extended in this particular category. The same is true for the treatment of services salespersons.

Exceptions to this level of uniformity of commitments are inevitable, but they do not represent major enhancements to the overall level of obligations assumed by certain countries. For example, three countries made commitments associated with services supplied without the affiliate office but through a contract with a host country service entity. In the extended negotiations, the European Union (EU) undertook additional commitments covering a list of specified licensed and unlicensed professionals who had a contract to work within the EU. The visa was subject to an economic needs test, and, where necessary, possession of the requisite professional credentials recognized by host country authorities. Nevertheless, the EU commitments in this regard were substantially conditioned by reservations taken by its individual member states, which have final control over visa policy in the EU. The United States bound its H1B visa category, which permits U.S. firms to offer temporary employment to foreign nationals with "highly specialized knowledge." The U.S. obligations are qualified by an annual quota of visas granted, as well as wage parity and labor disruption safeguards.

This is not to say that commitments under the other three modes represented a significant success story in trade liberalization. Generally, for all the modes the maximum level of obligation assumed by participants coincided with the requirements of the laws and regulations in place during the negotiations. In virtually no instance did a commitment require the enactment of new measures or changes to existing measures to bring about conformity with WTO obligations. (Some measures enacted autonomously during the course of the Uruguay Round were captured in schedules, which arguably represents a form of rollback to regimes that preceded the round. On the basis of the Uruguay Round experience, however, some observers have wondered whether the role of GATS will be limited to acting as, in the words of Aaditya Mattoo in a draft of Chapter 1, "the grim harvester of autonomous liberalization" rather than a catalyst for generating multilateral liberalization.) In numerous instances, participants did not bind the full measure of market access extended by existing law or regulation. Thus if the standard for measuring the quality of commitments among the four modes depends on the extent to which participants bound existing measures, those taken under the first three modes are generally superior to those assumed under the fourth mode. This is largely attributable to the exceptionally high skill and management levels that were included in bindings, despite existing visa systems that provide a basis for access in other skill levels.

It is not easy, however, to make such a generalization. For example, in the first mode of supply—the provision of a service across a border—most countries did not assume obligations, except in specified situations in which there is no regulation that prohibits the service from being supplied electronically. Generally, participants paid less attention to this mode of supply, because it offered more limited circumstances in which a service could actually be provided across borders, with the notable exception of telecommunications. (The Uruguay Round preceded the full development of the Internet, making the provision of services via electronic commerce a less important issue than it is today.)

The GATS is the only legal framework that provides for obligations related to the establishment of an enterprise abroad (called a "commercial presence"). Indeed, the commercial presence mode became the principal focus of request and offer negotiations, because most services that were the focus of attention in the Uruguay Round were generally provided through some form of establishment abroad. Numerous restrictions associated with the form of commercial presence (subsidiary, branch, representative office) and the percentage of foreign equity allowed made up the conditions and limitations to schedules of commitments under this mode of supply. A comparison of industrial and developing countries reveals that the most restrictions to commercial presence were assumed by the developing countries; nevertheless, the industrial countries assumed their share of restrictions to mode 3. This conclusion is based both on the overall number of restrictions to commercial presence, as well as on the universe of service sectors incorporated in country schedules. (In the GATS scheduling methodology, exclusion of a sector means that there are no obligations assumed for that sector under the four modes of supply.) Despite the reticence of the developing countries to consider investment as part of a trade negotiation, most of their services commitments were confined to mode 3. India, for example, limited all of its commitments (except telecommunications) to mode 3, despite its position throughout the negotiations that establishment-based trade was not trade at all.

Although commitments undertaken in mode 4 generally captured all service sectors included in the schedule, these commitments, when compared with those of commercial presence, did not capture the universe of temporary entry. Temporary entry regimes contain numerous visa categories that govern the different skill levels of the work force and the level of management within company organizations. As indicated earlier, GATS commitments were limited to a very small number of people compared with the large work force pool that falls outside the category of "senior managers, executives, and specialists who possess an advanced level of continued expertise and who possess proprietary knowledge of the organization's services." For all of the political sensitivity associated with binding lower job categories, any objective assessment of commitments that countries assumed under the four modes of supply would conclude that commitments under the fourth mode—the provision of a service through the temporary presence of natural persons in another Member's country—were the least extensive.

Perhaps it is too simplistic to compare levels of commitments among the four modes as one significant measure of the "balance" of benefits assumed by some countries compared with others. There clearly is no statistical basis for doing so unless and until improved data on the services trade are available. In the final analysis, the inevitable asymmetries in commitments among the various modes reflected the prerogatives of different regulatory cultures, which have little or no relationship to one another. Those responsible for negotiating commitments had a finite amount of control over these regulatory prerogatives. What seems clear, however, is that commitments under mode 4 were the least substantive of all the modes. Nevertheless, the intervening period between the Uruguay Round and the negotiations that resumed in 2000 has seen much greater attention paid to both the first mode of supply (owing largely to the development of electronic commerce) and, to a lesser extent, the fourth mode, because service industries have assessed their needs in doing business abroad. As a result of these developments, there is a greater equality of interest among countries in all of the modes, with the possible exception of mode 2.

Assessment of the Political and Regulatory Dynamics Affecting Mode 4 Commitments

Various issues are associated with assuming international legal obligations for the temporary entry and stay of natural persons. Two underlying factors probably have contributed to the relatively limited commitments in the Uruguay Round: enforcement concerns and protection of labor markets.

Enforcement Concerns.   Countries seek to ensure that their laws governing temporary entry are properly implemented. Immigration authorities have reported widespread abuse of visa systems by individuals purportedly traveling for tourist or business reasons, but whose intention is to gain permanent residence. Because this abuse has become a sensitive political issue in some countries, there is considerable sentiment in favor of measures that have the intent or effect of making it more difficult for visitors to obtain a visa for temporary entry. Many of these measures are overtly discriminatory and effectively deny market access to legitimate service suppliers. One aspect of the enforcement mechanism enables authorities to treat applicants from certain countries less favorably than those from other countries on the basis of a pattern of abuse demonstrated by visa applicants of specific countries. Visa authorities respond by requiring more data from visa applicants from these countries, arguably violating the most-favored-nation (MFN) spirit that is fundamental to the GATS.

Any assessment of enforcement concerns must take into account the exceptions in the GATS framework that permit discriminatory treatment in specified situations. The GATS provides for many of these measures in its Annex on Movement of Natural Persons Supplying Services under the Agreement. The annex clearly excludes any measure related to citizenship, residence, or permanent employment from the provisions of the agreement. It further provides for the right of governments "to regulate entry of natural persons . . . including those measures necessary to protect the integrity of, and to ensure the orderly movement of natural persons across, its borders." Therefore, through the annex the GATS provides member countries with considerable flexibility to enforce measures that address abuse of the visa system. Yet authorities remain concerned that bound commitments in country schedules will undermine their flexibility to administer temporary entry measures in a responsive way. These concerns contributed to the relatively modest commitments under mode 4 in the Uruguay Round.

Protection of Labor Markets.   A second principal factor is the protection of labor markets, which, under the GATS, relates solely to situations involving temporary periods of stay. The high skill levels authorized in country schedules reflect this concern, which emerged as an issue for all countries regardless of their level of development. There are sound economic arguments for creating an environment conducive to the most competitive wages and salaries possible. In addition, countries can more effectively address the problem of labor shortages in some of the lower-skill categories through the use of more liberal regimes that provide for the temporary entry of persons in these categories. The political side of this issue is much less manageable for most countries. Fears about job stability, wage and salary erosion, and loss of the associated social benefits remain the paramount concern for governments whose political accountability will always take precedence over economic logic (and associated labor shortages) on such an issue. Thus the principal issue for trade negotiations is what is politically feasible in the way of binding skill levels that are to be covered under the fourth mode of supply.

Industrial and developing countries differ over this issue. Developing countries have a comparative advantage when calculating skills and remuneration and can be expected to push for the lowest skill levels possible in the environment of trade negotiations. Industrial countries have their own limitations, which are dictated by powerful political interests with concerns about employment stability. Any success in progressively liberalizing commitments covering the temporary entry of natural persons will rest on the capacity of all participants to strike the right balance on this issue—that is, to progress from the existing level of "senior managers and executives" to a more expanded, but realistic, work force universe.

The Issues and Challenges in Current Negotiations

The Negotiating Mandate

Article XIX of the GATS lays down the rules of engagement for further liberalization of trade in services, based on the notions of gradual liberalization and a balance of benefits in the exchange of concessions. For this purpose, the negotiating guidelines and procedures approved closely track the provisions of Article XIX. Under these guidelines, the scope of negotiations has to be comprehensive without a priori exclusion of any service sector or mode of supply. Though nothing specific to mode 4 negotiations appears in the guidelines, special attention to sectors and modes of supply of export interest to developing countries is envisaged. The principal negotiation technique is request and offer, although other possible negotiating techniques are described in this chapter. The guidelines also envisage negotiations on Article II (MFN) exemptions in the current schedules.

Because scheduling of commitments under the GATS is a complex task that calls for a comprehensive understanding of the agreement's architecture and specific provisions, guidelines on scheduling of specific commitments were drawn up during the Uruguay Round. Nevertheless, the initial commitments have been found wanting in both clarity and precision. Good examples of this in the current schedules are the limitations imposed by various types of needs tests. The current schedules do not indicate any criteria for their application. One reason for this shortcoming was the little time available during the Uruguay Round for meaningful scrutiny of draft schedules.

Building on the earlier guidelines and the actual scheduling experience in the Uruguay Round, Guidelines for Scheduling of Commitments for the Current Round have been approved (WTO 2001). The guidelines address two main questions: *What* items should be put on a schedule? *How* should they be entered—that is, the limitations to be placed, if any, on market access and on national treatment and scheduling of additional commitments that are not restrictions on market access and limitations on national treatment under Articles XVI and XVII. In addressing these questions, the guidelines cover all relevant issues, from the scope of coverage under each mode, to the relationship between different modes for effective access, to issues related to horizontal and sector-specific commitments. These guidelines should go a long way toward ensuring greater clarity and precision in recording specific commitments. The negotiating process in this round will have to pay much greater attention to draft country schedules to ensure this outcome.

The Current Negotiating Environment for Mode 4

As noted earlier, the Uruguay Round produced modest commitments under mode 4. The question, then, is whether the present environment is a better one for generating more substantive commitments in the current negotiations. Generally, the conditions appear to be much more favorable for a more ambitious outcome in this area of activity.

For most of the Uruguay Round mode 4 issues were framed—rhetorically—as differences between industrial and developing countries. Many delegations envisioned a rough balance of concessions measured by commitments developing countries would undertake under the commercial presence mode and those taken by industrial countries under mode 4. The debate polarized countries unnecessarily and provoked a more defensive posture on both sides. Industrial countries generally feared the worst from such a result, requiring concessions at lower skill levels of workers that they knew were not politically sustainable. In pressing their negotiating leverage, developing countries that placed a premium on this issue did nothing to assuage these fears. As the debate matured, however, some developing countries revealed that they were having the same problems that industrial countries were having with this issue.

But the very modest results in mode 4 cannot be attributed to this dynamic alone. During the Uruguay Round, few stakeholders pressed their interests on their own governments as well as others. One notable exception was the Indian National Association of Software and Service Companies (NASSCOM), which actively (and effectively) devoted time and resources to persuading countries to make commitments affecting software engineers and their freedom of temporary entry under the GATS. In the United States a very powerful and diverse lobby used the GATS negotiations to generate a U.S. binding of the H1B visa provision covering the temporary employment of highly skilled foreign workers in U.S. companies and firms. By contrast, mode 3 (commercial presence) stakeholders were widespread and well organized. That mode 3 commitments were broader and deeper than those for mode 4 has much to do with the stakeholders who convinced governments of their needs.

Since the Uruguay Round, many countries have undertaken a more comprehensive assessment of their specific needs in the area of temporary entry and stay. In addition to the more traditional market access issues, they have paid greater attention to issues such as transparency, where market access is frequently denied because authorities are less than clear about application requirements and the data needed to gain temporary admission to a country. A related issue is that of utilizing new technologies to make temporary entry requirements more easily obtainable. Finally, these countries are paying more attention to the absence of criteria that govern admission based on economic needs.

In addition, the number of stakeholders in both industrial and developing countries has grown. As the world economy has become more globalized, companies and firms find increasingly that they need to deploy personnel on a short-term basis to meet specific project and contract requirements in different countries, often within short deadlines. These companies and firms are frustrated with visa procedures that can delay the entry of personnel by months, frequently resulting in the loss of business. The result is that the United States Coalition of Services Industries and the European Services Forum have endorsed improved mode 4 commitments by all countries to expedite the movement of professional-level personnel. These needs are incorporated in an effort to benefit companies and firms with overseas affiliates, as well as enterprises that do not have overseas operations, thereby expanding the benefits of such undertakings for all countries. The specific developments mentioned here do not capture the objectives of all stakeholders with an export interest. However, mode 4 has clearly emerged as a strategic component of trade in services in many countries, in sharp contrast to the environment that existed in the Uruguay Round.

In the current negotiations, delegations have presented "negotiating proposals" that indicate their interests in further liberalizing trade in services. Only six delegations have made specific proposals in the area of temporary entry. Objectives varied widely in these proposals, some of which stopped short of advocating improvements in market access. Four of these proposals are summarized briefly here:

- The *U.S. proposal* focuses on improving the transparency of procedures to make the process of applying for temporary entry easier and more predictable. More specifically, it proposes improved transparency in responses by authorities to visa applications and their reasons for denying visas. It also points to the need for additional regulatory disciplines to ensure implementation of existing commitments. The U.S. proposal does not include suggestions for expanded commitments to market access.
- The *EU proposal* calls for expanding market access commitments beyond current levels, although it does not specify those areas in which improvements could be made. In addition to a call for improved transparency of procedures, greater access to information, and published criteria for economic needs tests, the EU proposal places considerable emphasis on the harmonization of definitions of mode 4 categories, including common terms for intracorporate transferees.
- The *Canadian proposal* calls explicitly for expanded market access commitments and specifies areas in which countries should improve their schedules. These areas include expansion of coverage to include professionals, including employees of companies and firms that do not have foreign affiliates. Canada's proposal also calls for improved transparency of procedures for obtaining temporary entry, as well as the obligation to specify the criteria governing economic needs tests.
- The *Indian proposal*, the most comprehensive of the mode 4 proposals put forward during the negotiating proposal exercise, incorporates ideas found in a paper by Chanda (2001). India proposes improved market access commitments to the movement of individual professionals, technicians, and "assistant professionals," both on a horizontal and sector-specific basis. It also calls for a more disaggregated set of categories for scheduling purposes, suggesting ISCO-88 (International Standard Classification of Occupations) as a possible reference point. And it proposes improved administrative procedures for obtaining visas and work permits, together with published criteria that define needs tests. In addition, it calls for the binding of bilateral totalization agreements affecting social security payments, with exemption from social security contributions for developing country professionals. Finally, it proposes norms that establish the basis for the mutual recognition of the education and qualifications

of professionals, thus joining the harmonization of professional qualifications with visa requirements as part of the mode 4 exercise.

It is too early to use these negotiating proposals as a measure of member countries' newfound interest in mode 4. It will be more interesting to assess Members' level of interest after requests are tabled in June 2002 and offers are submitted in March 2003. Generally, governments have shown a greater willingness to engage the issue in a far more substantive and detailed manner, free of some of the old rhetoric and more focused on specific improvements that can be realized in schedules. It is less than clear, however, just how far governments are willing to commit to binding their systems of temporary entry into international legal obligations. Much will depend on the willingness of stakeholders in every country to present their case to member governments and to develop the same constituency other services areas have achieved in the past.

Substantive Market Access Issues

The earlier analysis in this chapter of the current level of scheduled commitments under the GATS revealed that, except for telecom services and to some extent financial services, the actual commitments to liberalizing trade were modest. For mode 4, it was even more so—that is, there was hardly any liberalization. The analysis attributes this disappointing outcome to several factors such as the new and unfamiliar nature of the GATS, the paucity of services trade statistics, the relative lack of interest of stakeholders in pressing their interests in this area, and the political and regulatory dynamics of mode 4 commitment negotiations. This time around, however, a positive outlook exists on all these elements. The framework agreement is better understood today thanks to the scrutiny of trade policy experts and academics. There may not be a consensus on its shortcomings as a trade agreement, but there is recognition of the need for greater clarity in rules and in scheduling commitments. Industry stakeholders also need greater clarity and transparency in the implementation of rules governing temporary movement.

Even though the political and regulatory dynamics for the exchange of concessions in this round have yet to emerge, there is an underlying assumption that the outcome under mode 4 will have to be significant if the round is to deliver a big package of liberalized trade. Yet it would not be realistic to expect any revolutionary developments in liberalizing mode 4 movement. As in all efforts to liberalize trade, the outcome is likely to be evolutionary and incremental. The challenge is to find the right balance between ambition and reality. It is in this context that the rest of this section looks at ways in which mode 4 negotiations may yield significant market opening measures.

Wider and Deeper Commitments under Mode 4. As explained earlier, countries have addressed mode 4 commitments by undertaking specific obligations that extend horizontally to all of the service sectors included in their schedule of commitments. However, it may be necessary to supplement this liberalization technique with commitments that pertain to the peculiar regulatory circumstances that govern temporary entry in different categories of sectors in order to deepen the extent of obligations under the temporary entry mode of supply. Sector-specific commitments can be used to impart greater precision to manpower categories, thereby improving transparency and reducing the scope for discretionary action to deny temporary entry. Proposals to this effect are already on the table and will have to be negotiated. Because horizontal commitments are limited to service sectors included in country schedules, the inclusion of additional sectors and subsectors, particularly skill-intensive ones (e.g., health, education, and other knowledge-based service sectors), might be needed to widen the scope of commitments under mode 4.

Classification of Natural Persons as Service Providers and Issues Pertaining to Skill Levels. A common understanding of categories of natural persons as service providers will help to promote the certainty and predictability of the commitments for the temporary movement of natural persons. As noted earlier, in the Uruguay Round negotiations it was proposed that an illustrative list of natural persons performing particular services in broad categories of sectors and skill levels be established and used for scheduling commitments. This illustrative list of natural persons was not established during the negotiations, in part because of lack of time and in part because of the negotiating fatigue generated by the marathon character of the round. However, as pointed out elsewhere in this chapter, the negotiating process, without a conscious effort, did produce for movement associated with mode 3 a more or less common nomenclature of natural persons in scheduled horizontal commitments. This nomenclature is not sufficient, however, to address the basic concerns about certainty and precision in scheduling mode 4 commitments.

One proposal calls for using the International Labour Organisation's ISCO-88 for scheduling mode 4 commitments. ISCO covers the entire range of occupations from top company executives to unskilled labor. Nevertheless, the comprehensive nature of the ISCO classification and its coverage of unskilled categories are viewed as an impediment to its adoption for scheduling purposes. There also is some industry concern that many of the job categories will become obsolete because of changes in job classifications stemming from technological change. Yet with adaptation and some degree of customization, it could serve as a basis for negotiations and scheduling of commitments. Classification of natural persons on an occupational basis should be treated as a procedural issue for imparting precision, specificity, and predictability to commitments under mode 4, much along the lines of the financial services classification in the Annex on Financial Services in the GATS. Such a classification also will help in segregating occupations and skills for conditions such as the economic needs test and the criteria for the application of such tests to ensure they are relevant and specific to a particular occupational category.

Although the agreement covers all categories of natural persons and although economists make a good case for the movement of even unskilled categories across borders, there are sensitivities about job security and the movement of low-skilled and unskilled service providers. Yet it may be possible to expand the scope of temporary movement to levels below those now covered by the GATS schedules. Some skill shortages in industrial countries could be relieved by the temporary movement of natural persons with such skills from developing countries. In fact, a great deal of seasonal labor, even unskilled, is moving between Members on a bilateral basis and in the context of economic integration agreements. Winters and others (2002) have suggested that some of the bilateral seasonal labor movement agreements be shifted to a multilateral basis in the current negotiations. At any rate, negotiators will have to strike the right balance between job security sensitivities and liberalization expectations under this mode.

Among the conditions attached to the access commitments under mode 4 in the current schedules are economic needs and other tests such as local market needs and management needs. As currently framed, they appear to be inconsistent with the letter and the spirit of the GATS framework because the schedules do not bring out the criteria for the application and administration of such tests. Some studies have made the case for multilateral guidelines on the criteria for applying such tests (see, for example, Chanda 2001). The criteria themselves must be clear and explicit and included in the commitment schedules, as is envisaged in the negotiating guidelines. Other improvements in this area must aim at reducing the occupational categories to which such tests may be applied.

Horizontal versus Sector-specific Commitments: A Flexible Approach.   As noted earlier, commitments under the temporary entry mode have been made in a horizontal fashion, producing the same level of obligation for all the sectors that Members have entered into their schedules. The horizontal form of commitment, which is reflected in the "Headnotes to Schedules," follows national laws and regulations, which generally classify temporary entry procedures according to job skills rather than specific service sectors. The question is whether this approach should remain the preferred one in the current negotiations, or whether some, if not all, undertakings should be made on the basis of individual sectors. Such a flexible approach might improve the overall level of commitments for mode 4.

Members have not bound the full measure of their existing laws when making commitments horizontally for the service sectors included in their schedules of commitments. At a minimum, horizontal scheduling should be considered through a top-down approach, where all service sectors except those that are specifically excluded would be covered by commitments under mode 4. This approach is certainly feasible because most measures affecting temporary movement do not distinguish among given sectors. For some sectors, this may represent the only commitment to market access and national treatment under the four modes of supply. However, it would be a more faithful reflection of existing law in the member country.

Several delegations, as part of the negotiating proposal exercise, indicated a preference to include both sectoral and generic configurations of coverage. For many participants, certain sectors may fall under a different set of temporary entry rules, requiring separate entries in schedules. Inevitably, some sectors may present a level of sensitivity that requires their exclusion from coverage. The goal should be to establish a negotiating framework that yields the greatest possible liberalization, regardless of how a Member assumes obligations.

Where horizontal scheduling is the rule, some delegations have urged that participants work from a common format of job classification categories, using ISCO-88, which breaks down nine occupational groups. However, the ISCO categories, while useful in their own right, do not necessarily follow the skill structures in national laws that establish the framework for temporary entry. Inevitably, some customization may be necessary among participants to fully reflect their own regimes. For all of the uniformity in the existing schedules covering the senior manager and executive category, it may be more onerous to negotiate other job categories that do not fit the peculiar standards set by national laws.

Formula Liberalization/Model Schedule Approach: Problems and Prospects. Since preparations began for the current GATS negotiations, delegations have considered more efficient ways of negotiating commitments. Service sectors present challenges because they lack a single instrument of protection—the tariff serves as such an instrument for goods. Moreover, considerable differences exist among service sectors and the unrelated regulatory environments in which each must operate. Nevertheless, some success has been achieved in negotiating around common parameters in individual sectors, as was the case for the "reference paper" commitments in basic telecommunications (WTO 1996). A similar effort was made in maritime services. As for temporary entry, it is worth exploring common approaches, because most countries basically use the same systems of regulation to control such entry. The question is: What areas of temporary entry lend themselves to a common approach, and how can it be utilized among the participants to further progressive liberalization?

A formula approach, the most ambitious of these techniques, aims to achieve identical commitments from all, or nearly all, participants. Yet a formula aimed at achieving identical commitments to market access under mode 4 might prove to be counterproductive because legal regimes for meeting temporary entry standards differ among countries. Inevitably, some countries will be prepared to do more than others in capturing the range of job skills that have different political dynamics in different countries. However, formula approaches to greater transparency of procedures may be more successful in gaining identical levels of obligation.

A more flexible negotiating tool would be the "model schedule" approach, which sets common negotiating objectives around which participants assume commitments. The formula and model schedule approaches are similar in that they propose a single set of obligations. The difference is that a model schedule is a template around which participants may bind levels of obligations that may differ from the specific goal of the model schedule. At the same time, each participant bears a certain burden in demonstrating why it cannot bind according to the model schedule. Such an approach encourages greater uniformity of scheduling (but inherently does not propose it), and it can lead to a better climate for negotiations than the more traditional request and offer method.

Negotiating through a formula or model schedule will only succeed, however, if the proposal reflects the delicate combination of ambition and realism and addresses the totality of regulatory issues of concern to all participants. Generally, the model schedule approach might be the better negotiating tool in dealing with levels of market access in mode 4. A formula effort, which would imply uniformity of scheduling, would seem useful in addressing transparency and other obligations related to "best practices."

Overcoming the Barriers to Effective Access

Authorization of Entry.   A major objective of all immigration rules and regulations is to control and eliminate unauthorized entry of natural persons. These laws and regulations give regulators a large measure of discretion in dealing with the new ways found to circumvent the regulations prohibiting unauthorized entry. While perhaps necessary for preventing unauthorized entry, this discretion erodes the value of a scheduled commitment for temporary entry of natural persons under the GATS by creating delays in processing visa applications and issuing visas. The rules were not meant originally to address trade needs, and certainly not the needs of a multilateral trade commitment. Toward the end of the Uruguay Round negotiations, the delegation from India introduced the idea of Members establishing separate fast-track procedures for granting visas for the movement of natural persons under their commitments, but there was no time to pursue this idea. Since then, the idea has been revived and discussed in the literature at great length. It does make sense to separate temporary movement under a GATS commitment from other kinds of movement. It also makes sense to provide for quicker procedures and elimination of much of the discretion to the issuing authorities, subject to safeguards for joint monitoring and cooperation between the home and host countries to prevent abuse. The host and the home countries have a common interest in ensuring that the movement of natural persons under the GATS remains temporary and is not abused for securing permanent entry into the labor market of the host country. This common interest can become the basis for establishing a separate set of procedures for granting visas for the movement of natural persons related to Members' GATS commitments.

Recognition of qualifications has emerged as an issue in the implementation of mode 4 commitments. Although this issue has proved difficult even in the context of economic integration agreements, it does, nevertheless, deserve attention.

Article VII of the GATS envisages transparency, nondiscrimination, and objectivity in granting recognition of qualifications and encourages member countries to enter into mutual recognition agreements or to extend recognition autonomously to other member countries. Yet it appears that so far nothing much has happened by way of recognition. The obligation under Article VI.6, requiring member countries to "provide for adequate procedures to verify the competence of professionals" of other member countries where specific commitments have been made to professional services, has by and large not been discharged. One problem is the absence of any incentives for Members to accord such recognition in sectors where mutual benefit in terms of access is not apparent. The suggestions made in the Indian proposal aimed at improving this situation deserve consideration.

The relationship of harmonized professional qualifications and improved access under mode 4 presents a different situation. Aside from the challenge of the WTO taking on the task of encouraging and engaging in bargaining over regulatory changes related to the professions, there is some question about how often qualifications are a condition for entry. As pointed out elsewhere, most professionals provide their services, through temporary entry and stay, as consultants and advisers, leaving such things as signing audits and engineering plans to locally licensed persons. All the issues related to this process, such as improved transparency of procedures, needs tests, and recognition of qualifications, will have to be explored, including the possibility of a set of multilateral disciplines along the lines of the WTO's reference paper on telecommunications services (WTO 1996). The outcome of the work in the Working Group on Domestic Regulation has some relevance in this context.

A "GATS Visa."   One of the growing problems in providing services through mode 4 is the length of time required for visa approval. Service enterprises face time-sensitive client obligations that require their presence in other countries. Indeed, as international trade and investment have expanded over the years, these enterprises have found that their customers reside increasingly outside their borders. Frequently, then, these enterprises lose business because the current visa regimes make it impossible for them to deploy resources to meet business needs. The idea of a single visa available for entry in all WTO member countries was discussed during the Uruguay Round, but the concept was at the time more than countries were ready or able to discuss.

Nevertheless, the GATS visa idea has been elaborated both in the negotiating proposal by the government of India, as well as in a model schedule approach endorsed by the services industry bodies of the United States and the EU. In the proposal by the services industry coalitions, the "permit" would not provide automatic access to every WTO member country; it would require application and approval by the member country to whom application is made. Once visa authorities have granted approval to the employee of the enterprise concerned, that employee would have the right to enter the foreign country for the life of the visa without seeking reapproval. Although the proposal has other features, it is intended to cover professional employees at all levels, requiring a university degree as an educational minimum.

The features of the GATS visa in the Indian proposal are very similar to those in the U.S. and European industry proposal. India would use the GATS visa as a way of separating persons seeking temporary entry from those interested in a permanent stay. The procedures for temporary and permanent entry would be separated, with the objective of streamlining those for temporary entry. India proposes strict time frames for obtaining the GATS visa, with easier renewal and transfer procedures. It also calls for GATS visas that can be issued to select enterprises for use by their employees sent abroad temporarily. It suggests, but does not specify, "adequate in-built safeguard mechanisms" against efforts to enter the permanent labor market.

Many countries already operate visa systems similar to the permit idea—that is, once a visa has been obtained, it is usable for an unlimited number of entries over the life of the visa. For other countries the permit idea would represent a substantial improvement in the effort to deploy persons on a time-sensitive basis when needed.

The GATS visa, however it is formulated, could bring about measurable improvements to the current system used by service providers to gain temporary access in other WTO countries, and it could greatly facilitate market access opportunities that otherwise could not be realized. It must, however, respect law enforcement and other regulatory needs or it has very little chance of acceptance among a critical mass of WTO participants. As indicated earlier in this chapter, immigration authorities contend constantly with the problem of visa abuses in which the granting of temporary stay results in efforts by the visa holder to gain permanent stay. To be feasible, the concept must enable authorities to complete the initial screening process in a manner that meets legitimate problems of abuse. It also must recognize the need to streamline the current environment with its repetitive, time-consuming procedures. The concept of expedited entry after initial screening is a feasible way of addressing this problem. Another critical issue is the skill levels of persons to whom the permit applies. As indicated earlier in this chapter, negotiating history has demonstrated that it is more difficult to incorporate lesser skilled persons into GATS commitments, in part because of the perceived effects on labor markets and wages. This will be a critical aspect of any such negotiation.

"Best Practices" that Address Issues of Transparency.   Persons seeking temporary entry are frequently denied timely visas because of the lengthy, onerous procedures in place in most WTO member countries. The visa application process in many countries lacks the transparency needed to enable applicants to provide the information requested by authorities—that is, information requirements may exist in writing but are impossible to obtain because no system is in place to ensure widespread public availability. This situation is particularly burdensome for employees of small enterprises that cannot afford to employ specialists to process visa applications and anticipate the needs of regulators on the basis of experience. In other instances, applicants are victims of egregious requests for information that could not have been anticipated and have very little relevance to the applicant's suitability for obtaining such a visa. This issue is not an easy one to address, because regulatory authorities deserve some flexibility in asking for supplementary information when questions arise about individual applicants. Nevertheless, anecdotal stories abound about requests for information that seem clearly designed to discourage or otherwise delay the process of obtaining a visa for temporary entry. Examples include family histories of the applicant, including formal evidence of birth by distant relatives and their spouses. Furthermore, too many countries refuse to provide information about the status of a visa application—another lack of transparency.

GATS transparency rules, which simply require publication or public availability of measures, are not adequate to meet these procedural problems. It is critical that member countries assume additional commitments under GATS Article XVIII that reflect "best practices" of greater transparency and predictability. The following elements might be included in a "best practices" set of commitments by all parties, regardless of the level of market access and national treatment obligations they have assumed:

- Public availability of a full and complete set of procedures that describe in sufficient detail the information and supporting documentation associated with a visa application, along with a description of the complete process for obtaining a visa. Authorities, where possible, should make this information available electronically in consolidated form.
- The establishment of deadlines for the completion of applications, together with written explanations for the denial of visas or the failure of visa authorities to provide information required for the application.
- A full description of the limitations to market access and other procedures, such as wage parity requirements, quota restrictions, and economic needs tests.
- An opportunity for interested parties to comment on regulations prior to their entry into force in member countries that have procedures governing prior comment on regulations.
- In those member countries in which economic needs tests are entered as a limitation to market access, establishment for public availability of the conditions governing economic needs, including the quantitative or qualitative criteria that establish the basis for such needs.
- Cooperation arrangements among the parties to enable both the home and host country to monitor the return of the visa applicant at the end of the temporary period.

These suggested best practices rules are hardly exhaustive, but they do bring greater predictability and therefore greater speed to the visa approval process. It is hoped that they will provide a basis for discouraging some requirements clearly intended to delay indefinitely an applicant's ability to obtain a visa. As stated earlier in this chapter, the needs of law enforcement and safety must be respected to achieve significant improvements in the granting of temporary entry visas. However, a more transparent and predictable system, stripped of redundancy, surely will complement, not compromise, efforts to improve security and safety, as well as prevent abuse.

Issues Related to Article VI.4

Domestic Regulations: Article VI.4.   Regulation is a sine qua non for liberalization in services, whether undertaken nationally or internationally to address market failures and public and social policy concerns. In its preamble, the GATS explicitly recognizes Members' freedom to regulate and to introduce new regulations in services. This freedom is practically unrestrained save the transparency obligation of publication and notification of regulations and their reasonable and impartial application. In addition, there is regulatory freedom in certain respects under the general exceptions clause (Article XIV) and, in the case of financial services, freedom in prudential regulations.

Article VI.4 focuses specifically on certain types of regulations to do with consumer protection and related public policy concerns. It mandates development of the disciplines needed for qualification requirements and procedures, technical standards, and licensing requirements with the objective of ensuring that such requirements are:

a. based on objective and transparent criteria, such as competence and the ability to supply the service;
b. not more burdensome than necessary to ensure the quality of the service;
c. in the case of licensing procedures, not in themselves a restriction on the supply of the service.

Under a ministerial decision made at Marrakech in April 1994, a working party was mandated to examine and report with recommendations on the disciplines necessary to ensure realization of the objectives of Article VI.4 in the case of professional services, with priority being given to the accountancy sector. Based on the recommendations of this working party, the decision on "Disciplines on Domestic Regulation in the Accountancy Sector" was adopted by the Council for Trade in Services on December 14, 1998 (WTO 1998b). The acceptance of the decision by Members is on a voluntary basis for the present. Subsequently, by a decision on April 26, 1999, the Council for Trade in Services set up a Working Party on Domestic Regulations to develop any necessary disciplines under the Article VI.4 mandate (WTO 1999). The working party is directed to develop generally applicable disciplines for all sectors, but it also may develop disciplines as appropriate for individual sectors or groups of sectors, keeping open the issue of application of disciplines on a horizontal or sectoral basis.

The working party is currently identifying and exploring issues relevant to its mandate. On the basis of the text of Article VI.4, accountancy sector disciplines, and the provisions of other WTO agreements on regulation of goods—specifically the Agreement on Technical Barriers to Trade and the Agreement on the Application of Sanitary and Phytosanitary Measures—it has been suggested that disciplines be developed in four areas: necessity, transparency, equivalence, and international standards. The WTO Secretariat has drawn up a checklist of issues on these and related issues such as the scope of ArticleVI.4 itself.

It is not possible to go into the merits of the issues in the checklist within the scope of this chapter, except to suggest that strong and enforceable disciplines are critically important in exploiting market opportunities in professional services. There is merit in developing a common set of disciplines applicable to all the professional services.

Meanwhile, some questions have been raised about the relationship between Articles XVI and XVII, on the one hand, and Article VI.4, on the other. In the GATS there is a fundamental legal distinction between these two sets of provisions. Articles XVI and XVII belong to Part III on Specific Commitments, and Article VI belongs to Part II on General Obligations and Disciplines. As a result, the elimination of restrictions on market access and national treatment is subject to the negotiation of specific commitments, and the obligation to minimize the trade-restrictive elements of domestic regulations is a general obligation that would be subject to the disciplines developed under Article VI.4. The legal status of these measures naturally differs. Measures restricting market access and national treatment are prohibited, unless scheduled, in sectors in which specific commitments have been undertaken, whereas they can be maintained in sectors that are not committed.

Other Relevant Issues.   These issues relate to applying conditions to the access of natural persons to such things as wage parity and social security contributions and benefits. A case has been made for developing a multilateral understanding on the application of these conditions along the lines of such guidelines for other conditions.

Conclusions and Recommendations

This chapter has offered suggestions for how the current GATS negotiations might bring about improvements in the schedules of commitments by WTO member countries. These suggestions are largely drawn from the current environment of trade in services and the needs of service providers in a rapidly changing global economy. This analysis has been based on one fundamental conclusion: trade in services can be facilitated in measurable ways through more substantive commitments in the fourth mode of supply. The current environment is conducive to that purpose, which presents an opportunity for governments to address some of the more difficult political issues associated with the temporary entry issue. The challenge for WTO Members is to develop a negotiating framework that will produce the best possible outcome. However, specific suggestions are preceded by a summary of some important conclusions of this chapter.

First, the GATS architecture and its specific provisions, including the definition of trade in services and the annex on the movement of natural persons, are the product of a negotiating foray into what was until recently uncharted waters. It was an attempt to address and reconcile, through a single framework, the diverse and sometimes conflicting interests of participants at different levels of development in an area of great regulatory diversity and complexity. Although some of the North-South controversies in the negotiations look sterile now, the modal approach to definition reflects, for developing countries, acceptance of their central concern about parity/symmetry in the treatment of the factor movement of capital and labor, and, for industrial countries, assurance that investment in services can be part of a trade framework. The notion of parity was, in the ultimate analysis, to find reflection in market access opportunities under modes 3 and 4, notwithstanding the problems of measurement.

Second, the current level of scheduled commitments, except in the telecom and financial services sectors, represents modest liberalization. In the case of mode 4, there has been little liberalization.

Third, the outcome has to produce significant improvements in mode 4 liberalization (by way of providing effective market access), if there is to be a big liberalization package overall. Otherwise, the GATS might end up as a "harvester of autonomous liberalization in services" rather than a catalyst for future liberalization,"as observed in Chapter 1 of this report.

Last, fortunately the present is a propitious time to attempt this liberalization because of developments in the areas of technology and demographics, greater interest among stakeholders, and increasing discourse between trade experts and regulators on how to implement commitments and prevent abuse. A better understanding also has been gained of the scope of the movement under mode 4 and the common interest of host and home countries in keeping the movement temporary.

It is against the backdrop of these conclusions that the following steps are proposed to realize greater liberalization and effective market access under mode 4:

1. Negotiate market access and national treatment commitments from a common template that is sufficiently flexible for parties with differing interests and varying levels of ambition.
2. Mount a priority effort to gain a single text of agreed-upon commitments that would improve the transparency of granting temporary entry to services providers.
3. Aim to arrive at a generally agreed-upon formulation of the skill levels of workers affected by the temporary entry negotiations as a part of the negotiating process itself. This will be a difficult issue to reconcile among participants, but an early consensus, however informally reached, might help to expedite the overall level of improved commitments.
4. Impart greater clarity to rules and commitments by negotiating guidelines for the application of rules and conditions to market access commitments.

References

Chanda, R. 2001. "Movement of Natural Persons and Trade in Services: Liberalizing Temporary Movement of Labor under the GATS." *World Economy* 24 (5).

Winters, L. A., T. L. Walmsley, Z. K. Wang, and R. Grynberg. 2002. "Liberalising Labour Mobility Under the GATS." Economic Paper No. 53. Commonwealth Secretariat, London.

WTO (World Trade Organization). 1996. "Telecommunications Services: Reference Paper." Negotiating Group on Basic Communications. April 24 <*www.wto.org/english/tratop_e/serv_e/telecom_e/tel23_e.htm*>.

———. 1998a. "Council for Trade in Services—Presence of Natural Persons (Mode 4)—Background Note by the Secretariat." Document S/C/W/75, December 8 <*www.wto.org*>.

———. 1998b. "Disciplines on Domestic Regulation in the Accountancy Sector—Adopted by the Council for Trade in Services on 14 December 1998." Document S/L/64, December 17 <*www.wto.org*>.

———. 1999. "Decision on Domestic Regulation—Adopted by the Council for Trade in Services on 26 April 1999." Document 2/L/70, April 28 <*www.wto.org*>.

———. 2001. "Trade in Services—Guidelines for the Scheduling of Specific Commitments under the GATS—Adopted by the Council for Trade in Services on 23 March 2001." Document S/L/92, March 28 <*www.wto.org*>.

4

THE ECONOMIC IMPLICATIONS OF LIBERALIZING MODE 4 TRADE

L. Alan Winters[*]

This chapter sets out the economic case for liberalizing the temporary flow of labor between countries for the purpose of providing services. In fact, this is the subject of the negotiations currently under way on mode 4 of the General Agreement on Trade in Services (GATS). Mode 4 is one of the four modes of supplying services recognized by the GATS and refers explicitly to the temporary movement of natural persons. Until now a mere bit player in the GATS drama, mode 4 is at last starting to command some attention from negotiators and policymakers. This chapter, and some more detailed companion pieces,[1] argue that this attention is long overdue and that serious efforts to liberalize the temporary movement of natural persons (TMNP) from developing to industrial member countries could generate very large mutual benefits.

The very heart of international trade, be it in goods or in factors, lies in exploiting differences. The larger the differences, the larger are the potential gains from opening up international trade. For TMNP, potentially large returns would be feasible if medium and less skilled workers, who are relatively abundant in developing countries, were allowed to move and provide their services in industrial countries. The review of the existing empirical studies of factor mobility and the new estimates described in this chapter agree that even relatively small movements of labor would produce huge returns. An increase in industrial countries' quotas on the inward movements of both skilled and unskilled temporary workers equivalent to 3 percent of their work forces would generate an estimated increase in world welfare of more than US$150 billion a year.[2]

[*]L. Alan Winters is a professor at the School of Social Sciences, University of Sussex. He is grateful to his coauthors of a major study for the Commonwealth Secretariat (Winters and others 2002)—Terrie Walmsley, Zhen Kun Wang, and Roman Grynberg—for inputs and discussions on mode 4; to Antonia Carzaniga and J. Michael Finger for comments on mode 4; to Aaditya Mattoo and an anonymous referee for comments and advice on this chapter; and to Angelica Mayorga and Reto Speck for logistical help.

These gains are widely shared within the world economy. Moreover, as their populations age and their average levels of training and education rise, industrial countries will face an increasing scarcity of less skilled labor. Given that, at least in some occupations, there is really no substitute for human labor, the demand for and benefits of allowing TMNP will increase through time. Thus, although TMNP poses formidable political challenges, it actually offers a strong commonality of interest between developing and industrial countries.

Unlike the concerns associated with the mass migration of less skilled workers, fears for cultural identity, problems of assimilation, and the drain on the public purse are hardly relevant to TMNP. The biggest concern it raises is its competitive challenge to local less skilled workers. But this challenge is no more imposing than that presented to such workers by imports of labor-intensive goods from developing countries, which has been overcome by the weight of economic gain that trade can deliver and by policies to ease adjustment among local less skilled workers in industrial countries. Applied with the same sensitivity and the same sorts of policies as trade policy reform in goods has received in the past, the temporary movement of less skilled workers between countries would offer those countries the chance to reap some very large gains from trade.

The chapter is divided into three parts. The first part discusses ways in which one might think about and model the liberalization of mode 4. This discussion is based on two polar forms—treating mode 4 as perfectly akin to goods trade and treating it as perfectly akin to labor migration. The first part then discusses the ways in which these polar forms may be relaxed in future empirical exercises to try to estimate the effects of liberalization. The second part summarizes a new estimation exercise on the benefits of mode 4 liberalization, treating it as akin to migration. Such a treatment is argued to be a reasonable assumption in the context of the kind of models that economists have to use for this sort of exercise, and it suggests the very large economic benefits already noted. More details of the estimation exercise are available in the original sources. Finally, the third part of this chapter considers briefly the arguments for and technicalities of compensating domestic workers who are disadvantaged by inflows of workers from abroad. As just noted, these are mainly unskilled workers, who have proved adept at resisting goods market liberalization, and it is argued here that mode 4 will need to treat them with as much consideration as they received from goods market liberalization.

The Economic Case for Labor Mobility

To date, the TMNP has defeated attempts to fit it into a robust analytical model. At one extreme, it appears to be no different from cross-border services trade (mode 1), which, in turn, is often argued to be analytically no different from ordinary goods trade. For example, an academician traveling to Geneva to deliver a paper in person is analytically close to that paper being sent in hard copy form, electronic form, or even by video link. Thus one part of the "mode 4 story" is the familiar trade story.

At the other extreme, mode 4 has much in common with "regular" migration, in which workers actually relocate from one country to another. This commonality is particularly true where periods of stay are long or where a particular job in country B is filled by a continuous flow of temporary workers from country A, each being replaced by another as his or her contract expires. Although such a "revolving door" provision has different implications for social integration, network formation, and intergenerational spillovers from education, the basic fact that B gains a worker and A loses one is akin to migration. This model could be particularly relevant to agency-provided flows of midlevel professional workers such as nurses and teachers. Thus a second strand of thought about mode 4 is based on the economics of factor mobility. Because this strand of thought is less familiar to trade negotiators than the trade literature, some space is devoted to it here.

Yet neither of the polar models—trade or migration—seems to capture the full essence of mode 4 mobility. Therefore, a small portion of this chapter is devoted to extensions and refinements to those models in an effort to devise a more satisfying analysis. Because ultimately the questions at stake are empirical, the last subsection focuses on how the benefits of mode 4 liberalization might be estimated in practice. But its musings on this subject are very preliminary, and improving them would seem to be a very high priority for further research.

International Trade

At its simplest, trade in services is no different from trade in goods, for which there is now widespread acceptance of the benefits of a relatively liberal trading regime. These benefits include:

- Reaping economies of scale
- Gaining the benefits of specialization according to comparative advantage
- Learning by doing and developing expertise by concentrating on particular sectors
- Importing better technologies
- Creating stronger competition.

All of these benefits apply equally to services as well as goods. Indeed, there are good reasons to expect greater gains from trade liberalization in the service sectors than in goods:

- Barriers are generally greater in services than in goods, although, of course, there are exceptions such as in agriculture.
- Many barriers explicitly and dramatically reduce competition in the services sector, which can be most costly in terms of efficiency.
- Many services are needed to sustain efficiency and competition in other parts of the economy—for example, communications, transportation, or banking. Liberalization in these sectors can have broad and deep, but essentially indirect, effects. For example, improved services can create completely new markets for other goods, which, as Romer (1994) shows, can induce dramatic improvements in welfare: improved transport and communications can allow peripheral farmers to sell in the cities or to obtain previously unavailable credit that could dramatically increase their output.
- Services as a whole account for a greater share of income (and, frequently, employment) than industry and agriculture together.

Thus, for example, Hertel and others (1999) suggest that, while 40 percent liberalization in agriculture and manufacturing will each raise global welfare by about $70 billion a year, similar liberalization in services could contribute more than $300 billion. These modeling estimates should not be taken too literally—TMNP is only part of service delivery—but the orders of magnitude are striking and even a small share of so large a benefit renders mode 4 significant. Some observers might counter that TMNP currently accounts for only 1.4 percent of the value of services trade (Karsenty 2000), which demonstrates that it has little promise for large gains. In fact, it shows the very opposite: the low figure arises from the very high barriers to TMNP, and so TMNP offers the greatest potential returns to liberalization.

None of this argues for wholly unregulated international trade in services. Governments will always have a fiduciary role in regulating many services to counter the problems that arise from market failures such as moral hazard or asymmetric information. Rather, services trade liberalization, including that of mode 4, calls for ensuring that such regulations are geared to solving market failures rather than to protection, that they do so in "trade-efficient" ways, and that, *above all*, they enhance rather than curtail competition (Mattoo 2000).

The parallel with goods trade liberalization does, however, call for a very close look at the arguments that services require generalized infant industry protection or that they have national security dimensions. These seem more like the traditional objections to trade liberalization based on special interests than analytical solutions to specific problems.

Here it is worth a reminder that although goods trade liberalization is widely accepted as one of the key components of the policy cocktail required for growth and efficiency, it is not without its challenges. Trade reform is strongly redistributional, both among producers, governments, and consumers, and within those groups. Although widespread reform seems likely to benefit nearly everyone eventually—what Max Corden (1984) called the "Hicksian optimism"—there are likely to be short-term hardships, and long-term casualties cannot be ruled out. The political economy literature on the way in which these redistributions affect the prospects of reform—for example, Rodrik (1995)—is substantial. Additional literature discusses the need for, and design of, complementary and compensatory policies to counteract their adverse effects—see, for example, DFID (2000) and Sapir (2001). McCulloch, Winters, and Cirera (2001) offer a detailed discussion of the way in which trade liberalization might affect poverty, while Winters (2002) considers the Doha Development Agenda and poverty. All of these issues are likely to be as relevant to mode 4 as to goods market liberalization, and the lessons learned from the latter should be considered.

Trade and Factor Rewards (Wages)

The fundamental premise of the neoclassical theory of international trade is that the incentive to trade arises from differences in countries' relative costs of producing different goods. These differences, in turn, arise from differences in countries' endowments of various factors of production. These endowments are assumed to be immobile between countries but mobile between sectors within any country. In its purest form, the theory generates the remarkable prediction that free (and costless) trade in goods between countries whose endowments are, in a technical sense, "not too different" would be sufficient to ensure that their factor prices are equalized—the so-called factor price equalization (FPE) theorem of Nobel Laureate Paul Samuelson (1949). If this were true, trade in goods and the movement of factors of production would be substitutes: as trade is freed, the incentives for labor migration and capital movement would decrease, ultimately to zero. Intuitively, one can think of goods as bundles of their constituent factors. Therefore, trade in goods and the migration of factors are two means to the same end. More technically, the result arises because under suitable assumptions factor prices are uniquely determined by goods prices; free, costless trade equalizes goods prices and, through that mechanism, factor prices.[3]

The basic idea of FPE is a powerful motivator of trade policies in the real world. For example, the North American Free Trade Agreement (NAFTA), the European Union (EU)–Mediterranean agreements, and the EU–Central Europe agreements were all promoted partly as solutions to migration pressures (see Chapter 5 for a description of these agreements). However, no one (not even Samuelson) takes the prospect of complete FPE seriously—the casual evidence against it is just overwhelming, even in the absence of barriers to mobility such as within the EU.

Moreover, once one moves beyond the strictly neoclassical theory, to allow trade to be determined by things such as technology differences or tax structures, trade and migration become complements rather than substitutes, and wage differences can persist indefinitely in the absence of factor movements (Markusen 1983).

Within the neoclassical framework, FPE may fail because there are more factors than goods (this is particularly likely if some factors are specific to particular industries—that is, are not intersectorally mobile—which is true of almost all in the short run); or because not all countries produce all goods (so-called complete specialization); or because technology is such that the same goods prices are consistent with different factor prices (the case of so-called factor intensity reversals). And, of course, in reality many barriers to trade persist, some are of a policy nature, but many that are natural, such as cultural and physical distance and geography. Extending neoclassical theory in a practical direction, FPE can fail because the productivity of factors varies systematically between countries, possibly because of unobserved differences in their quality or in the set of complementary inputs that is available; economies of scale may allow larger economies to pay higher wages, and the taxes that influence rewards differ by country. Finally, Rauch (1999) argues that trade and migration are complementary because expatriate communities are instrumental in creating trade links, a view validated empirically by Dunlevy and Hutchinson (2001).

All of this analysis suggests that international factor mobility will remain an important feature of the world economy even as trade barriers decline. Indeed, Wong (1986) shows that, whatever the reason, trade and migration are positively associated under most sets of realistic circumstances in the United States, and Lopez and Schiff (1998) find complementarity between trade and unskilled labor movements. Williamson (1998) suggests that migration was a much greater source of economic integration in the nineteenth century than was international trade, accounting perhaps for 70 percent of the observed convergence of real wage-rental ratios.

Even with perfectly unfettered migration—the nineteenth-century situation—one would not expect the complete equality of real wages. Many nonpolicy discouragements to labor mobility exist, including genuine preferences for home, the costs of establishing new social or production networks, and the fixed costs of migration. Recent developments in the theory of economic geography have explored some of these—see, for example, Fujita, Krugman, and Venables (1999), and the discussion of the brain drain in Commander, Kangesniemi, and Winters (2002).

Factor Mobility

This section describes the second analytical approach to TMNP, which is to treat it as parallel to migration. TMNP is *not* international migration—that is, it has none of cultural, social, or political dimensions associated with international migration, because it explicitly does not entail shifts in residence. However, its direct economic consequences can be thought of as those of migration. Workers enter a country temporarily to carry out particular jobs and thus labor inputs in one economy are reduced while those in another are increased.

At its simplest, the motive for workers to work abroad is that their real wages are higher there. Corresponding to these different wages are different productivities. In reasonably competitive labor markets, workers are paid their marginal products—that is, firms pay workers the value they generate—and even where this is not true, the differences between wages and productivity are not usually very large. Thus one can be very confident that when a worker moves from a low-wage to a high-wage country, his or her productivity increases and world aggregate output rises, offering scope for economic gains.

In the extreme case in which workers from different countries are identical and productivity is purely a function of location-specific characteristics, the increment in output when a worker moves is equal to the difference in wages between the two countries involved. In an early model of this situation, Hamilton and Whalley (1984) suggest that if labor were able to move between regions sufficiently to equalize wages around the world, world income could increase by 150 percent or more! Varying the assumptions—for example, to reflect higher dependency ratios in developing countries, different costs of living in different countries, or incomplete wage equalization—would still allow huge gains, far in excess of anything observed elsewhere in the trade liberalization literature.

In a much later, back-of-the-envelope calculation of a different nature, I suggested the possibility of gains of more than $300 billion a year from increased labor mobility (Winters 2001). Suppose, very conservatively, that when a worker moves from a low- to a high-income country, he or she could make up only one-quarter of the productivity or wage gap between the two countries—that is, assume that three-quarters of observed wage gaps stem from differences in individual characteristics such as health, education, or culture, and thus that they would persist even after developing country workers started to work in the rich countries. Suppose also that 50 million additional developing country workers worked abroad in any year, equivalent to an increase of about 5 percent in the population of industrial countries. With a wage gap of, say, $24,000 a year, the gains would be $300 billion a year![4]

The next major section discusses some new estimates combining these two methodologies on the basis of work by Walmsley and Winters (2002). These estimates also suggest huge returns to even relatively small movements of natural persons. Increasing industrial countries' quotas for the incoming temporary movement of natural persons by 3 percent of their labor forces generates gains of more than $150 billion a year.

Under the general heading of labor mobility, it is useful to identify three particular dimensions: the flow of unskilled workers from developing to industrial countries; the flow of skilled and professional workers from industrial to developing countries; and the flow of skilled, professional, and particularly business workers from developing to industrial countries. Of course, there are flows between pairs of developing countries and between pairs of industrial countries, but they are not the North-South movements that are of concern in this paper.

Industrial to Developing Country Labor Flows.   The main issue here is the ability of industrial country firms to send their specialists to their plants in developing countries, so-called intracorporate transfers. In some cases, highly skilled technical workers are required, often at short notice and for short periods. Such workers are needed to commission new plants and equipment, repair and maintain such equipment, and provide intrafirm services such as accounting, designs, or legal advice. In other cases, the interest is in the mobility of managers—either senior managers to oversee major functions or the regular rotation of middle management. Firms already see these various flows as a means of increasing local efficiency and of integrating their operations on a global scale, and one must presume that such flows increase global output (as well as the multinationals' profits). Indeed, these flows are central to the dissemination of both hard and soft technologies to the developing world, and so, apart from very long-run concerns about the incentives they create or destroy for human capital formation, they are an important contributor to development.

Tang and Wood (1999) have shown in a simple model that, like for most migration driven by wage differences, business mobility increases world output. Not surprisingly, they found that such mobility narrows the skills gap (the difference between skilled and unskilled wages) in the developing host countries and unskilled wages rise, while widening it in industrial countries. In the latter, home country unskilled workers suffer from having fewer skilled workers to work with. In the developing country, the gross domestic product (GDP) increases, and although part of it accrues to the mobile skilled workers who are domiciled in the industrial country, part accrues at home in terms of higher unskilled wages and tax revenues. Yet such mobility might reduce the developing country's skilled wage and so reduce the incentive for education. This possibility is reinforced by the fact that, once mobility is permitted, the multinational corporation might be able to do less local training. Thus longer-term costs to the developing country are possible. But such a result is far from certain, and apparently has never been examined formally. Analytically, the arguments associated with this situation have parallels with the arguments surrounding the "beneficial brain drain," which is the subject of the next section.

Developing to Industrial Country Flows: Skilled Labor.   The second element of labor mobility is the flow of skilled workers from developing countries. The value of skilled labor to a well-functioning economy has never been plainer, and in certain sectors such as information technology, education, and health, industrial countries are now seeking to recruit from abroad.

An immediate reaction to this situation might be to point out that if the advanced economies gain, the developing countries from which these skilled workers emigrate must necessarily lose. Indeed, this is not an implausible scenario, and it is one that should worry development specialists. The loss of the services of skilled people, even temporarily, reduces total output and therefore the tax base and scale economies. Depending on the length of the skilled workers' absences, such a loss also could reduce an economy's entrepreneurship, the ability to absorb new technologies, and various positive spillovers from skilled to other workers and to society in general.

But, in fact, straight loss is far from inevitable and is much less likely with TMNP than with permanent migration. For example, skilled workers from developing countries are likely to be more productive and have higher earnings in advanced economies, and the share of their higher earnings that they bring home may more than fully offset the loss of their services locally. This is particularly true if the developing country had not been making optimal use of the skilled labor initially, say for bureaucratic reasons or because the necessary complementary inputs were not available. These arguments have been made previously about remittances from permanent or quasi-permanent migrants, but they apply with far more force to TMNP.

Workers abroad also are likely to be a source of ideas, technology, markets, or networks for those who remain, increasing their productivity and market opportunities. Again this applies to permanent migrants, but the spillovers are likely to be much stronger if the workers with foreign experience spend more time living and working in their home economies. Under these circumstances, TMNP will boost local productivity as returning skilled workers instruct or inspire local colleagues. It is true, however, that TMNP may be less effective at building up foreign networks than permanent migration. Workers who are abroad only temporarily also may be subject to income tax in their home rather than their host countries. In many countries, their tax status depends on how temporary they are, and taxation is potentially a major consideration in the allocation of the benefits of TMNP between host and home countries.

Another possibility is that TMNP increases the returns to education and that the resulting increase in the supply of skills exceeds the actual loss of skilled inputs through TMNP, leaving the domestic economy in the developing country with a net gain in skills. Commander, Kangesniemi, and Winters (2002), who analyze these arguments in some detail, find them quite plausible and uncover several reasons why again TMNP offers greater scope for gains than does permanent migration. They caution, however, that the better the receiving (host) country screens potential immigrants so that it admits only the ablest, the weaker the beneficial brain drain argument becomes. The argument relies on the fact that the chance to migrate makes education more attractive to people who would otherwise have remained uneducated, and that, on the whole, these people will be less capable than those who would find education profitable on the basis of only domestic opportunities. If effective screening means that only the latter group are candidates for migration or TMNP, the incentives for others to acquire education are not affected, and thus there is no additional formation of human capital.

Clearly, developing countries' policies toward the temporary movement of skilled natural persons should depend heavily on the net balance of these effects, which is currently very uncertain. Moreover, the balance is likely to vary by country. For example, highly skilled workers may benefit from clustering, so that the larger the market in which they operate, the greater their worth (because there are more people to benefit from their good ideas). Thus one can imagine the following taxonomy of countries:

- Very small economies that could never generate the market or society size to make acquiring skills very profitable. They gain from migration via remittances, network effects, and so forth.
- Large economies that can reliably create the mass of skilled workers needed for efficiency. Although migration may reduce their local supplies of skills, it does so only at the margin, and its effects may be offset by things such as remittances.
- Medium-size economies that may be prevented by migration from reaching the critical mass of skills necessary to achieve local "takeoff" in high-skill activities. These economies suffer a quantum decline in local value added that no remittance or networking could ever overcome.

All this is speculation, of course, and it is not clear what small, medium, and large mean in this context, but this speculation does at least serve as warning that attitudes to migration could differ between developing countries.

Developing to Industrial Country Flows: The Unskilled. Although they are not entirely frictionless, flows of skilled workers are much easier than general migration for industrial countries to handle politically. But the real gains from trade, whether in goods or in factors, come from exploiting *differences*. Therefore, it is the flow of unskilled (or, strictly, less skilled) workers from developing to industrial countries that promises the larger returns. Not only is the proportionate gap in productivity between host and home countries likely to be largest here, but so too are the numbers of people available to move. The large benefits cited earlier come mainly from the mobility of less skilled workers.

But formidable political problems are associated with large-scale, permanent, unskilled migration. Host countries fear cultural and integration problems because the unskilled are less likely to adapt to Western culture. These countries also fear drains on the public purse, and they worry that the jobs taken by unskilled immigrants will not command immediate respect and will appear to be at the expense of the employment of local unskilled workers. Given the ability of various lobbies to ensure that protection in the member countries of the Organisation for Economic Co-operation and Development (OECD) is skewed toward supporting unskilled wages and employment, it is not surprising that the same forces have been able to resist immigration so effectively.

TMNP offers a way out of this dilemma. Although it will clearly deliver only some of the economic benefits of straight migration in terms of output and income, it avoids most of the latter's political costs. Temporary movers pose no cultural or integration threat and make virtually no call on public services. Thus the only major challenge posed by well-run TMNP schemes is the increase in competition that they pose for indigenous low-skill workers. This challenge is neither more nor less than the one posed by imports of labor-intensive goods from the developing world, and it has the same aggregate gains and distributional consequences (losses for the low-skilled, gains for everyone else). As formidable as it has been, the resistance to the liberalization of imports of labor-intensive goods has been at least partly overcome in the past by the weight of the economic gain that trade can deliver and by policies designed to ease adjustment among the local unskilled workers. If it is applied with the same policies and sensitivities that trade policy reform in goods has received in the past, TMNP offers less skilled workers a chance to reap some of the large gains described earlier.

Moreover, as developed countries' populations age and as average levels of training and education rise, the scarcity of less skilled labor in those countries will worsen. And given that at least in some occupations there is really no substitute for human labor—for example, in the caring occupations, personal services, and delivery of goods—the benefits of TMNP will increase through time. Thus although TMNP poses formidable political challenges, it actually offers a strong, long-run identity of interest between developing and industrial countries.

Developing the Empirical Model.   The major challenge to modeling the effects of mode 4 liberalization as a simple trade liberalization is the complete absence of information about size of the barriers to services trade. (This is true of virtually all services trade, not just that delivered by TMNP.) The use of TMNP to deliver services involves both para-tariffs—such as the costs of visas, additional health insurance, and registering qualifications—and quantitative restrictions. Such restrictions come in both a specific form, such as the failure to accept foreign qualifications as equivalent to the domestic qualifications necessary for delivering a particular service, and the general form of immigration restrictions. Often both will have to be relaxed before trade can increase. Because many of the pseudo quantitative restrictions (QRs) are prohibitions, they preclude the direct collection of data on their restrictive effects in the form of the differences between delivered and border prices—that is, there are no data from which to infer directly the tariff equivalents of services QRs. Clearly, one way of unlocking the empirical estimation of the costs of mode 4 restrictions is to seek alternative ways of quantifying these barriers for specific sectors.

This approach amounts more or less to preparing a "business plan" for the provision of service X in market A by country B residents. Taking the wage in B for the workers concerned as given, one would have to quantify the additional costs of providing the service in A. Some costs would be obvious—for example, subsistence, insurance,[5] travel—while others could be less so—for example, the need for advertising or discounts to assuage customer uncertainty about quality or reliability. Some costs would be policy related. For example, current regulations might require electricians to complete a full training course in country A, but if objective criteria were applied with goodwill officials might conclude that merely reexamining foreign-trained electricians was sufficient. Whether these barriers are costed at their actual or perspective rates would depend on whether one is considering their relaxation.

The next step is to compare the cost to residents of country B of supplying a service in market A (which will clearly depend on the scale of operations assumed) with the existing price in market A. A small relaxation in the quota of TMNP would then generate rent equivalent to the difference between the two—which would presumably be shared between the mobile workers and the firms or institutions facilitating their mobility. If the relaxation in quota were nonmarginal, then estimates of the elasticities of supply of temporary workers and demand for the service would be needed in order to calculate the new equilibrium. The latter is not beyond imagination, but the elasticity of supply is extremely difficult to estimate, despite the fact that modelers occasionally make assumptions about it.

Clearly, any exercise such as this will be highly sector-specific and subject to very wide margins of error. Moreover, while it might indicate possible changes in trade volumes, it would not necessarily immediately generate estimates of the overall welfare benefits of liberalization, because many of the monetary costs of TMNP—for example, those related to training and testing workers—are for rents or subsidies. The per unit rents and subsidies need to be quantified and the new volumes of activity to which they apply predicted in order to calculate the gross losses or gains they imply. In addition, the location in which the rents accrue needs to be identified.

Moving to the opposite end of the spectrum, the problems with modeling TMNP as migration are: (a) the transactions costs associated with temporary mobility are ignored, (b) the elasticity of supply of mobile workers is unknown, and (c) the implicit assumption is that the work force of permanent and temporary workers is costlessly distributed across sectors within the economy according to labor demand. Items (a) and (b) come back to the "business plan" exercise just discussed; item (c) requires some discussion, however.

Virtually all trade liberalization modeling exercises involve the assumption of perfect long-run mobility of each kind of labor between sectors and the consequent equalization of real wages for each kind across sectors. Some models allow for nominal wage differences between sectors that reflect the sectors' nonpecuniary advantages or disadvantages. These nonpecuniary factors are assumed to be unvarying and proportional to the wage, so that, in fact, all wages move up and down together. Other models allow for upward sloping aggregate supply curves of labor to reflect the way in which higher real wages will attract more people into the work force. None of these, however, addresses the issue that seems most pertinent to TMNP: the frictions on moving between sectors.

Suppose some temporary workers are allowed in to work in a particular sector j. If, on the one hand, the labor for this sector were wholly specific to that sector, wages would fall and employment and output could rise. There would also be spillovers to other sectors via the consequent changes in output prices—the additional output would drive down prices and therefore cut the demand for other goods—but no direct spillover to other sectors' labor markets. If, on the other hand, labor were perfectly mobile between sectors, the incipient wage decline induced by the extra workers in sector j would immediately drive some existing workers out of j into other sectors, reducing wages in other sectors. Ultimately, wages would fall by the same proportion in all sectors and, if demand factors are not unduly biased, all sectors would experience an increase in employment and output. The output shock would be spread throughout the economy, and the shock to sector j would be much smaller in this case than in the sector-specific case.

Which of these stories is more plausible? In the very short run, labor is fairly sector-specific, especially if workers have sector-specific skills, so that impacts are deep and narrow. Kletzer (2001), for example, finds quite long-lived unemployment and wage cuts for some of the workers losing their jobs in import-competing sectors. In the longer run, however, most economies show a good deal of flexibility and so impacts are broader and shallower. Borjas and Freeman (1992) show that U.S. regions that attract large immigrant inflows experience corresponding declines in internal inflows or increases in worker outflows, because in the long run their work forces seem to be no different from what would be expected in the absence of immigration. Given that it is probably less costly to change one's sector than one's location (especially for the less skilled), this finding might be taken as evidence to support the single labor market assumption. The fact that workers' attitudes toward globalization owe more to their skills levels than to their sectors of employment (Schreve and Slaughter 2001) also suggests fair degrees of mobility.

Clearly, the truth lies somewhere between the two polar extremes, and while I am inclined to the view that, subject to suitable compensatory polices, the flexible labor market approach is adequate for most policymaking jobs, there is obviously room for additional research on how to model intersectoral mobility. One approach that might yield fruit would be to examine the price relativities between different services across countries to determine whether they could be related to the openness of the economies to sector-specific migration or temporary mobility. If sectors differ in their openness but relativities do not, that finding may indicate that labor is relatively mobile between sectors. As with any price comparison, it will be difficult to ensure that like is being compared with like, but there should be fairly standard tasks that can be compared, and one could try to choose countries that have similar levels of income and other demand conditions. One also might try to get around some of these difficulties by considering a whole range of services or occupations and by estimating wage equations that explain earnings in terms of the individuals' characteristics and occupational/sectoral location. Such an approach might identify outlying sectors whose openness could be investigated, and a comparison of such wage gradients over countries might reveal anomalies even more efficiently.

A long-run analysis—of the sort that trade liberalization requires—means identifying not so much the costs of moving sectors (a transitory phenomenon), although these affect the net benefits of liberalization, as the costs of being in the "wrong sector"—that is, the permanent loss of productivity implied by a worker leaving his or her preferred sector for another. To my (imperfect) knowledge, no evidence exists on this loss at all, although ultimately, over the space of several generations, it might be assumed to be very small.

The Gains from Temporary Movement— New Estimates

Who would benefit from liberalizing the restrictions on the temporary movement of natural persons and by how much? This section summarizes some recent modeling results derived from a global applied general equilibrium model of the temporary movement of labor from South to North.[6] The method is to fit a computable model to data from a base year (1997) and then ask how the outcome would have differed had there been freer labor mobility in that year.[7] Thus the results are not unconditional predictions of the effects of future policy changes, but rather quantitative thought experiments to suggest possible orders of magnitude.

In the absence of quantifiable data on restrictions to services trade per se, TMNP is modeled merely in terms of the movement of workers from one country to another. This approach clearly overlooks a huge array of institutional details in actual and potential schemes for the temporary mobility of labor. However, as argued earlier, in terms of the effects on narrowly defined economic variables, it is not seriously misleading, especially in the sort of model used. Ultimately, TMNP means that fewer workers produce at home and more do so in the host country.

The bottom line of the modeling exercise is that increased mobility equivalent to 3 percent of the receiving countries' work forces would generate $156 billion a year in extra economic welfare. These gains are shared between developing and industrial countries and owe more to unskilled than to skilled labor mobility. These results are informative, although one cannot rely on the specific numbers.

The Model

The model and data used in Walmsley and Winters (2002) are based on the static version of the GTAP (Global Trade Analysis Project) model and database developed by Hertel (1997). GTAP is a standard applied general equilibrium model that assumes perfect competition. Consequentially, this exercise contains none of the scale or clustering effects that often figure in the skilled migration literature. In each of several regions, a single household is assumed to allocate income across private and government consumption and saving in fixed proportions. Demand for domestic and imported goods then depends on income and relative prices. Firms minimize the costs of production. They combine intermediate inputs, from domestic and imported sources, with primary factors to produce commodities for the domestic and export markets. Demand for factors of production (land, skilled and unskilled labor, capital, and natural resources) depends on output and relative prices. Prices adjust to ensure that demand equals supply in every market.

Walmsley and Winters modified the standard GTAP model and incorporated the movement of natural persons as follows. They began by distinguishing the terms *temporary migrant* and *temporary worker*:

"A temporary migrant leaves his or her home region to become a temporary worker in a host region."

Walmsley and Winters undertake considerable efforts to identify the stocks of temporary workers and migrants by country in 1997. Because no bilateral information is available, however, they can say nothing about where existing temporary migrants from a given home region are temporary workers, or where new migrants become workers. Thus they postulate a global labor pool, which collects the temporary migrants from all home regions and then allocates them across host regions. The temporary workers add to the supply of labor in the host region and are allocated across sectors within the region according to labor demand. In the host country, temporary workers earn a wage for their labor, related to their productivity. Part of this wage is then sent back to the home region via the global pool as remittances. Within a country, the income of permanent and temporary residents plus net remittances received is then allocated across consumption, saving, and government spending to maximize utility.

Walmsley and Winters characterize changes in policies toward TMNP as increases in industrial countries' quotas on inflows of temporary workers. Assuming that the quotas are always binding—that is, that there is excess demand for places in the host countries—they can do this exogenously without having to model the incentives to move very precisely. They then assume that the new migrants are drawn from various home countries (mostly developing) according to the latter's labor force shares.

Having determined the number of temporary migrants leaving the home region and the number of temporary workers entering the host regions, they need to calculate how these changes affect the effective supply of skilled and unskilled labor in terms of productivity units. Because they have no data on bilateral flows of workers, they have to assume that a temporary worker initially has the same productivity as the average temporary migrant in the pool of mobile labor. The latter merely reflects the productivities of these workers in their home countries and the shares of each home country in the overall total of temporary migrants. Once working in the host region, however, the temporary worker acquires some of the productivity of the host region, and his or her productivity is assumed to equal the average productivity of a temporary migrant plus half the difference between that and the host region's productivity. By working in such productivity-adjusted "equivalent-worker" terms, Walmsley and Winters are able to combine indigenous and migrant unskilled workers into a single aggregate with a single wage (per equivalent worker)—and similarly for skilled workers.

Once the temporary workers have left their home regions and entered the work force of the host region, they are allocated across sectors—in both countries. In the standard model, labor moves freely between sectors until wages are equalized across sectors for each type of worker. In the host regions, where the supply of labor has increased, wages are expected to decline, whereas in the home (sending) regions, they will rise. The extent of the change in wages will depend on the demand for labor, which, in turn, depends on the demand for production. That demand is driven by prices and income, both of which depend on wages.

Changes in the supply of labor and wage rates will ultimately affect the demand for other factors of production, notably capital. In the standard GTAP model, income includes all factor incomes (skilled and unskilled labor, land, capital and natural resources) net of depreciation and taxes. In the Walmsley and Winters model, factor incomes have to reflect the distinction between the incomes of temporary and permanent labor, and have to be adjusted for the remittances sent by temporary workers to their home countries. The income of temporary workers in an economy is assumed to consist of the income from their labor less remittances sent home (which, in turn, are assumed to be a given share of the wage). All other income, including that from land, capital, taxes, and remittances received, is assumed to be earned by permanent labor alone. Because they do not have data on bilateral labor movement or remittances, Walmsley and Winters have to base remittances received on average remittances from all temporary workers. Given that temporary workers in different host countries remit at different rates, changes in the geographical distribution of temporary workers may therefore lead to changes in the average remittance rate. To calculate the effects of TMNP on the migrants from a particular home country, one must aggregate across all host regions the income of the temporary labor by host region and labor type, and then distribute the aggregated income across home regions according to their numbers of temporary migrants in productivity equivalents.

Changes in the economic welfare of permanent and temporary workers are related to their income flows deflated by prices in their place of residence (work).[8] The welfare of temporary migrants is found by summing the welfare changes of temporary workers across host countries and sharing it out over the various home countries, according to their shares in total TMNP. Once the welfare changes of temporary migrants are determined, welfare by home region, regardless of temporary residence, also can be calculated by simply summing the relevant changes. Table 4.1 summarizes the way in which income and welfare changes are summed to obtain national totals. Walmsley and Winters distinguish home and host country concepts. The former refers to all people starting off in a particular country— essentially a nationality concept. The latter refers to all people actually located in a country after mobility has occurred—essentially a residence concept. At a practical level the only difference is the treatment of the income retained by temporary workers, which is attributed to the host country when the "host country" concept is used and the home country when the "home country" concept is used.

The Experiments

The main simulation conducted by Walmsley and Winters is that of an increase in the quotas for inflows of skilled and unskilled temporary workers into industrial countries.

TABLE 4.1 Home and Host Concepts: Accounting Concepts for the Temporary Flow of Labor from Country A to Country B

Income Flow	Host Concept	Home Concept
PL_j	B	B
K_B	B	B
TL_B retained	B_T	A_T
TL_B remitted	A	A
K_j	A	A
PL_A	A	A

Note: PL_j = permanent labor in country j; K_j = other factors in country j; TL_B = temporary workers in B = temporary migrants from A; Retained = earnings retained in B by temporary workers; Remitted = earnings of temporary workers remitted to country A; A = included in country A's total for permanent residents; B = included in country B's total for permanent residents; A_T = included in A's accounts under temporary migrants; B_T = included in B's accounts under temporary workers.
Source: Walmsley and Winters (2002).

After looking at this simulation, this section will examine the effects of other issues, such as the relative importance of skilled versus unskilled mobility and the sectoral allocation of the mobile workers.

Quotas on the movement of natural persons are assumed to increase in a number of regions that traditionally import labor, supplied by temporary migrants from a number of countries that traditionally export labor, according to the labor force shares of both sets of countries. Table 4.2 divides the regions used in this analysis into labor-importing and labor-exporting regions (the nonzero entries in columns II and III, respectively). The quotas are increased by an amount that would allow the quantity of labor supplied to the host (or labor-importing) countries to increase by 3 percent.[9] For example, for the United States the increase in the quota would amount to 2.7 million unskilled temporary workers and 2.4 million skilled temporary workers. China, as a supplier of temporary workers, would then supply 2.4 million of the total 8.5 million unskilled workers required and 0.49 million of the total 8 million skilled workers required worldwide. Columns II and III of Table 4.2 give the assumed changes to regions' labor forces.

Increasing industrial countries' quotas on both skilled and unskilled temporary workers increases world welfare by an estimated $156 billion—about 0.6 percent of world income in 1997. Tables 4.3 and 4.4 give some geographical details, but for these, care must be taken to distinguish between "home" country residents—those who start off in a country but some of whom move temporarily—and "host" country residents—the set of people who end up there *after* movement has occurred. Region A "as a home country" refers to A's permanent workers who

TABLE 4.2   Regions and Sectors

I All Regions	II Labor Importers (Thousands)[a]	III Labor Exporters (Thousands)[a]	IV European Union (EU) Partners[b]	V North American Partners[c]	VI Sector	VII Service Sectors
United States	5,165.36				Crops	
Canada	573.00				Livestock	
Mexico		375.90		✓	Meat	
United Kingdom	1,134.00				Dairy	
Germany	1,665.00				Food	
Rest of EU	4,713.10				Other primary products	
Rest of Europe	234.12				Wood and paper products	
Eastern Europe		538.37	✓		Textiles and wearing apparel	
Former Soviet Union		1,563.65	✓		Petroleum, chemical, and mineral products	
Australia–New Zealand	435.90				Metals	
China		2916.65		✓	Autos	
Japan	2,610.00				Electronics	
Rest of East Asia		509.80		✓	Other manufacturing	
Southeast Asia		1,709.02		✓	Household utilities	✓
India		2,844.72	✓	✓	Construction	✓
Rest of South Asia		661.84	✓	✓	Trade	✓

TABLE 4.2 *(Continued)*

I All Regions	II Labor Importers (Thousands)[a]	III Labor Exporters (Thousands)[a]	IV European Union (EU) Partners[b]	V North American Partners[c]	VI Sector	VII Service Sectors
Brazil		654.46		✓	Transport	✓
Middle East and northern Africa		1,259.69	✓		Financial services	✓
South Africa		1,810.28	✓		Insurance	✓
Rest of world		546.61			Business services	✓
Total	16,530.48	165,30.49			Other services	✓

a. The figures in this column are the inflow or outflow assumed in the simulations that follow.

b. EU partners are the group of countries or regions from which most of the temporary labor in the EU currently comes.

c. North American partners are the group of countries or regions from which most of the temporary labor in North America currently comes.

Source: Walmsley and Winters (2002).

TABLE 4.3   Economic Welfare by Region and Class of Worker (millions of U.S. dollars)

I Region	II Welfare of Temporary Workers	III Welfare of Temporary Migrants	IV Welfare of Permanent Residents[a]	V Welfare by Home[b] Region III + IV	VI Welfare by Host[c] Region II + IV
Developed countries	175,960	68,577	6,982	75,559	182,942
Developing countries	–5,002	98,984	–20,685	78,301	–25,688
FSU and CEE	–25	12,511	–4,991	7,521	–5,017
East and Southeast Asia	–762	29,647	–12,192	17,456	–12,955
South Asia	–53	4,158	16,377	20,535	16,325
Latin America	–718	30,980	–12,457	18,523	–13,175
Africa	–3,444	21,688	–7,422	14,266	–10,866
Total[d]	170,932	170,704	–14,626	156,078	156,306

Note: FSU = former Soviet Union; CEE = Central and Eastern Europe.

a. Permanent residents who do not move temporarily.

b. "Home" refers to people originating in the specified country regardless of where they work or live.

c. "Host" refers to people living in the specified country regardless of their place of origin.

d. Includes a small "rest of the world" region.

Source: Walmsley and Winters (2002).

TABLE 4.4 Percentage Change in the Real Wages of Skilled and Unskilled Workers

I Region[a]	II Percent Change in Real Wage of Skilled Labor	III Percent Change in Real Wage of Unskilled Labor	IV Percent Change in Rental Price of Capital	V Percent Change in Real GDP[b]	VI Percent Change in Terms of Trade
Developed countries	-1.02	-0.61	0.78	1.05	-0.24
Developing countries	5.13	0.12	-0.52	-0.91	0.53
FSU and CEE	4.40	-0.48	-0.70	-1.03	0.18
East and Southeast Asia	4.94	0.02	-0.49	-0.88	0.28
South Asia	5.92	0.60	0.59	-0.48	4.55
Latin America	4.67	-0.21	-0.63	-0.88	0.06
Africa	5.75	0.20	-1.02	-1.39	0.37

Note: In this table percentage change means the percentage change in variable from base case. FSU = former Soviet Union; CEE = Central and Eastern Europe.

a. Weighted averages of results for the regions distinguished in the model. Weights are skilled workers, unskilled workers, GDP (gross domestic product), GDP, and GDP, respectively, for columns II–VI.

b. Real GDP is not a measure of welfare; it is a measure of production, and welfare is a measure of the utility achieved from consumption, which depends, among other things, on remittances received.

Source: Walmsley and Winters (2002).

never leave plus its temporary migrants who work abroad—loosely speaking, a nationality-based concept. A "as a host country" refers to the permanent workers plus the temporary workers from elsewhere who work there—a residence-based concept.[10]

In aggregate terms, the main gainers from liberalizing mode 4 are the initial residents of the developing (labor-exporting) economies—see column V in Table 4.3, developing countries as "home" countries. Most of this increase is the result of the higher incomes earned by the people who can become temporary migrants as a result of the relaxation in quotas (column III in Table 4.3). They are now able to earn higher wages in the industrial countries, as shown in column II of Table 4.3, "welfare of temporary workers." (Recall that each mobile worker is both a "temporary worker and a temporary migrant," so columns II and III in Table 4.3 report the welfare of the same set of people allocated once by residence and once by nationality.)

Despite the remittances they receive, permanent residents in the developing countries generally lose from the outflow of temporary migrants (column IV in Table 4.3) because the decrease in the labor supply reduces the returns to capital and other factors of production (column IV in Table 4.4). Combining the results for permanent residents and (the few) temporary workers already located there gives the outcomes for developing countries as host countries (column VI of Table 4.3). In general, these economies record losses, but recall that this result excludes the benefits experienced by the temporary migrants who are working abroad. The loss of labor reduces aggregate output—that is, real GDP—in the labor-exporting countries (column V in Table 4.4), and because the outflow of labor is biased toward skilled labor, skilled workers' real wages rise in developing countries (column II in Table 4.4).[11] Developing economies generally experience improvements in their terms of trade because the fall in their GDP reduces the supply of the varieties of goods that they produce and so drives up their prices.

There are exceptions to these trends, however, especially in India, where the welfare of permanent residents increases because the increase in remittances outweighs the declines in labor and capital income. This increase in income elevates the demand for domestic goods and attenuates the decline in production in the economy. Moreover, it allows the real wages of both skilled and unskilled workers to rise.

Although the developing countries are the main beneficiaries of the increase in quotas, the initial residents of most of the industrial countries also experience increases in welfare from the higher returns to capital and increased taxes collected. In fact, the estimates in Table 4.3 for the welfare of permanent residents of industrial countries are understated. The database available for this exercise shows the United States subsidizing output and factor use, so that an expanding U.S.

economy causes its welfare to fall, which is manifestly absurd. When the data are overridden and the United States is given the average OECD tax structure, industrial country permanent residents gain about $11 billion rather than the $7 billion shown. Real GDP increases substantially in the industrial economies (column V in Table 4.4), but in most cases the terms of trade decline as higher output drives down the prices of exports relative to imports.

One number of note in Table 4.3 is the strong gains for industrial countries' temporary migrants—that is, those who have left an industrial country to work abroad. This finding reflects the fact that more than half of the stock of skilled temporary migrants identified in the database comes from the "rest of the EU" region (the European Union less the United Kingdom and Germany). By means of the unavoidably crude way of allocating these migrants over destinations, many of them are allocated to developing countries (mostly in the Middle East), where they benefit from the strong increase in skilled wages.

Among sectors, agriculture is the least affected by the temporary movement of labor in both the industrial and developing economies. In industrial economies, the output of services (particularly trade, business services, and other services) and of most manufacturing sectors increases significantly with the labor inflows, while primary sectors and utilities show only small increases. The impact on production in developing countries is almost the mirror image, with the manufacturing and services sectors experiencing most of the decline because of the loss of skilled labor and smaller changes in utilities and the unskilled-intensive sectors.[12]

Table 4.5 considers the effects of relaxing the skilled and unskilled quotas separately. Notably, both the industrial and developing countries would benefit more from the liberalization of restrictions on unskilled labor than on skilled labor. For developing (labor-exporting) countries, the reason is that, while skilled temporary migrants can greatly increase their earnings by moving, the negative effect of their loss on their home economies is considerable. Thus, for example, although the skilled temporary workers improve their welfare by $61 billion, permanent residents in the developing world lose $34 billion, while those in the industrial world break even (although this last figure is too pessimistic because of the U.S. data problem).

As for the mobility of unskilled workers, the temporary migrants from developing countries gain $38 billion in all, and their remittances more than offset their original (low) contribution to home output, so that the welfare of those who remain behind also rises. For the developed (labor-importing) regions, higher quotas on unskilled labor also are more beneficial in terms of welfare than those on skilled workers, although most of the effect comes from the welfare of industrial countries' temporary migrants, an effect that is not convincingly modeled. The increases in supplies of unskilled labor reduce unskilled wages and stimulate

TABLE 4.5 Welfare Decomposed According to Effects of Increasing Skilled and Unskilled Quotas (millions of U.S. dollars)

I Region	II Welfare of Permanent Workers (Unskilled[a])	III Welfare of Permanent Workers (Skilled[b])	IV Welfare of Temporary Migrants (Unskilled[a])	V Welfare of Temporary Migrants (Skilled[b])	VI Welfare by Home Region (Unskilled[a]) II + IV	VII Welfare by Home Region (Skilled[b]) III + V
Developed countries	6,860	121	50,587	17,989	57,447	18,111
Developing countries	13,097	−33,781	37,676	61,309	50,773	27,528
FSU and CEE	205	−5,196	3,418	9,094	3,622	3,898
East and Southeast Asia	2,331	−14,523	9,558	20,089	11,889	5,566
South Asia	9,295	7,083	1,789	2,369	11,084	9,452
Latin America	−158	−12,298	13,216	17,763	13,059	5,465
Africa	1,424	−8,846	9,695	11,993	11,119	3,147
Total[c]	20,181	−34,807	89,346	81,358	109,527	46,551

Note: FSU = former Soviet Union; CEE = Central and Eastern Europe.

a. Welfare of the whole population when only quotas on unskilled workers are relaxed.

b. Welfare of the whole population when only quotas on skilled workers are relaxed.

c. Includes a small "rest of the world" region.

Source: Walmsley and Winters (2002).

most sectors (agricultural, manufactures, and some services), whereas the benefits of increased supplies of skilled labor are concentrated in just a few service sectors. The main effect, however, is again on their existing migrants.

Walmsley and Winters (2002) also provide some alternative estimations. In doing so, they confirm that the precise details of the experiment do not undermine the basic results of their work—that is, that mode 4 offers potentially huge gains to liberalization.[13]

In one experiment they confine the inflow of labor to the industrial countries' service sectors. They do this by postulating two separate labor markets between which there is no labor mobility and thus wages can vary between them. The inflows of labor to the services sector results in a large expansion of the services sector in the industrial economies at the expense of the other sectors. In the services sector the wages of skilled and unskilled labor decline by between 1 and 2 percent, and in the other sectors they increase substantially, by between 1 and 3 percent. Capital is replaced with the cheaper skilled labor in the services sector, allowing it to move to other sectors—agriculture and manufacturing. Developing countries see the opposite result. Their service sectors decline by more and their nonservice sectors by less than in the unrestricted increases case (or even expand).

It is not surprising that restricting the sectors that can use temporary labor reduces the benefits for all the major groups distinguished, for the restriction frustrates one of the routes through which economies maximize the benefits of the inflow of labor. However, the loss from the restriction is not very large—benefits of $152 billion compared with $156 billion. Moreover, the assumption of completely separate labor markets is too extreme. Thus, at least in the initial stages of liberalization, restricting new temporary labor to the services sector (as mode 4 will do) will not seriously reduce the gains from those available under unrestricted mobility.

The main results also are basically unaffected if labor flows are restricted to the traditional bilateral flows (for example, from Mexico to the United States, from the southern Mediterranean to the EU), although, of course, their distribution over countries is affected. Essentially, the differences in productivity between source countries are small relative to the differences between source and recipient countries, so shifts in the allocation of a given temporary flow between source countries have only small aggregate effects. The results are largely the same if it is assumed that developing countries have perfectly elastic supplies of unskilled labor.

Walmsley and Winters also show that the gains are more or less proportional to two critical parameters. If it is assumed that incoming workers catch up to only one-quarter of the gap between their home and host country productivities (rather than one-half), the benefits are roughly halved. Similarly, if it is assumed that there is a three-quarters catch-up, the benefits are increased by 51 percent.

Walmsley and Winters have rather little information on productivity catch-ups, but Borjas (2000) has shown that for permanent migrants it eventually reaches and exceeds 100 percent of the gap (also see Hendricks 2002). Overall, the assumption of 50 percent for temporary movers seems about right. The gains are similarly proportional to the size of the liberalization, very nearly doubling if quotas expand by 6 percent rather than 3 percent of the work force.

Finally, by way of comparison, Walmsley and Winters find that the complete abolition of all goods trade restrictions in the model generates only $104 billion in welfare gains compared with $156 billion from a limited relaxation of restrictions on labor movement.

It bears reiterating: do not take these numbers literally; they are mere orders of magnitude. They are not subject to much uncertainty in terms of the experiments that were run, but they are broadly uncertain once certain factors are recognized: the inadequacies of the original data, the crudity of treating temporary mobility as a mere change in countries' labor endowments, and the extremity of the modeling assumptions. Nevertheless, the results suggest startlingly large benefits to freeing up the temporary movement of labor. Even for a limited liberalization, they are far larger than the benefits available to a complete goods market liberalization and they also are larger for unskilled than for skilled labor mobility. If they do nothing else, these results should challenge negotiators to think hard about the priorities they bring to the new round of GATS negotiations.

Compensatory Policies

It was argued earlier in this chapter that admitting less skilled workers under a mode 4 liberalization is fundamentally no different from admitting imports of labor-intensive goods under a General Agreement on Tariffs and Trade (GATT) liberalization. Both raise general welfare but threaten indigenous less skilled workers. This section briefly considers the strength of that parallel and what lessons goods market liberalization has for mode 4.

The postulated equivalence seems to be a good one for the nature of the shock. However, questions arise about whether the scale is equivalent. In industrial countries, services are substantially larger employers than manufacturing and the primary sector, and although services employ large numbers of highly skilled workers, they also employ a high proportion of societies' less able members. Sectors such as personal care, janitorial services, and much hotel work offer havens for the unskilled, and given that any society will have some people in such categories, they play a role in terms of both providing these people with income and allowing them the self-respect of contributing. Indeed, these sectors have often been characterized as providing the jobs to which displaced unskilled manufacturing employees can be moved when their sectors have been liberalized, although Kletzer (2001) suggests this is much less true in reality than in perception. However, the existence of these sectors has helped to ease adjustment in goods sectors in a way that will not be feasible when they themselves come under pressure.

If all low-grade service jobs in the industrial countries were costlessly contestable by residents of the poorest developing countries at those countries' wage rates, the indigenous unskilled would indeed be squeezed very hard. However, that is clearly too extreme a view, because the natural protection of distance, culture, and experience will all maintain wage premia in the industrial countries relative to the developing world. And at least for the moment only partial liberalization is up for discussion. Nevertheless, it does seem reasonable to expect that a vigorous mode 4 liberalization will pose significant adjustment strains.

What could be done? In the long run it is important to realize that the displaced unskilled workers could be compensated out of the general gains from liberalization. But that would require the willingness of the more able majority to be taxed and make transfers, and the construction of a tax system that does not seriously discourage effort. If there are significant numbers of natives who cannot make a "decent living" in the sheltered sectors, more or less permanent transfers would have to be made on a large scale, and it is not clear that societies have yet really mastered this technically or would adopt it ideologically (think of the social dysfunction and distress among many indigenous peoples at present). Subsidies might take the form of housing subsidies for nationals or income top-ups to bring a national's wage up to acceptable levels if his or her employer paid only the developing country wage.

This discussion suggests that there is a huge return to trying to ensure that fewer nationals are on the bottom rungs of the skills ladder. This point, in turn, suggests ever-increasing use of the education sector to increase individuals' endowments of human capital, and might also entail finding ways of allowing all nationals to hold a reasonable stock of other capital. Capital owners are major beneficiaries of the inflow of workers from abroad. Therefore, if profit streams were equitably distributed, nationals would have reasonable living conditions even if they have low earning power. But careful thought would have to be given to exactly how such capital transfers are handled in order to balance freedom and personal responsibility with assurance that the income flow would remain intact. Indeed, this is exactly the debate that industrial countries are having over pension plans, and one could think of giving nationals a capital grant as being akin to a lifetime pension.

Turning to the shorter term and recognizing that even the most aggressive liberalization will proceed relatively slowly compared with the size of the overall economy, one can draw better parallels with goods trade liberalizations. Broadly, four approaches deserve comment. First, sensitive sectors could just be left out of the process of liberalization, but this does not make it good economics. If WTO member countries are serious about mode 4—and they should be for the sakes of both industrial and developing countries—they should tackle some of the major sectors early on.

Second, liberalization can proceed slowly. This does not mean so much taking a small step and then waiting before deciding to take another, but rather planning a long transitional period for a known adjustment. The key is credibility. If the liberalization is not credible, long adjustment periods are an invitation to lobby for their reversal, but if the end point is firmly expected at a date certain in the future, the gradual introduction of change can give people a chance to adjust more gently. Indeed, slow adjustment is not always better. Rather, unless there are obvious externalities, it is better to give private actors the information and let them decide the best speed of adjustment. Also related to timing is the macroeconomic cycle. It is manifestly more difficult to gain acceptance of liberalization if the economy is weak; the costs of employment change are greater because transitional unemployment spells are longer in depressed economies. Thus there is something to be said for scheduling a mode 4 liberalization during a boom rather than a recession. This point raises the question of whether services require a safeguards clause such as the one goods have in the GATT. Such clauses are likely to be subject to a good deal of abuse, but in terms of political reality, they may be desirable.

The third approach to compensation is specific trade-related compensation schemes. Among the best known is the U.S. Trade Adjustment Assistance Act (TAA). This act offers a composite of measures to support an industry damaged by liberalization with loans and assistance, plus measures to compensate the displaced workers, including benefits to support income and training services.

The TAA was established by the John F. Kennedy administration in 1962 as a quid pro quo for the wave of liberalization stemming from the U.S. Trade Expansion Act (TEA) and the Kennedy Round in the GATT. It provides trade-displaced workers with extended unemployment benefits, relocation expenses, and (compulsory) training as a bridge to a new job with similar levels of income and benefits.[14] Several evaluations of the TAA program have shown that it provides additional income for temporarily displaced workers, many of whom obtain alternative employment relatively quickly anyway. But it fails to assist significantly those permanently displaced by trade-related closures. In addition, Decker and Corson (1995) suggest that training does not increase the future earnings of displaced workers.

Nevertheless, the TAA forms the basis of the North American Free Trade Agreement Transitional Adjustment Assistance (NAFTA-TAA) program established in 1993. This program assists workers who lose their jobs, or whose hours of work and wages are reduced as a result of trade with Canada or Mexico, by providing them with the opportunity to engage in long-term training while receiving income support.

Canada and Australia have operated similar schemes at various times in the past—the General Adjustment Assistance Programme (GAAP) in Canada and the Special Adjustment Assistance (SAA) program in Australia—with similarly unconvincing effects. Overall, experience with trade adjustment assistance has not been particularly happy. Schemes are often bureaucratic, providing limited benefits to a small category of workers who might well have found alternative jobs anyway, while providing little long-term assistance to the permanently displaced. Decisions on whether a worker is displaced because of a government trade policy or some other shock have inevitably been rather arbitrary, leading to resentment among workers who fail to qualify for the benefit. In some cases, such schemes have assisted firms in moving to activities better reflecting comparative advantage; in others, they have inhibited such a move.

The Europeans and Japanese have no such specific compensation schemes. The reason, Sapir (2001) argues, is in part that their less effective markets have given them a degree of insulation against trade shocks, and in part that they have much deeper general social protection systems. In fact, these systems are the fourth of the approaches to adjustment. They avoid the problem of attributing an individual's problems to trade and of giving priority to trade-related losses above those associated with other causes, but they are expensive and arguably bad for incentives. The preservation of the social security system is often quoted as one of the aims behind Europeans' resistance to immigration, but in fact, TMNP, which offers foreign workers no rights under the system, helps to get around these fears. Nevertheless, the European models are under budgetary pressure, and their future is not entirely secure. A major shock from a mode 4 liberalization, even if temporary, could pose serious problems if not appropriately anticipated.

In summary, the adjustment stresses that mode 4 liberalization could engender are real. They cannot be wished away, because they will be both large and concentrated on a vulnerable section of society. In the short run, sensitivity about the timing and extent of liberalization may contain the pressures, and existing compensatory schemes can cope with those that actually arise. In the longer run, when deeper liberalization has been achieved, more active redistribution will be required to try to ensure that fewer nationals of industrial countries are actually in the sectors competing with foreign workers. Such an approach will require education and training as well as giving thought to asset distribution.

Notes

1. Winters recently directed a study funded by the Commonwealth Secretariat; see Winters and others (2002) and Walmsley and Winters (2002). This chapter represents a distillation of some of that study, and also includes some new analysis of the economics of mode 4 liberalization.

2. All dollar amounts are in 1997 U.S. dollars.

3. Winters (1991), for example, gives an elementary textbook treatment of FPE, and Bowen, Hollander, and Viaene (1998) give a more advanced one.

4. Labor costs per manufacturing worker, which are an indicator of productivity, were about $32,000 in the United States in 1990–94, compared with $1,192 in India, $1,442 in Lesotho, $5,822 in China, and $6,138 in Mexico. The population of high-income countries was 927 million in 1997 (World Bank 1999).

5. Winters and others (2002) argue that temporary workers should seek private medical insurance.

6. This section is based on Winters and others (2002) and Walmsley and Winters (2002), from which more details of the modeling and results may be obtained. I am extremely grateful to Terrie Walmsley for her inputs to the modeling exercise.

7. Details of the data are available in Walmsley and Winters (2002).

8. Walmsley and Winters used the Hicksian Equivalent Variation to measure changes in economic welfare. This measure expresses changes in money terms, which can be summed across classes of workers to derive national aggregates.

9. In other words, the number of workers (actual bodies) increases by 3 percent of the labor force. Because relative productivities differ, this does not mean that the labor force increases by 3 percent; it increases by the number of equivalent workers.

10. Note, however, that in Table 4.3 even "labor exporters" record effects on temporary workers. Most labor exporters have some temporary workers in their economies, and, as wages change, so does the economic welfare of these workers. The changes parallel those of permanent residents in these countries. A similar explanation applies for labor importers and temporary migrants.

11. By assumption, the relaxation of quotas reflects the skills mix of industrial countries and so is substantially more skill-intensive than the typical developing country's labor force endowment.

12. Walmsley and Winters (2002) discuss the reason for these effects.

13. Robustness with respect to the details of the experiment is not the same as robustness with respect to the details of the model, however.

14. See Kapstein (1998) for a history of the TAA.

References

The word *processed* describes informally produced works that may not be commonly available through libraries.

Borjas, G. J. 2000. *Labor Economics*. 2d ed. Boston: McGraw-Hill.

Borjas, G. J., and R. B. Freeman, eds. 1992. *Immigration and the Work Force: Economic Consequences for the United States and Source Areas*. Chicago: University of Chicago Press.

Bowen, H. P., A. Hollander, and J-M. Viaene. 1998. *Applied International Trade Analysis*. Ann Arbor: University of Michigan Press.

Commander, S., M. Kangesniemi, and L. A. Winters. 2002. "The Brain Drain: Curse or Boon? A Survey of the Literature." Paper presented at the International Seminar on International Trade, Stockholm, May.

Corden, W. M. 1984. "The Normative Theory of International Trade." In R. W. Jones and P. Kenen, eds., *Handbook of International Economics*. Amsterdam: North Holland.

Decker, P. T., and W. Corson. 1995. "International Trade and Worker Displacement: Evaluation of the Trade Adjustment Assistance Program." *Industrial and Labor Relations Review* 48: 758–74.

DFID (Department for International Development). 2000. *Eliminating World Poverty: Making Globalisation Work for the Poor*. London: Her Majesty's Stationery Office.

Dunlevy, J. A., and W. K. Hutchinson. 2001. "The Pro-Trade Effect of Immigration on American Exports during the Late Nineteenth and Early Twentieth Centuries." Discussion Paper 375. IZA (Institute for the Study of Labor), Bonn.

Fujita, Masahisa, Paul Krugman, and Anthony J. Venables. 1999. *The Spatial Economy: Cities, Regions and International Trade.* Cambridge, Mass.: MIT Press.

Hamilton, C., and J. Whalley. 1984. "Efficiency and Distributional Implications of Global Restrictions on Labour Mobility: Calculations and Policy Implications." *Journal of Development Economics* 14(1–2): 61–75.

Hendricks, L. 2002. "How Important Is Human Capital for Development: Evidence from Immigrants' Earnings." *American Economic Review* 92(1): 198–219.

Hertel, T. W., ed. 1997. *Global Trade Analysis: Modelling and Applications.* Cambridge: Cambridge University Press.

Hertel, T. W., et al. 1999. "Agricultural and Non-agricultural Liberalisation in the Millennium Round" <www.worldbank.org/research/trade/archive.html/>.

Kapstein, E. 1998. "Trade Liberalisation and the Politics of Trade Adjustment Assistance." *International Labour Review* 137: 501–16.

Karsenty, G. 2000. "Assessing Trade in Services by Mode of Supply." In P. Sauvé and R. M. Stern, eds., *GATS 2000: New Directions in Services Trade Liberalization.* Washington, D.C.: Brookings Institution Press.

Kletzer, L. 2001. *Job Loss from Imports: Measuring the Costs.* Washington, D.C.: Institute for International Economics.

Lopez, Ramon, and Maurice Schiff. 1998. "Migration and the Skill Composition of the Labor Force: The Impact of Trade Liberalization in LDCs." *Canadian Journal of Economics* 31 (2): 318–36.

Markusen, J. R. 1983. "Factor Movements and Commodity Trade as Compliments." *Journal of International Economics* 14: 341–57.

Mattoo, A. 2000. "Developing Countries in the New Round of GATS Negotiations: Towards a Pro-Active Role." *World Economy* 23: 471–90.

McCulloch, N., L. A. Winters, and X. Cirera. 2001. *Trade Liberalisation and Poverty: A Handbook.* London: CEPR (Centre for Economic Policy Research).

Rauch, J. E. 1999. "Networks versus Markets in International Trade." *Journal of International Economics* (48)1: 7–35.

Rodrik, D. 1995. "Political Economy of Trade Policy." In G. M. Grossman and K. Rogoff, eds., *Handbook of International Economics.* Amsterdam: Elsevier.

Romer, P. 1994. "New Goods, Old Theory, and the Welfare Costs of Trade Restrictions." *Journal of Development Economics* (43)1: 5–38.

Samuelson, P. A. 1949. "Factor Price Equalisation Once Again." *Economic Journal* 59: 181–97.

Sapir, A. 2001. "Who's Afraid of Globalisation?" In P. Sauvé and A. Subramanian, eds., *Efficiency, Equity and Legitimacy: The Multilateral Trading System and the Millennium.* Chicago: University of Chicago Press.

Schreve, K. E., and M. J. Slaughter. 2001. "What Determines Individual Trade Policy Preferences?" *Journal of International Economics* 54: 235–66.

Tang, P. J. G., and A. Wood. 1999. "Globalisation, Co-operation Costs and Wage Inequalities." Institute of Development Studies, University of Sussex, January. Processed.

Walmsley, T. L., and L. A. Winters. 2002. "An Analysis of the Removal of Restrictions on the Temporary Movement of Natural Persons." University of Sheffield. Processed.

Williamson, J. G. 1998. "Globalisation, Labour Markets and Policy Backlash in the Past." *Journal of Economic Perspectives* 12(4): 51–72.

Winters, L. A. 1991. *International Economics.* London: Routledge.

————. 2001. "Assessing the Efficiency Gain from Further Liberalization: A Comment." In P. Sauvé and A. Subramanian, eds. *Efficiency, Equity and Legitimacy: The Multilateral Trading System and the Millennium.* Chicago: University of Chicago Press.

————. 2002. "Doha and the World Poverty Targets." Paper presented to the Annual World Bank Conference on Development Economics. April *<econ.worldbank.org/view.php? type=5&confid=2579&id=14983>.*

Winters, L. A., T. L. Walmsley, Z. K. Wang, and R. Grynberg. 2002. "Liberalising Labour Mobility Under the GATS." Economic Paper No. 53. Commonwealth Secretariat, London.

Wong, K-Y. 1986. "Are International Trade and Factor Mobility Substitutes?" *Journal of International Economics* 21(1/2) (August): 25–43.

World Bank. 1999. *World Development Indicators, 1999.* Washington, D.C.

5

LABOR MOBILITY IN REGIONAL TRADE AGREEMENTS

Julia Nielson[*]

T his chapter explores the coverage and treatment of labor mobility in regional trade agreements (RTAs) and compares them with that found in World Trade Organization (WTO) agreements—that is, under mode 4 of the General Agreement on Trade in Services (GATS). Although mode 4 under the GATS is limited to the temporary movement of service suppliers, this chapter refers to "labor mobility" because many of the agreements examined are broader in their coverage of movement of workers than the relatively narrow definition of mode 4 in the GATS.

The chapter has three parts. The first part provides an overview of the key points emerging from this study of the various agreements. It is followed by a summary of the provisions of WTO agreements related to labor mobility. The third part outlines the coverage of labor mobility in 22 regional trade agreements. A glossary of regional trade agreements that includes the members of each agreement appears in the appendix to this chapter.

Overview

Regional trade agreements approach the movement of workers, or labor mobility, in a wide variety of ways. Some agreements cover the mobility of people in general, including permanent migration and nonworkers; others offer free movement of labor, including entry to the local labor market; some are limited to facilitate

[*]Julia Nielson is with the Trade Directorate of the Organisation for Economic Co-operation and Development (OECD). The views expressed in this paper are the author's alone and do not bind the member states of the OECD in any way.

movement for certain kinds of trade- or investment-related activities; and still others, such as the GATS, are confined to temporary movement and only for service suppliers (and explicitly exclude entry to the labor market or permanent migration). Some agreements cover workers at all skill levels; others are limited to higher skilled workers.

The different approaches in RTAs to labor mobility reflect a range of factors, including the geographic proximity of the parties, their similarities in levels of development, and cultural and historical ties. Generally, agreements among countries enjoying geographic proximity and similar levels of development have a more liberal approach to labor mobility—for example, the European Union (EU), European Free Trade Agreement (EFTA), Agreement on the European Economic Area (EEA), and Trans-Tasman Travel Arrangement——as compared with agreements between geographically distant members of differing levels of development— such as the Asia Pacific Economic Cooperation (APEC) forum and the U.S.-Jordan Free Trade Agreement). But such a characterization is not always the case—for example, the Southern Common Market Agreement (MERCOSUR) and South Asian Association for Regional Cooperation (SAARC).

Determining whether the RTAs examined offer greater liberalization than that offered by the same countries under the WTO agreements can be difficult. Labor mobility provisions under the WTO are limited to those related to movement of service suppliers under the GATS, and access under the GATS is determined by Members' individual commitments. For example, although the GATS includes service suppliers of all skill levels, Members' commitments are generally limited to the higher skilled workers. Indeed, an RTA that provides for general access for certain categories of personnel but excludes certain sectors may offer additional liberalization or may simply reflect a country's existing level of GATS commitments (in terms of actual commitments, RTAs among WTO Members would not normally offer less access than that accorded under GATS commitments, for obvious reasons). Assessment of whether the access offered by individual parties goes beyond their GATS commitments would thus depend on a case-by-case analysis.

This chapter therefore looks at whether the regional trade agreements include elements that are not covered by the general GATS provisions rather than at the specific commitments of WTO Members. Additional elements might include: access to the labor market (EU, EFTA, EEA, Trans-Tasman Travel Arrangement); full national treatment and market access for service suppliers (Australia–New Zealand Closer Economic Relations Trade Agreement—ANZCERTA); commitments on visas (North American Free Trade Agreement—NAFTA), including for groups beyond service suppliers (U.S.-Jordan); special market access or facilitated access for certain groups, including beyond service suppliers (Caribbean Community— CARICOM, NAFTA, Canada-Chile, Europe Agreements, APEC); separate chapters dealing with all temporary movement, including that related to investment (Japan-Singapore) or to trade in goods or investment (Group of Three); specific reference to key personnel in relation to investment (EU-Mexico, FTAA); extension of WTO treatment to non–WTO Members (ASEAN [Association of Southeast Asian Nations] Free Trade Area—AFTA); or nondiscriminatory conditions for workers, including beyond service suppliers (Euro-Med—Morocco and Tunisia).

In addition, the provisions related to labor mobility in RTAs were read in conjunction with provisions in the same agreements related to supply of services. Facilitated movement of people does not always automatically entail the right to provide specific services; actual opportunities also will depend on the degree of liberalization in particular service sectors. This is true not simply of agreements in which labor mobility is covered only by mode 4 in the services chapter (e.g., MERCOSUR, EU-Mexico, U.S.-Jordan); it also is true of agreements that provide for broad freedom of movement (e.g., the EU) or in which the movement of natural persons related to services and investment is the subject of a separate chapter (Japan-Singapore). Moreover, some agreements exclude certain service sectors from coverage (e.g., ANZCERTA, EU-Mexico, Europe Agreements) or apply special rules to certain sectors (e.g., EU, EU-Mexico). Generally, right of labor mobility does not automatically entail the right to practice a certain profession; national regulations for licensing and recognition of qualifications are still applied and candidates must meet all criteria and conditions.[1]

Assessment of the degree of liberalization offered by different agreements also is complicated by the very different approaches taken—it is easy to fall into the trap of comparing apples and oranges. Comparison of the types of exceptions in different agreements reveals little: certain types of restrictions are unnecessary when the agreement does not offer a certain kind of access. For example, because the EU provides a general right to move and work anywhere in the EU, it specifies that certain jobs in public services are reserved for nationals. But such provisions are not found in other agreements, because they do not offer a level of general access to the labor market that would make such an exception necessary. Similarly, care is needed in comparing the liberalization offered by agreements providing for broad labor mobility, but excluding some sectors, with that offered by agreements including all sectors, but limiting mobility to certain defined groups.

Those agreements that do not provide for full labor or service supplier mobility (e.g., EU-Mexico, NAFTA, Canada-Chile, U.S.-Jordan, MERCOSUR, Japan-Singapore, Group of Three) tend to use GATS-type carve-outs, often using GATS language verbatim. These agreements generally exclude permanent migration and access to the labor market (although NAFTA and Canada-Chile allow temporary entry to the labor market for some categories), and do not impinge on the right of countries to regulate the entry and stay of individuals, so long as such regulations do not nullify or impair specific commitments undertaken. Some agreements (e.g., EU-Mexico and a proposal in the FTAA) seem to carve out a slightly broader regulatory prerogative for parties, including regulations also related to work, labor conditions, and the establishment of natural persons, in the general formulation of measures that members can apply, provided that they do not nullify or impair specific commitments undertaken (per paragraph 4 of the GATS Annex on Movement of Natural Persons Supplying Services under the Agreement).

Although some agreements, such as the EU, allow the general mobility of people and confer immigration rights, the majority provide only special access or facilitation of existing access within existing immigration arrangements. In most agreements, labor mobility does not override general migration legislation, and parties retain broad discretion to grant, refuse, and administer residence permits and visas. Some agreements, such as Euro-Med (Morocco and Tunisia), specify that liberalizing provisions of the agreement cannot be used to challenge immigration decisions refusing entry, or that dispute settlement under the agreement can be invoked only in cases in which the matter involves a pattern of practice and local remedies have been exhausted (e.g., Canada-Chile, NAFTA).

Occasionally, an agreement (e.g., the draft FTAA), while including mode 4 in the services chapter, will also include provisions in the investment chapter on companies' needs to bring in key personnel. Similarly, the ASEAN Investment Framework Agreement calls for the promotion of freer movement of skilled labor and professionals; the US-Jordan agreement includes visa commitments for investors; and the EU-Mexico agreement section on financial services includes provisions on the nationality of key personnel. Although these provisions may be more concerned with mode 3 (establishment), they illustrate the linkages between modes 3 and 4. And although such provisions may go beyond the GATS in specifying treatment of key personnel, they also may simply reflect the reality of WTO Members' GATS commitments, many of which provide better access for mode 4 movement linked to mode 3 (e.g., intracorporate transferees). Other agreements devote a separate chapter to the temporary movement of all types of businesspeople (e.g., the Group of Three and some bilateral agreements in Latin America), or group intracorporate transferees, service suppliers, and investors in a separate chapter on movement of natural persons (e.g., Japan-Singapore).

Finally, the symbiotic relationship between the GATS and RTAs is evident in the agreements chosen. NAFTA provided the model for language in the GATS on temporary entry, including the negative definition of "temporary," and, in turn, other RTAs use the GATS model (EU-Mexico, U.S.-Jordan, MERCOSUR), sometimes simply by reference (U.S.-Jordan). RTAs also feed off each other—Canada-Chile draws heavily on the NAFTA model; many of the agreements among Latin American countries closely mirror each other; and the influence of both NAFTA and EU-Mexico can be seen in some proposals on the table in the FTAA. For labor mobility, RTAs basically take two general forms—free labor mobility (or close to it) or provision of certain forms of mobility for some categories of persons related to trade. Within each of these forms, the agreements generally contain basic types of similar provisions, with differences reflecting the depth and extent of commitments rather than fundamentally different approaches.

Provisions in WTO Agreements

There are no provisions on labor mobility in the WTO agreements. However, movement of natural persons as service suppliers is covered by mode 4 of the GATS, which is defined as "the supply of a service . . . by a service supplier of one Member, through presence of natural persons of a Member in the territory of another Member." Service suppliers include independent service suppliers and the self-employed, as well as foreign employees of foreign companies established in the territory of a member.[2] The GATS applies to nationals, or to permanent residents where a member does not have nationals, or accords substantially the same treatment to permanent residents and nationals (however, in such cases the Council for Trade in Services must be notified).

The GATS Annex on Movement of Natural Persons Supplying Services under the Agreement contains two important limits on mode 4. Paragraph 1 of the annex states that the GATS does not apply to "measures affecting natural persons seeking access to the employment market of a Member, nor . . . to measures regarding citizenship, residence or employment on a permanent basis." The GATS is thus limited to temporary movement, although "temporary" is not defined and members have adopted a range of approaches.

Paragraph 4 of the annex notes that the GATS shall not prevent a Member from applying measures to regulate the entry of natural persons into, or their temporary stay in, its territory, including those measures necessary to protect the integrity of, and to ensure that orderly movement of natural persons across, its borders, provided that such measures are not applied in such a manner as to nullify or impair the benefits accruing to any Member under the terms of a specific commitment.

Discriminatory visa requirements are not per se regarded as nullifying or impairing such benefits.

The GATS provides no guaranteed access for mode 4 suppliers; access is determined by the nature of each member's specific commitments. Generally, mode 4 commitments are quite restrictive, tend to concern mostly intracorporate transferees, and often are subject to economic needs tests. Although mode 4 covers service suppliers at all skill levels, members' commitments tend to be limited to higher skill categories such as managers, specialists, and professionals. Access under mode 4 also can be affected by most-favored-nation (MFN) exemptions and licensing requirements, including recognition of qualifications, as well as restrictions under mode 3. The GATS contains no specific provisions for facilitated entry, although individual countries' specific commitments may include measures to facilitate entry.[3]

Provisions in Regional Trade Agreements

The RTAs described in this section have been divided into seven broad groups, according to the approach they take to labor mobility. Groupings are based on the agreements' text, not on what has actually been implemented, because such an assessment is beyond the scope of this study. Thus the Common Market for Eastern and Southern Africa (COMESA) is included under the heading "full mobility of labor" because that is the objective of the agreement, although progress toward that objective appears to have been limited to date. Even though some agreements have built-in future work (e.g., the Euro-Med agreements commit to exploring ways to achieve progress on the movement of workers, and the Group of Three and other Latin American agreements create working groups on temporary entry), the separate category of "works in progress" is used for those agreements still being negotiated (e.g., FTAA, Southern African Development Community— SADC). For the former, the parties have clearly agreed to something that they have yet to implement, or they have agreed to a process; for the latter, it cannot be stated with any certainty to what the parties will agree. Finally, the groupings used are indicative only, and some similarities exist between agreements in different groupings—for example, NAFTA and U.S.-Jordan both contain visa arrangements.

Agreements Providing Full Mobility of Labor

European Union (EU).   The EU provides for a broad right to labor mobility. As one of the four fundamental freedoms of the single market, Article 18 of the European Community treaty gives every EU citizen a fundamental, personal right to move and reside freely within the territory of the member states (subject to some limitations and conditions). In addition, treaty provisions apply to movement of workers, the self-employed, and service suppliers, including those posted temporarily to another member state:

- Freedom of movement of workers (Article 39) includes access to employment in other member states; residence rights (with family) in other member states (for those seeking employment, a six-month time limit normally applies); and equality of treatment in working conditions and employment-related benefits.

- Right of establishment (Article 43) includes the right to work as a self-employed person, by establishing either the main professional center or a subsidiary, under the same conditions applying to nationals (subject to provisions relating to capital).
- Freedom to provide services (Article 49) covers commercial and industrial activities, craftsmen and the professions on a temporary[4] basis, under the same conditions as for nationals (or, where a service has not been liberalized, restrictions must apply equally to nationals and other EU citizens).

No visas or work permits are required, although residence permits may be.[5] Even within the very liberal EU regime, there are exceptions to free movement on the grounds of public policy, public security, or public health. However, any measures taken must be: (a) justified by a real and sufficiently serious threat to a fundamental interest of society; (b) in conformity with the European Convention for the Protection of Human Rights and Fundamental Freedoms and the proportionality principle; and (c) not invoked to service economic ends. Limits on the freedom to provide services also can be determined by the degree of liberalization in a given service sector. Special conditions apply for transport, banking, and insurance services, and some public service posts may be reserved for nationals.

The EU treaty on the free movement of persons has been expanded, under the EEA agreement, to include the EFTA-EEA states.

Agreement on the European Economic Area (EEA). The agreement allows EEA nationals to enter any member state of the EU as workers, self-employed, service providers, or recipients.[6] Workers can stay or move freely within EU and EFTA states for the purpose of employment and remain in the territory of those states after being employed. Discrimination based on nationality in employment, remuneration, and other conditions of work and employment is forbidden. However, employment in the public service—that is, the exercise of official governmental authority—is excluded. Rights of establishment also are guaranteed, including for self-employed persons. Exceptions relate to public policy, public security or public health, and the exercise of official authority. There are no restrictions on the freedom to provide services, and temporary service providers receive national treatment. Special conditions apply to transport, financial, audiovisual, and telecommunications services.

European Free Trade Association (EFTA). Similar arrangements are provided under the Agreement Amending the Convention Establishing the EFTA, signed on

June 21, 2001, and set to enter into force in parallel with the Swiss-EU bilateral agreements.[7] These amendments largely extend to all EFTA members, including Switzerland, the arrangements existing among the EFTA-EEA states (Iceland, Liechtenstein, Norway). The agreement introduces free movement for workers, the self-employed, and persons with no gainful employment who otherwise have sufficient financial means, including, under certain conditions, their family members. It confers the right of access to work, entry/exit, and establishment (residence); the right to provide services for a period of up to 90 days a year; and the right of equal treatment. These rights cover all persons, regardless of nationality, who are integrated into the regular labor market of one of the EFTA states. No visas are required. However, some limits and transition periods apply,[8] and special rules govern frontier workers, public service and public authority activities, and the acquisition of real estate in Switzerland.

Common Market for Eastern and Southern Africa (COMESA). The COMESA treaty envisions a community within which goods, services, capital, and labor are free to move across national borders. The complete COMESA mandate is regarded as a long-term objective; establishment of a monetary union and the free movement of bona fide persons, including right of establishment (economic community status), is planned for 2025. In the interim, COMESA is implementing a protocol on the gradual relaxation and eventual elimination of visa requirements and a protocol on the free movement of persons, labor, and services, and the right of establishment and residence.

Australia–New Zealand Closer Economic Relations (ANZCERTA). The Services Protocol of ANZCERTA provides both full market access (Article 4) and full national treatment (Article 5) for all service suppliers.[9] Because all service suppliers are covered, the agreement does not feature detailed definitions of types of personnel, nor does it distinguish between different modes of delivering services. However, certain service sectors[10] are excluded from coverage by the parties, and the agreement also is subject to the foreign investment policies of the member states (Article 2). ANZCERTA does not cover general labor mobility, but probably does not need to do so, because, under the Trans-Tasman Travel Arrangement, Australians and New Zealanders are free to live and work in each other's countries for an indefinite period. Limited exceptions apply, however, such as people with criminal records. This arrangement is not expressed in the form of any binding bilateral treaty, but rather is a series of immigration procedures applied by each country and underpinned by joint expressions of political support. This arrangement does not form part of ANZCERTA.

Agreements Providing Market Access for Certain Groups or a Separate Chapter on Mobility

Caribbean Community (CARICOM). Under CARICOM, Protocol II, Establishment, Services and Capital (1998) provides for the free movement of university graduates, other professionals and skilled persons, and selected occupations,[11] as well as freedom of travel and exercise of a profession. In doing so, it eliminates passport requirements, facilitates entry at immigration points, and eliminates work permit requirements for CARICOM nationals. National treatment is guaranteed (although specific reservations can be made), but there is currently no MFN provision. Exceptions, per the GATS, cover activities involving the exercise of governmental authority and measures to protect public morals, human, animal, and plant life, and national security; maintain public order and safety; and secure compliance with the laws of a member state. Progress has been solid, but implementation is incomplete.

North American Free Trade Agreement (NAFTA) and Canada-Chile Free Trade Agreement. NAFTA predated and informed the development of the GATS. Chapter 16 of NAFTA facilitates the movement of businesspeople, and the corresponding part of the Canada-Chile Free Trade Agreement, Chapter K, is modeled on it. Both agreements are limited to temporary entry, defined negatively as being "without the intent to establish permanent residence," and apply only to citizens of parties. Access is basically limited to four higher-skill categories: traders and investors, intracorporate transferees, business visitors, and professionals (detailed definitions are provided). However, these groups are not limited to services and may include persons in activities related to agriculture or manufacturing. Labor certification or labor market assessment/tests are removed for all four groups,[12] and work permits are required for traders and investors, intracorporate transferees, and professionals, but not business visitors (see note 11). Although visas are still required, fees for processing applications are limited to the approximate cost of services rendered.

Under both agreements, existing general immigration requirements (e.g., related to public health or national security) still apply. Both agreements also refuse entry if it may adversely affect settlement of a labor dispute in progress at the intended place of employment, or the employment of any person who is involved in such a dispute. Equally, both specify that dispute settlement provisions cannot be invoked for a refusal to grant temporary entry, unless the matter involves a pattern of practice and the businessperson has exhausted the available administrative remedies.

Under NAFTA, the United States provides "Trade NAFTA" (TN) visas for professionals, which are valid for one year and are renewable.[13] Canadians can receive

TN status at the port of entry on presentation of a letter from a U.S. employer, but until January 1, 2004, Mexicans must arrange for their employer to file a labor condition application, and then must apply for a visa at the U.S. embassy in Mexico. There are no provisions for facilitated entry under the Canada-Chile agreement, although Chilean businesspeople can apply for an extension of the employment authorization while in Canada.

Under NAFTA, until January 1, 2004, the United States applies a quota of 5,500 a year to Mexican professionals. The Canada-Chile agreement does not permit either party to impose or maintain any numerical restriction on the temporary entry of any category.

Europe Agreements.   In the agreements concluded by the EU with Bulgaria, Czech Republic, Estonia, Hungary, Latvia, Lithuania, Poland, Romania, Slovak Republic, and Slovenia, there is no general freedom of movement for workers.[14] However, parties are to allow the nationals of, or companies established in, the parties to progressively supply services, taking into account the development of the service sectors. Temporary entry is provided for natural persons providing a service, key personnel,[15] and representatives of a company or national of an EU or Central or East European country who are negotiating for the sale of services or entering into agreements to sell services, provided they are not engaged in direct sales to the public or supplying services themselves. A horizontal transition period of 10 years applies. General exceptions cover public policy, public security or public health, and activities connected to the exercise of official authority. Sectoral exclusions also can apply, varying between countries (e.g., transport for Poland). Rights of establishment, including on a self-employed basis, also are extended without discrimination, and key personnel can be posted on a long-term basis, provided a real and continuous link with the home country is demonstrated.

Japan-Singapore Free Trade Agreement.   Chapter 9 (Movement of Natural Persons) of the Japan-Singapore Free Trade Agreement applies to measures affecting the movement of natural persons of a party (nationals of Japan and nationals and permanent residents of Singapore) who enter the territory of the other party for business purposes, including as investors. Exclusions are similar to those in the GATS Annex on Movement of Natural Persons Supplying Services under the Agreement—that is, regarding nationality, citizenship, residence, or employment on a permanent basis. Conditions for entry and stay are governed by specific commitments covering short-term business visitors and intracorporate transferees (Annex VI, Part A) and investors and independent service suppliers[16] (Annex VI, Part B). Specific commitments apply only to those sectors in which commitments have been made under Chapter 7 (Services) and in which no specific restrictions have been made under Chapter 8 (Investment). [17] The agreement includes the general exceptions of GATS Article XIV (with the exception of XIV.d and XIV.e relating to taxation) and includes the language from the GATS annex (paragraph 4) about measures to regulate the entry and stay.

Group of Three.   For the Group of Three—Colombia, Venezuela, and Mexico—temporary entry for businesspersons is the subject of Chapter XIII, which refers to the preferential trading relationship between the parties, the desirability of facilitating temporary entry on a reciprocal basis and of establishing transparent criteria and procedures for temporary entry, and the need to ensure border security and to protect the domestic labor force and permanent employment in their respective territories.[18] (GATS carve-outs related to access to employment markets or permanent employment are found in Chapter X on services.) The agreement requires each party to apply expeditiously measures related to such entry in order to avoid unduly impairing or delaying trade in goods or services or conduct of investment activities. The parties also endeavor to develop and adopt common criteria, definitions, and interpretations for implementation of the chapter. The agreement creates a Temporary Entry Working Group, including immigration officials, which must meet at least once a year.

Similar provisions are found in the Mexico-Nicaragua Agreement, the Agreement between Central America and the Dominican Republic, the Chile-Mexico Agreement, the Mexico-Bolivia Agreement, and the Mexico-Costa Rica Agreement.

Agreements Using the GATS Model with Some Additional Elements

U.S.-Jordan Free Trade Agreement.   In this agreement labor mobility is covered under the section on trade in services (Article 3), which uses the GATS as a frame of reference. Indeed, unless otherwise stated, all terms in Article 3 and the accompanying schedules have their GATS meanings *mutatis mutandis* (Article 3.4[a]). Treatment of mode 4 is also modeled on the GATS; the GATS Annex on Movement of Natural Persons gives rise to rights and obligations under the U.S.-Jordan agreement (Article 3.2[c][ii]), and specific commitments appear in schedules annexed to the agreement.[19] However, the agreement goes further than the GATS in specifying visa commitments (Article 8) for both independent traders (Article 8.1) and persons linked to investment (Article 8.2),[20] beyond service suppliers. Nationals of Jordan are eligible for U.S. treaty-trader (E-1) and treaty-investor (E-2) visas, and similar treatment is guaranteed for U.S. nationals seeking entry to Jordan.

However, these provisions are subject to the laws relating to entry, sojourn, and employment of aliens of the parties.

EU-Mexico Free Trade Agreement.   The EU-Mexico Free Trade Agreement addresses labor mobility through trade in services. The agreement provides for the creation of a GATS Article V agreement, based on principles of market access, MFN, and national treatment. Negotiations on modalities are to take place within three years of the date of entry into force of the agreement. The negotiated commitments are to be implemented over a transition period of up to 10 years from that date. The agreement is not intended to cover movement beyond service suppliers under the GATS. Like the GATS, mode 4 access will not include access to the labor market (Article 3[c][i]), and parties maintain their right to regulate the entry and stay of individuals—although, unlike the GATS, the EU-Mexico agreement also specifies regulations on "work, labour conditions and establishment of natural persons" (Article 27 [Exceptions]). Access is limited to nationals of the parties (Article 3[f]). Some service sectors are specifically excluded from the scope of the negotiations: audiovisual, air transport services not currently covered under the GATS, and maritime cabotage.

A separate section on financial services (Chapter III) states that parties may not require that managerial or key personnel be of a particular nationality, or that more than simple majorities of boards of directors of financial service suppliers of the other party be nationals or residents of a party (Article 16). However, parties may maintain measures inconsistent with this provision, provided they are scheduled and subject to review with a view to their modification, suspension, or elimination (Article 17). Although these are technically requirements related to mode 3 (establishment) rather than mode 4, they illustrate the linkages between these two modes, in particular the impact of mode 3 restrictions on mode 4 (see also FTAA).

ASEAN Free Trade Area (AFTA).   AFTA contains no specific provisions on labor mobility, although mode 4 is included under the general coverage of trade in services. The 1995 ASEAN Framework Agreement on Services committed members to negotiations aimed at achieving commitments beyond those in their existing GATS schedules. Packages of offers were finalized in 1997 and 1998, respectively, covering all modes of supply and including service sectors not previously included in GATS commitments. The 1998 package also provided for member states that were WTO Members to extend their GATS specific commitments to ASEAN member states that were not WTO Members. Indonesia and Lao People's Democratic Republic have yet to ratify this agreement. The Framework Agreement on the ASEAN Investment Area (1998) commits members to promoting the freer flow of capital, skilled labor, professionals, and technology among ASEAN member states.

Euro-Mediterranean Association Agreements (Morocco and Tunisia). The Euro-Mediterranean Association Agreements with Morocco and Tunisia (Title III, Right of Establishment and Services) simply reaffirm each party's obligations under the GATS.[21] However, they provide for future widening to cover rights of establishment and supply of services through the establishment of an "economic integration" type of agreement, with progress to be reviewed no later than five years after the agreement's entry into force. In addition, under Title VI (Cooperation in Social and Cultural Matters), Chapter II (Dialogue on Social Matters), the parties agree in Article 69.2 to pursue on a regular basis ways in which to achieve progress on the movement of workers—that is, all workers, not just service suppliers. The same title, under Chapter I, Workers, also includes stipulations for nondiscriminatory treatment. It covers working conditions; remuneration; dismissal, including for temporary workers (Article 64); and social security (Article 65). However, nondiscrimination obligations with regard to redundancy cannot be invoked to obtain renewal of a residence permit. The granting, renewal, and refusal of residence permits continue to be governed by the legislation of each party or by any bilateral agreements. Nationals residing or working illegally in another party are excluded from this agreement (Article 66); bilateral agreements between individual member states and Morocco/Tunisia may provide more favorable treatment (Article 68).[22]

New Zealand–Singapore Closer Economic Partnership. Labor mobility is included in Part 11 (General Provisions), Article 72 (Movement of Natural Persons), which mirrors almost exactly the language of the GATS annex on the same subject. Movement of service suppliers is covered by Part 5 (Services), which adopts the GATS framework. Parties undertake to review their schedules of commitments at least every two years (earlier if so agreed) and to progressively expand these initial commitments as well as expand market access or national treatment between them in accordance with the APEC objective of free and open trade in services by 2010 (Article 20.4). In specific commitments, both Singapore and New Zealand have scheduled horizontal commitments for mode 4, limited to certain categories.[23]

Agreements That Use the GATS Model

Southern Common Market Agreement (MERCOSUR). MERCOSUR also directly replicates the GATS model. GATS carve-outs related to access to the labor market and permanent migration and the right of members to regulate the entry and stay of foreigners in their territory are included verbatim. Market access is based solely on specific commitments, covering the movement of all categories of natural person who provide services within the framework of the protocol. Movement of natural persons is not specified under the Bolivia-MERCOSUR Agreement or the Chile-MERCOSUR Agreement (see www.oas.org).

Agreements Providing No Market Access but Facilitated Entry

Asia Pacific Economic Cooperation (APEC) Forum.   APEC does not contain any specific market access arrangements related to labor mobility. Periods of, and conditions for, temporary entry vary among economies. However, APEC does include arrangements aimed at facilitating labor mobility by information exchange; dialogue with business; development and implementation of immigration standards; and capacity building to help streamline temporary entry, stay, and departure processing for businesspeople. In-principle agreements have been reached to improve application processing times for temporary entry permits for executives and senior managers on intracorporate transfers and for specialists.[24] APEC arrangements exclude the self-employed and unskilled or semiskilled labor.

Although APEC does not grant any right of entry, it has established a scheme to facilitate the entry of business visitors under the APEC Business Travel Card Scheme. The APEC Business Travel Card is valid for three years and provides multiple short-term business entries, with stays of two or three months on each arrival. Cardholders are required to present their passports, but receive expedited airport processing and are not required to submit separate applications for business visitor visas.[25] Participating economies commit to implement the scheme on a best endeavors basis and are free to maintain existing visa requirements for business visitors.[26] All economies retain the right to refuse an individual a card without providing reasons or to refuse entry to APEC Business Travel Card holders at the border.

South Asian Association for Regional Cooperation (SAARC).   The South Asian Preferential Trading Arrangement does not cover trade in services, but a South Asian Free Trade Area was supposed to be developed by 2001. However, under a Visa Exemption Scheme (1992) visa requirements are waived for 21 categories of persons. Simplification of visa procedures and requirements also is under way to help businesspeople to accelerate promotion of trade and tourism within the region.

Agreements without Provisions on Labor Mobility or Services

Central European Free Trade Agreement (CEFTA).   CEFTA contains no provisions on labor mobility or trade in services (and thus mode 4), and there are no plans at this stage to expand the scope of the agreement.

Agreements That Are Works in Progress

Free Trade Area of the Americas (FTAA). The FTAA is still very much in the negotiations stage, but proposals on the table seem to reflect provisions in agreements to which putative FTAA members are already party.

At this stage of the FTAA, mode 4 is included in the draft services chapter in terms similar to those found in the GATS. Coverage is proposed for citizens/nationals and possibly permanent residents. Proposed exceptions are also similar to those found in the GATS—for example, permanent migration and access to the labor market, and requiring that the agreement be subject to members' laws and regulations, including those on labor and the entry and stay of foreigners. One proposal calls for adding elements from the EU-Mexico agreement related to requirements connected with "work, labour conditions and establishment of natural persons." Another proposal would exclude government procurement in services and certain public services from the agreement.

Provisions on "Key Personnel" appear in the draft chapter on investment, covering nationality requirements for senior management and boards of directors, and the ability of companies to bring in key personnel, including management and persons with specialized knowledge or skills or considered indispensable to the proper control of an investment. It is proposed that key personnel be exempted from labor certification tests or numerical restrictions.

Southern African Development Community (SADC). The ultimate aim of SADC is to promote the free movement of goods and services within the region. In 2002 SADC trade and industry ministers approved the development of an Annex on Trade in Services to the SADC Protocol on Trade. The draft annex includes a provision along the lines of GATS mode 4. Ministers are currently awaiting members' comments on the draft. Work is also under way on a study of labor market issues, including migrant labor and mobility of high-level personnel. The study will explore development of a subregional classification of occupations to facilitate mobility of labor.

Appendix: Glossary of Regional Trade Agreements

AFTA (ASEAN Free Trade Area): Brunei Darussalam, Indonesia, Lao People's Democratic Republic, Malaysia, Myanmar, Philippines, Singapore, Thailand, Vietnam.

ANZCERTA (Australia–New Zealand Closer Economic Relations Trade Agreement): Australia, New Zealand.

APEC (Asia Pacific Economic Cooperation Forum): Australia; Brunei Darussalam; Canada; Chile; China; Hong Kong, China; Indonesia; Japan; Republic of Korea;

Malaysia; Mexico; New Zealand; Papua New Guinea; Peru; Philippines; Russian Federation, Singapore; Taiwan, China; Thailand; United States; Vietnam.

ASEAN (Association of Southeast Asian Nations): Brunei Darussalam, Cambodia, Indonesia, Lao PDR, Malaysia, Myanmar, Philippines, Singapore, Thailand, Vietnam.

CARICOM (Caribbean Community): Antigua and Barbuda, the Bahamas, Barbados, Belize, Dominica, Grenada, Guyana, Haiti, Jamaica, St. Kitts and Nevis, St. Lucia, St. Vincent and the Grenadines, Suriname, Trinidad and Tobago. The Bahamas does not participate in the common market and Haiti is not yet a full member.

CEFTA (Central European Free Trade Agreement): Bulgaria, Czech Republic, Hungary, Poland, Romania, Slovak Republic, Slovenia.

COMESA (Common Market for Eastern and Southern Africa): Angola, Burundi, Comoros, Republic of Congo, Djibouti, Arab Republic of Egypt, Eritrea, Ethiopia, Kenya, Madagascar, Malawi, Mauritius, Namibia, Rwanda, Seychelles, Sudan, Swaziland, Zambia, Zimbabwe.

EEA (Agreement on the European Economic Area): Austria, Belgium, Denmark, Finland, France, Germany, Greece, Iceland, Ireland, Italy, Liechtenstein, Luxembourg, Netherlands, Norway, Portugal, Spain, Sweden, United Kingdom.

EFTA (European Free Trade Association): Iceland, Liechtenstein, Norway, and Switzerland.

EU (European Union): Austria, Belgium, Denmark, Finland, France, Germany, Greece, Ireland, Italy, Luxembourg, Netherlands, Portugal, Spain, Sweden, United Kingdom.

Europe Agreements: The EU has concluded these with Bulgaria, Czech Republic, Estonia, Hungary, Latvia, Lithuania, Poland, Romania, Slovak Republic, Slovenia.

Euro-Med (Euro-Mediterranean Association Agreements—first generation): The EU has concluded these with Cyprus, Malta, Turkey.

Euro-Med (Euro-Mediterranean Association Agreements): The EU has concluded these with Algeria, Israel, Jordan, Lebanon, Morocco, Palestinian Authority, Tunisia.

Euro-Med (Euro-Mediterranean Co-operation Agreements): The EU has concluded these with Algeria, Egypt, Jordan, Lebanon, Syria.

FTAA (Free Trade Area of the Americas): Antigua and Barbuda, Argentina, the Bahamas, Barbados, Belize, Bolivia, Brazil, Canada, Chile, Colombia, Costa Rica, Dominica, Dominican Republic, Ecuador, El Salvador, Grenada, Guatemala, Guyana, Haiti, Honduras, Jamaica, Mexico, Nicaragua, Panama, Paraguay, Peru, St. Lucia, St. Kitts and Nevis, St. Vincent and the Grenadines, Suriname, Trinidad and Tobago, Uruguay, United States, República Bolivariana de Venezuela.

Group of Three: Colombia, Mexico, República Bolivariana de Venezuela.

MERCOSUR (Mercado Común del Sur/Southern Common Market Agreement): Argentina, Brazil, Paraguay, Uruguay.

NAFTA (North American Free Trade Agreement): Canada, Mexico, United States.

SAARC (South Asian Association for Regional Co-operation): Bangladesh, Bhutan, India, Maldives, Nepal, Pakistan, Sri Lanka.

SADC (Southern African Development Community): Angola, Botswana, Republic of Congo, Lesotho, Malawi, Mauritius, Mozambique, Namibia, Seychelles, South Africa, Swaziland, Tanzania, Zambia, Zimbabwe.

Trans-Tasman Travel Arrangement: Australia, New Zealand.

Notes

1. Provisions facilitating mutual recognition are included in some agreements (e.g., EFTA). Others have complementary arrangements. For example, the ANZCERTA Services Procotol, the Trans-Tasman Travel Arrangement, and the Trans-Tasman Mutual Recognition Arrangement together provide that persons registered to practice an occupation in one country can practice an equivalent profession in the other country.

2. There is some debate within the WTO Secretariat about whether foreign employees of domestic firms are covered by mode 4. The secretariat's background note on mode 4 concludes that foreigners working for host country companies would fall under mode 4 if they are working on a contractual basis, but not if they are employees of those firms (WTO 1998). However, others have argued that, because the schedules of many WTO Members refer to short-term employment and schedules form part of the GATS, there is a degree of legal uncertainty on this point (Karsenty 2000). Nonetheless, it should be noted that the WTO Secretariat is not the legal interpreter of the GATS.

3. Disciplines that may later be developed under GATS Article VI.4 also may have implications for regulations affecting mode 4 movement.

4. Like the GATS, this refers to not seeking access to the labor market.

5. Residence permits must be granted for at least five years for workers; for temporary employment of less than one year a temporary residence permit can be issued for the expected duration of employment. Employees working for less than three months, cross-frontier workers, and seasonal workers (on specified terms) do not require residence permits. The cost of residence permits cannot exceed that of identity cards for nationals.

6. EEA nationals should have sufficient funds to support themselves without recourse to public funds.

7. The original Stockholm Convention was signed in 1960.

8. Freedom of movement *into* Switzerland from the other EFTA states is subject to transition periods of up to five years. Switzerland reserves special quotas for EFTA citizens.

9. Different treatment is permitted, provided that it is no greater than necessary for prudential, fiduciary, health and safety, or consumer protection reasons, and such different treatment is equivalent in effect to the treatment accorded by the member state to its ordinary residents for such reasons (Article 5.2[a] and [b]). Both subsidies and government procurement are excluded from the scope of national treatment (Article 5.4).

10. For Australia, these sectors are air services, coastal shipping, broadcasting and television (short-wave and satellite broadcasting); third party insurance; and postal services. For New Zealand, they are aviation (airways services) and shipping (coastal shipping). For many of these services only specific aspects or policies have been excluded.

11. Graduates of universities (several regional universities are named but others also are included), media workers, sports persons, musicians and artists, and workers in the entertainment and tourism industries.

12. Business visitors are exempt from labor market tests, because they receive no remuneration in the country they are entering and therefore are not viewed as entering the labor market.

13. Criteria include: the profession is on the NAFTA list; the candidate meets the specific criteria for that profession; the prospective position requires someone in that capacity; and the candidate is going to work for a U.S. employer.

14. The Europe Agreements reference and supersede previous bilateral labor agreements between some EU member states—in particular, Germany—and some Central and East European countries.

15. Key personnel are defined as senior employees of an organization who are primarily engaged in its management, and persons who possess high or uncommon qualifications, referring to a type of work or trade requiring technical knowledge essential to the organization's service, research, equipment, techniques, or management. They must have been employed by the organization for at least one year prior and must be nationals of the country in which they work.

16. The term *independent service suppliers* is not used; the actual terminology is: natural persons who engage in work on the basis of a personal contract with public or private organizations. Specific commitments for investors and independent service suppliers are to be implemented in accordance with each party's laws and regulations.

17. Singapore's specific commitments provide for entry for the following categories (all defined): business visitors—one month upon arrival, extendable up to three months on application; intracorporate transferees who are managers, executives, or specialists linked to mode 3 presence (12-month immediate preemployment requirement applies)—two-year period, extendable for periods of up to three years each time, for a total period not exceeding eight years (further extensions may be possible); investors—limited to a two-year period, extendable for periods of up to three years each time, for a total period not exceeding eight years (further extensions may be possible); and independent service suppliers (see note 16) limited to engineers recognized under the domestic laws and regulations of Singapore— two-year period, extendable for periods of up to three years each time, for a total period of not more than eight years (further extensions may be possible). Japan's specific commitments provide entry for short-term business visitors (defined)—a period not exceeding 90 days; intracorporate transferees (subject to an preemployment requirement of not less than one year)—no time limits specified, but the person must be engaged in certain types of activities (basically senior management or involving certain types of specialized skills); investors—for as long as the person continues to meet the criteria and conditions stipulated at the time of entry; and independent service suppliers (see note 16), limited to those engaged in work that requires technology or knowledge pertinent to engineering—for as long as the person continues to meet the criteria and conditions stipulated at the time of entry.

18. The Web site of the Organization of American States (*www.oas.org*) is the basis for material on this and the other agreements mentioned under this heading.

19. Mode 4 commitments are primarily horizontal, with sectoral commitments "[un] bound, except as provided for the horizontal section" but sometimes with additional requirements. Commitments cover: United States—service salespersons, intracorporate transferees (managers, executives, and specialists), personnel engaged in establishment, fashion models, and speciality occupations; Jordan—business visitors, intracorporate transferees, executives, managers, specialists, and professionals.

20. Independent traders must be engaged in substantial trade, including trade in services or trade in technology, principally between the parties. Persons linked to investment must be establishing, developing, administering, or advising on the operation of an investment to which they, or a company of the other party that employs them, have committed or are in the process of committing a substantial amount of capital or other resources.

21. Provisions on labor in the various types of Euro-Med agreements vary (see Appendix). There are no specific provisions on services in the Euro-Med agreement with the Palestinian Authority. The Co-operation Agreement with Algeria does not contain general provisions on services, but does include provisions similar to Articles 64 and 65 of the Agreements with Morocco and Tunisia on nondiscrimination and labor (Articles 38–41 in the agreement). Cooperation agreements with the Arab Republic of Egypt, Lebanon, and Syria contain no provisions on either services or labor/workers. The first-generation association agreement with Cyprus similarly contains no provisions on either services or labor/workers.

22. Migration issues more generally are raised in Article 69.3 (dialogue on migration issues) and in Article 71 (projects aimed at reducing migratory pressure) of Chapter III (Co-operation in the Social Field).

23. New Zealand also makes reference to the presence of natural persons under "dental services." National treatment on mode 4 "dental services" is limited to registered dentists who must satisfy the relevant registration board that they intend to reside and practice in New Zealand.

New Zealand has made no horizontal commitments other than on certain categories of intracorporate transferees (defined as natural persons employed by a service supplier of the other party supplying services through a commercial presence) and business visitors. Intracorporate transferees are executives, senior managers, specialists, or senior personnel (all defined and subject to 12 months' preemployment). They may stay initially up to three years. Installers and servicers (where such installation or servicing is a condition of the purchase of the machinery or equipment) may stay no longer than three months in any 12-month period. Business visitors may stay a period or periods not exceeding three months in any calendar year. Singapore also has also left the presence of natural persons unbound, except for intracorporate transferees and business visitors. Intracorporate transferees are limited to managers, executives, and specialists (all defined and subject to one-year minimum preemployment). Entry is limited to a three-year period that may be extended for two years, but the total period may not exceed five years. Business visitors are granted an initial stay of up to one month on arrival, extendable to a maximum of three months on request.

24. Guideline definitions have been developed for executives and senior managers. Specialists are defined by each economy and are included in economies' *APEC Travel Handbook* entry <www.apecsec.org.sg>.

25. There is no limit on the number of cards, and almost 4,000 have been issued to date. Fees vary among the participating economies. The scheme is open to citizens of participating APEC economies (or permanent residents of Taiwan, China and Hong Kong, China), who hold a valid passport or equivalent, have never been convicted of a criminal offense, and are bona fide businesspeople. The scheme does not include spouses and children; persons who wish to engage in paid employment or working holidays; and professional athletes, news correspondents, entertainers, musicians, artists, and persons engaged in similar occupations.

26. The participating countries are: Australia; Brunei Darussalam; Chile; Taiwan, China; Hong Kong, China; Republic of Korea; Malaysia; New Zealand; Peru, the Philippines, and Thailand. Neither the United States nor Canada is planning to participate in the business travel scheme.

References

Karsenty, G. 2000. "Assessing Trade in Services by Mode of Supply." In P. Sauvé and R. M. Stern, eds. *GATS 2000: New Directions in Services Trade Liberalization*. Washington, D.C.: Brookings Institution Press.

WTO (World Trade Organization). 1998. "Council for Trade in Services—Presence of Natural Persons (Mode 4)—Background Note by the Secretariat." Document S/C/W/75, December 8 <www.wto.org>.

6

CURRENT REGIMES FOR THE TEMPORARY MOVEMENT OF SERVICE PROVIDERS: CASE STUDIES OF AUSTRALIA AND THE UNITED STATES

*Julia Nielson and Olivier Cattaneo**

This chapter undertakes a preliminary exploration of the Australian and U.S. regimes for temporary entrants falling under mode 4 of the General Agreement on Trade in Services (GATS).[1] The first part of the chapter is an overview of the difficulties encountered in trying to map migration systems and regimes for temporary entry against mode 4 of the GATS. The second and third parts present case studies of the Australian and U.S. migration systems, respectively, providing some information on those entry categories that might be most relevant to mode 4. The third part also takes a closer look at U.S. specialty occupation (H1B) visas. This chapter, originally drafted in 2001, has been revised to include changes made since then to both the Australian and U.S. temporary entry regimes.

Overview

The task of exploring current migration regimes for mode 4 entry is not an easy one. The obvious starting point—the GATS commitments of Members of the World Trade Organization (WTO)—yields little in the way of useful information. GATS commitments generally do not reflect the current regime. Rather, they

*Julia Nielson and Olivier Cattaneo are with the Trade Directorate, Organisation for Economic Co-operation and Development.

reflect at best the state of play at the time of the Uruguay Round (1986–93), and generally not even that. Because GATS commitments are binding and cannot be changed unilaterally without cost, WTO Members have tended not to include their existing migration regime in detail in those commitments but to take advantage of the flexibility in the GATS to commit to less than the status quo. Most Members' GATS commitments represent a baseline or "floor" of practice. To obtain a picture of the actual regime for mode 4, one would have to look at the temporary entry schemes within the migration systems of WTO Members.

However, mode 4 is a trade, not a migration, concept. Because no migration category is associated directly with mode 4, it is necessary to identify which type of entrants might fall under mode 4 and which visa categories might be relevant. Mapping mode 4 against temporary entry categories necessarily involves some interpretation, particularly because the type of information required for migration purposes is not always the same as that required to judge the extent of mode 4 coverage.

Both the U.S. and Australian migration systems are sources of transparent and comprehensive data on the number and type of entries, as well as on the terms and conditions for entry. Both systems separate temporary from permanent entry, and, within temporary entry, distinguish between short-term visits (often three months or less) and longer-term (but still temporary) presence (e.g., up to four to five years). Both systems also distinguish between business visitors and tourists, and provide information on the country of origin of entrants and their type of occupation (in terms of skill level, sector, or specific profession). Yet even within these "state-of-the-art" systems, difficulties arise.

First, migration categories generally do not distinguish between service and nonservice activities. Categories such as "business visitors" generally do not include information on the sector in which the entrant is working, and these visitors could be involved in both service and nonservice (e.g., manufacturing, agriculture) activities. Although some visa categories are targeted toward certain sectors such as medical practitioners, other categories refer to more general skills or positions such as finance manager, company secretary, or human resources manager.

Furthermore, it is not always clear what might constitute a service. For example, should fruit pickers be viewed as temporary agricultural workers (outside the scope of mode 4) or as suppliers of fruit-picking services (covered by mode 4)? The answer may depend in part on how broadly WTO Members interpret the scope of the category "services incidental to agriculture" in the Services Sectoral Classification List (W/120).[2] However, even where a service sector is indicated, it may not correspond to the W/120 categories used by many WTO Members in making their GATS commitments.

Second, it is not always possible to judge whether the activities covered by some visa categories are truly commercial (i.e., constitute trade for GATS purposes).

In some cases, the extent to which the activity is commercial is unclear (e.g., sports visas can include both amateurs and professionals). In others, it is hard to judge whether the work would qualify as the supply of a service under the GATS (e.g., occupational trainees, professional exchange programs).

Third, some visa categories include persons both consuming and supplying services. For example, trainees may engage in some on-the-job activities, but also may fall under mode 2 (consumption abroad of training services). Exchange visitors could encompass both those consuming services (e.g., students participating in a given program) and providing services (e.g., visiting lecturers). Such "mixed mode" categories also can occur when those entering to consume a service are granted limited working rights. For example, overseas students in Australia are allowed to work up to 20 hours a week during the academic term and unlimited hours during term breaks (potentially mode 4). However, their primary reason for movement is consumption of education services (mode 2). Similarly, the primary purpose of movement of Australian Working Holiday Makers (WHMs) is consumption of tourism services (mode 2); however, they enjoy working rights while in Australia (temporary or casual work of up to three months with any single employer). Although their economic impact is limited at the national level, it has been argued that the substantial increase in WHMs, more than doubling in the 1990s, has had a significant impact on specific industries and specific areas (Hugo 2002).

Fourth, the boundaries of the definition of mode 4 itself may not be entirely clear. Although "business visitors" who receive no remuneration in the host country are clearly covered by mode 4, and foreign employees of foreign firms clearly fall under mode 4, the status of foreign employees of domestic firms may not be clear. The WTO (1998) has concluded that foreigners working for host country companies would fall under mode 4 if they are working on a contractual basis, but not if they are employees of those firms. However, Karsenty (2000) has argued that, because many WTO Members' schedules refer to short-term *employment* and schedules form part of the GATS, there is a degree of legal uncertainty on this point. Although the WTO Secretariat is not the legal interpreter of the GATS, there is perhaps some need for clarity on this point. After all, it might be difficult to know with certainty in every case whether a foreigner working for a specified period for a domestic company is to be considered as working on a contractual basis or as an employee. Even though from a GATS mode 4 perspective this distinction may be important, it is unlikely to be considered relevant information from a migration policy point of view. For the purposes of this chapter, foreign employees of domestic companies have been included in mode 4.

Notwithstanding these difficulties, some initial observations can be drawn. The actual U.S. and Australian migration systems for temporary entry are broader, more detailed, and more flexible than those countries' GATS commitments.

Actual trade under mode 4 is much greater than the commitments would suggest, with temporary entry increasing for both countries. In the United States, the fastest-growing categories are temporary visitors for business (4.5 million in 1999), temporary workers (including H1B visas) and trainees, and intracorporate transferees. In Australia, it is now estimated that at any one time 2–3 percent of the Australian work force is made up of people on temporary working visas (Hugo 2002).

Both the United States and Australia focus temporary entry on persons with a high level of skills or education. In Australia, 73.5 percent of entrants under the temporary business category fall into the two highest skill categories—managers/administrators and professionals—as compared with 38.8 percent of the total Australian population (Hugo 2002). In addition to managers, executives, and specialists, visa schemes tend to be geared toward those with recognized skills in certain areas such as the media, entertainment, or sports, or those with connections to investment such as investors, intracorporate transferees, or, in Australia, persons entering under Regional Headquarters (RHQ) Agreements. Although there is some provision for lower-skilled labor (e.g., Labour Agreements), the number of entrants is relatively small. Both the United States and Australia also offer special facilitation or entry schemes for nationals of certain countries, including on the basis of regional trade agreements.

In the United States and Australia, periods of stay for temporary entrants vary according to the category of entrant. Extensions are generally (but not always) possible and are usually subject to a maximum limit. All entrants are required to meet general visa conditions regarding, for example, good health and character. Both countries' systems also allow families to accompany many categories of temporary entrants.[3]

Sponsored workers in both the United States and Australia must be paid the same rates as nationals and benefit from the same working conditions. Both countries also stress the need to limit any possible negative impact on nationals by, for example, requiring labor market testing, or requiring companies seeking to employ temporary foreign workers to have a demonstrated record of training nationals, or prohibiting the hiring of temporary foreign workers during labor-management disputes in an industry.

Finally, both case studies underline the difficulty of identifying with precision visa categories of relevance for mode 4. Few if any categories are an exact fit—many are broader than mode 4, and in some cases the available information does not enable a judgment to be made about the extent of mode 4 coverage. Attributions in this chapter are thus indicative and preliminary only. These difficulties are sobering given that the United States and Australia have migration systems that are more detailed than those of many WTO Members. Both case studies therefore underline the need for dialogue at the national level among trade, migration, and labor authorities to gain an understanding of the relationship between temporary entry schemes and mode 4 of the GATS.

Australia: A Case Study

Australia has traditionally encouraged permanent migration rather than temporary residence. However, Australia also has been affected by the general trend toward increased mobility generated by (a) the development of high-skill regional labor markets that cross international boundaries; (b) the internationalization of capital; (c) the exponential development of communications and the exchanges it makes possible; (d) reductions in the time and cost of travel; and (e) the expansion of multinational corporations (Hugo 2002). As a result, Australia is increasingly attracting temporary workers, and a new temporary business entry visa category was created in 1996. But, even though temporary entry is increasing, it remains largely limited to the highly skilled.

Yet the Australian system for temporary entry still must be viewed in the context of an overall permanent migration program increasingly geared toward attracting skilled migrants. Indeed, some of the schemes for temporary entry (e.g., employer sponsorship, Labour Agreements) have counterparts enabling permanent migration.

An Overview of the Australian System

Australia has a highly developed visa system that differentiates among a wide number of categories (based both on length of stay and on type of entrant) and provides detailed information on the number, country of origin, and occupation of persons entering on a temporary basis. Generally, the Australian system allows for a range of temporary entry, with an emphasis, as noted, on the highly skilled. While detailed, the scheme retains the flexibility to allow skills shortages to be targeted and areas of oversupply to be removed from the gazetted list of occupations.[4] It aims, then, to meet shortfalls in the Australian labor market, while minimizing any negative impact on the domestic work force. Both minimum skills level and minimum salary requirements apply, and employers are obliged to comply with Australian industrial relations law and working conditions. Key features of the Australian system include:

- A special scheme for temporary (up to three months per visit) entry for business visitors, covering conferences, training, meetings, building inspections, equipment installation, or short-term projects requiring special skills. This scheme does not include employment by a company in Australia, and holders must not engage in work that might otherwise be carried out by an Australian. Special facilitation schemes (electronic travel authority and the APEC [Asia Pacific Economic Cooperation] Business Travel Card) exist for nationals of certain countries.

- A special "Service Sellers" category introduced specifically for the GATS, covering representatives of overseas suppliers of services seeking to negotiate, or enter into, agreements for the supply of services in Australia (but not actually supplying or directly selling those services), providing for stays of up to six months.
- RHQ Agreements enabling companies establishing such headquarters to transfer key expatriate executive and specialist personnel.
- A range of specific visa categories covering certain sectors, such as medical, educational (includes academics and occupational trainees but not students), entertainment, sports, and media and film staff.
- Some schemes aimed primarily at other purposes but that allow limited working rights, such as the WHM scheme and the Retirement visa.
- Business sponsorship for most categories of economic entrants planning to stay more than three months and up to four years, with approved sponsors often having to nominate specific positions to be filled by foreign workers. Labor market testing does not apply, but entry is limited to certain listed types of positions at the higher skill level.
- A requirement to demonstrate the benefits for Australia, including in terms of job creation and increased trade, that would stem from the temporary entry of foreign workers.
- An emphasis on minimizing any negative impacts for Australians. For example, in the context of applying to sponsor the entry of an overseas worker, companies have to demonstrate a record of employing and training nationals. Specific reference is made in certain categories (e.g., entertainment) to the need to protect the employment of Australians. Some visas are conditional on there being no qualified Australian applicants (e.g., educational visas) or other labor market needs (e.g., medical practitioner visas, including an emphasis on services for rural and remote areas).
- Some highly skilled occupations and some lower-skilled occupations subject to special Labour Agreements (reached between the government, employers, or industry representatives) where there is a demonstrated need for such.
- Allowance in most entry schemes for accompaniment by family members under the same visa conditions as the principal applicant.

Business consultation is another feature of the Australian system. Initiatives include a special business branch and a temporary entry branch within the Department of Immigration and Multicultural and Indigenous Affairs (DIMIA); business centers in state and territory offices providing advice; and external reference groups, formed to consider special areas and made up of experts in the field with an interest in the type of visas being examined.

The Australian scheme is also highly advanced in its use of technology to disseminate information and facilitate processing, with many application forms available online. Australia has a universal visa requirement for all countries except New Zealand; however, electronic visas are available for some nationalities.

All visitors to Australia, under all visa schemes, must meet criteria related to health, character, national security, unpaid debts to the Commonwealth, likelihood of overstaying, and periods of exclusion from Australia for previous breaches of immigration law. Applicants refused a visa are informed of the reasons for refusal and, if applicable, where they can apply for review of the decision. Reviews are available in three situations: (a) the applicant is applying for the visa within Australia; (b) the applicant is applying from outside Australia, but a criterion was that an Australian employer sponsor the applicant—in which case the sponsor may apply for a review; or (c) the application of an Australian business for sponsorship or nomination is refused.

Like many countries, Australia is experiencing particular shortages in information technology (IT). The growth in demand has been estimated at about 9 percent a year—an annual need of about 30,000 workers—which is not being met by current graduate levels. Temporary entry is playing a key role in addressing this demand. The number of computing professionals entering Australia under the temporary residence business visa in 1999–2000 was significantly higher than the number of those coming permanently (Hugo 2002). In 2000–01 almost 30 percent of employer-sponsored business entrants were in IT positions. Nurses are another key area of high demand. Although there is no specific visa for nurses, most visa applications under other categories (e.g., short- or long-stay business visas or WHM) from nurses receive priority processing.

But also like other countries, Australia is concerned about brain drain, particularly (but not only) to the United Kingdom and the United States. The number of Australians leaving for these countries has been increasing, and they are concentrated in the highly skilled occupations. However, the main finding of a recent report is that, over the past five years, Australia has registered a "brain gain" (Birrell and others 2001). Although there was a net loss of skilled Australian residents in some occupations, it was offset for almost every occupation by gains from settler movement and a net inflow of long-term temporary entrants. Similarly, in the IT sector there is some evidence that many Australians with IT skills who go overseas to work later return (Hugo 2002). Nevertheless, this situation is being monitored closely.

Temporary Entry: Visitors and Temporary Residents

There are five main types of temporary entrant: visitors (i.e., tourists); overseas students; WHMs; business; and other (includes economic, social/cultural, and international relations activities). For the purposes of mode 4, the main category of interest is business, which includes both short-stay and temporary residence.

However, WHMs also may be of interest. The WHM scheme allows young people (ages 18–30) from countries with bilateral working holiday arrangements[5] to holiday and work for short periods to supplement their funds. A 12-month stay is permitted, and visa holders can work on a temporary or casual basis for three months at a time with any one employer. Wages and conditions of WHMs should be consistent with Australian standards. The WHM program is argued to generate economic benefits for Australia and has been particularly important for the tourism industry. The government has now commissioned research on WHMs and their impact on the labor market. WHM appears to be a mixture of modes 2 and 4 and could potentially include activities falling outside mode 4, such as agricultural labor.

In addition, many of the categories under "other" may be relevant to mode 4, including some types of social/cultural entrant; domestic worker; educational entrant; medical practitioner; New Zealand citizen family relationship; retirement; and supported dependent.[6] These categories are discussed briefly below.

Social/Cultural Class.   *(This category appears to be mode 4.) Entertainment* visas (420) cover people involved in a wide range of social and cultural events and activities (including fashion models), taking into account the need to protect the employment of Australians. Sponsorship is required unless covered by a bilateral agreement, and visa holders may not change employer or times or places of engagements without prior permission. *Media and film staff* visas (423) cover correspondents or other professional media staff members posted to Australia by overseas news organizations, and photographers and film and television crews making documentaries or commercials for exclusive overseas consumption. A letter of support is required for stays of up to three months, or if the organization is not represented in Australia, or entry is under a bilateral agreement. Sponsorship is required in all other cases for stays of more than three months, and visa condition 8107 applies. This condition states that the visa holder must not cease to be employed or cease the activity for which the visa was granted; work in any other position inconsistent with that for which the visa was granted; or engage in other work while undertaking the activity for which the visa was granted.

Sports visas (421) cover amateur or professional sportspeople engaging in competition with residents in order to improve general sporting standards through high-caliber competition and training. Sponsorship, a letter of invitation, or both may be required, depending on the activity and length of stay. Visa condition 8107 applies. This category appears to be a mixture of mode 4 and non–mode 4 activities, because unpaid activities (e.g., amateur competitions) or activities consumed (e.g., training programs) would fall either outside the GATS or under mode 2, not mode 4.

Public lecturer visas (424) cover professional lecturers or experts invited to make public presentations. A letter of invitation is required for stays of up to three months or entry under a bilateral agreement; in all other cases sponsorship is required. Visa condition 8107 applies.

Exchange visas (411) allow temporary stay by skilled people seeking to broaden their work experience and skills under a reciprocal arrangement. A letter of invitation is required from the organization offering the position. Visa condition 8107 applies.

Domestic Worker Visa Class.   *(This category appears to be mode 4.) Domestic worker (overseas executive)* visas (427) cover the domestic staff of people holding long-stay temporary business entry visas (where necessary for the discharge of their representational duties). Visa condition 8107 applies, and visa holders may not remain in Australia after the permanent departure of their employer.

Educational Visa Class.   *(This category seems closely related to mode 4, although there could be some question if the entrants were seen as employees of, rather than contract service suppliers to, domestic companies.) Educational* visa (418) permits the temporary stay of staff for educational or research institutions to fill academic, teaching, and research positions unable to be filled from within the Australian labor market. A letter of appointment is required for stays up to three months, and sponsorship is required for longer stays. Visa condition 8107 applies. *Visiting academic* visas (419) cover people whose presence will contribute to the sharing of research knowledge. A letter of invitation is required from the institution involved, and the visa holder may not receive a salary from the host institution in Australia.

Occupational trainee visas (442) cover workplace-based (at least 70 percent) training compatible with an applicant's employment history. A visa holder may not work in Australia other than in relation to the course of training. This category may cover both modes 2 and 4.

Foreign government agency visas (415) cover foreign government employees conducting representative business or teaching duties on behalf of their government without diplomatic or official status (e.g., British Council, Alliance Française). These visa holders may *not* be covered by the GATS because they could be providing services in the exercise of governmental authority.

Medical Practitioner (422).   *(This category would seem to fall under mode 4, although there could be some question if the entrants are considered to be employees of, not contract service providers to, local companies.)* This visa allows temporary stay by suitably qualified medical practitioners where there is a demonstrated need to employ a medical practitioner from overseas on a full-time basis. Temporary resident doctors are recruited to fill identified "area of need" positions identified by state health authorities, and many are providing services in regional and remote areas of Australia. Applicants must be sponsored by an Australian organization; have sufficient qualifications; and have conditional registration to work. Employment must be based on relevant Australian legislation and awards and must be of benefit to Australia. Visa condition 8107 applies.

New Zealand Citizen Family Relationship (461).   *(This category might fall under mode 4 because work is permitted.)* This visa permits the temporary stay of family unit members of New Zealand citizen Special Category visa holders, with no conditions.

Retirement (410).   *(This category might fall under mode 4 because work is permitted.)* This visa permits an initial four-year stay by people who want to retire in Australia, with limited work rights (up to 20 hours). Visas for further stays are usually granted for two years at a time. Applicants must have no dependents (other than a spouse) and be self-supporting in Australia without cost to welfare services. Sponsorship or nomination is not required.

Supported Dependent (430).   *(This category might fall under mode 4 if the dependent is not an Australian citizen and if he or she supplies services.)* This visa permits the temporary stay of dependents of an Australian who are usually resident outside Australia. Visa condition 8107 may apply.

Business Entry

This section provides greater detail on the temporary entry schemes for business, because they are the most closely related to mode 4 of the GATS. These schemes fall into two main categories: business visitors (up to three months) and temporary business residents (more than three months but not more than four years).

Temporary business residents include personnel (executives, managers, and specialists) for companies operating in Australia; personnel from offshore companies seeking to establish a branch in Australia, participate in joint ventures, or fulfill a contract awarded to an offshore company; and personnel coming temporarily under a Labour or RHQ Agreement. A category for independent executives seeking to establish a new business or joining existing businesses in Australia has only recently been ceased, and thus is still included in the discussion of each of these categories and subcategories below.

Business Visitors. The Business (short-stay) visa (subclass 456) allows a bona fide businessperson to make a short visit of up to three months to conduct business— a conference, training, meeting, building inspection, equipment installation, or short-term project requiring a high level of skill. It does not cover employment by a company in Australia (456 visa holders are at all times paid by their overseas company), and visa holders must not engage in work that might otherwise be carried out by an Australian. The 456 category and its electronic equivalent (described later in this section) are the major categories clearly related to mode 4. To meet the threshold criteria the applicant must enter or remain in Australia temporarily for business purposes; propose to remain in Australia for not more than three months on any single occasion; and have adequate funds for personal support during the period of stay.

Visas may be issued for single or multiple entry. The latter remains valid for either up to five years or the life of the passport (maximum 10 years). Applications must be made from outside Australia; must describe the proposed business activity; and must include intended length of stay. A passport is required, with an application fee of $65,[7] and processing time is normally a few days. Accompanying family members can be included on the same visa application for no extra fee and are granted the same visa entitlements. Applications for an extension cannot be made within Australia; those wishing to stay on should apply for a longer-stay visa (described later in this section).

A Sponsored Business Visitor (short-stay) visa (subclass 459) exists for visitors sponsored by a federal, state, or territory member of Parliament; a government agency; or local government mayor. Sponsored Business Visitor visas, which can be applied for only from outside Australia, permit only a single entry for a stay of up to three months.

Nationals of eligible countries[8] may receive an *Electronic Travel Authority (ETA)*. There are two types of ETA for business. The Business Entrant (long-validity) ETA ($65) allows multiple entry for up to five years, but stays are limited to three months per visit; extensions may not be sought inside Australia. The Business Entrant (short-validity) ETA covers one entry within 12 months for a stay of up to three months at no fee. All the conditions attached to the 456 visa apply to these ETAs. Business ETAs can be arranged at participating travel agents when the ticket is purchased, or arranged online for a $20 service charge. Processing time in both cases is a few minutes. Family members accompanying holders of long-validity ETAs must each pay the fee. If they do not wish to do so, they can receive a tourist ETA.

APEC Business Travel Card holders from participating APEC economies[9] are not required to make a separate application for a subclass 456 business (short-stay) visa, or to produce evidence of such visa. They receive fast-track entry at airports. Cards are valid for three years and permit multiple entry (visits are limited to three months). The application charge is $150.

Temporary Business Residents.   The temporary residence business (long-stay) visa (457) allows employers to recruit key personnel from overseas to overcome temporary skilled labor shortages. Included in this category are personnel (executives, managers, and specialists) for companies operating in Australia; personnel from offshore companies seeking to establish a branch in Australia, participate in joint ventures, or fulfill a contract awarded to an offshore company; personnel coming under a Labour or RHQ Agreement; and, until recently, "Independent Executives" seeking to establish a new business or joining existing businesses in Australia.

The extent to which entrants under the 457 category fall under GATS mode 4 is not clear. Within the employer-sponsored category, foreign workers sponsored by foreign companies (Overseas Business Sponsorship) would seem to fall under mode 4; however, foreign workers sponsored by Australian companies may not if they are employees rather than working on a contractual basis. Similarly, workers entering under Labour Agreements may be deemed to be employees of domestic firms and not working on a contractual basis, and therefore perhaps are not covered by GATS mode 4. (It is unclear whether such agreements include foreign firms; workers for foreign firms would fall under mode 4.) RHQ Agreements would seem to be relevant for mode 4 because they cover intracorporate transferees (key executive and specialist personnel) of foreign firms. Service Sellers clearly fall under mode 4 of the GATS; indeed, the category "Service Sellers" was specifically developed as part of Australia's participation in the GATS. Independent Executives also are relevant to mode 4, but, being investors, they also are closely linked to mode 3. However, Independent Executives may go beyond the GATS because they are now more closely linked with applications for permanent visas (they also may include non–service sector activities).

The temporary residence business (long-stay) visa covers stays of more than three months but not more than four years. Visa holders are required to pay

Australian taxes, but they are not eligible for welfare or national public health coverage (citizens of countries with which Australia has Reciprocal Health Care Agreements are entitled to emergency medical coverage). Visa condition 8107 applies. Dependent family members have access to the same visa entitlements (same application, no fee) and can work and attend school. Most business (long-stay) visa holders are employed in professional or management positions, and they tend to have salary rates generally above the Australian average.

Conditions for the main categories of temporary business residents—sponsored temporary overseas employees (including RHQ and Labour Agreements), Service Sellers, and Independent Executives—are outlined in the rest of this section.

The first category, *sponsored temporary overseas employees*, includes employees who are employer-sponsored (either by an Australian or overseas business), or who are covered by Labour or RHQ Agreements.[10]

Businesses can sponsor personnel from overseas on a temporary basis to work in Australia for up to four years (labor market testing no longer applies, but entry is limited to positions gazetted by DIMIA. There are three types of business sponsors. *Pre-qualified Business Sponsors* (PQBS) seek approval to fill an unspecified number of vacancies over an initial two-year period, with the possibility of annual renewal (normally larger, established businesses). *Standard Business Sponsors* (SBS) seek approval to fill a set number of anticipated vacancies over a 12-month period. *Overseas Business Sponsors* are businesses with no formal operating base or representation that are bringing employees into Australia to establish a branch, joint venture, or agency distributorship and subsidiary branches, or to fulfill obligations for a contract or other business activity. Approval covers a specified number of temporary business entrants over 12 months or until the nominations are filled. A summary of conditions for sponsorship appears in Table 6.1.

Three steps are required for sponsored entry: (1) the firm applies to be a sponsor; (2) it nominates the positions for which temporary entrants are sought; and (3) the nominees for the positions apply for a temporary residence business (long-stay) visa.

To be approved as a sponsor, an applicant business must satisfy DIMIA that:

- It is a lawfully and actively operating a business—that is, it is not a paper or shelf company.
- It is the direct employer of the temporary business entrant—that is, it is not a recruitment agency.
- It has a record of compliance with immigration laws, with nothing adverse known.
- Australia will benefit from the business employing overseas personnel (e.g., it will create or maintain employment for Australians, expand trade in goods or

TABLE 6.1   Summary of Business Sponsorships, Australia

Sponsor Status	Sponsorship Fee	Nomination Fee	Status Length	No. of Positions
Pre-qualified Business Sponsor	$3,395	nil	Two years initially; possible annual renewal, $1,135	Unlimited
Standard Business Sponsor	nil	$235 per nomination	One year or until nominations are filled, whichever happens earlier	Fixed at time of approval
Overseas Business Sponsor	nil	$235 per nomination	One year or until nominations are filled, whichever happens earlier	Fixed at time of approval

Source: DIMIA (2003).

services, improve business links with international markets, or increase competitiveness within sectors of the Australian economy.

- It will advance skills through technology or training—that is, its Australian business operations will introduce, use, or create new or improved technology or new business skills or have a satisfactory record of training Australians.

    The supporting statement should include details of the number of Australian and non-Australian employees; evidence of cutting-edge technology or business skills, preferably supported by independent advice from a relevant government agency or industry body; and detailed information on the firm's training record (e.g., future recruitment plans, including the nature and duration of the training provided, annual training expenditure as a percentage of gross payroll, number of sponsored employees, and number of graduates/apprentices/trainees hired in the last two years).

- The business is able to comply with the sponsorship undertakings (e.g., compliance with Australian industrial relations laws, levels of remuneration, and conditions of employment—ensuring the salary paid is not less than the industry award or gazetted minimum salary, whichever is higher; assuming financial responsibility for medical costs; ensuring person holds any necessary license or registration; complying with migration requirements, including cooperation with monitoring and site visits).

In addition, businesses operating in Australia must accept as good practice that it is desirable to create career opportunities for Australians and that efforts to recruit labor from overseas must support government training policies and objectives to produce a highly skilled and flexible work force.

Next, employers must identify each of the positions to be filled with a temporary resident and the skills and experience required. Positions are limited to a minimum skill level—managerial, professional, associate professional, and tradespersons and related workers (major groups 1–4 of the Australian Standard Classification of Occupations), which are specified in a DIMIA *Gazette* notice.[11] The list of gazetted positions is subject to change, because groups may be added in times of shortage and removed in times of oversupply. A minimum salary level of $35,828 applies.[12] Certain employers can seek a waiver of minimum skills and salary levels if the position is located in a regional or low population growth area in Australia and cannot be filled from the local market. The salary should still be at least at the local market rate, and adherence to labor laws is required.

Finally, applicants must demonstrate that they have the skills to match those of the nominated vacancy; that they will be paid at not less than the minimum salary level; and that they have attributes consistent with their proposed employment. An application fee is payable (see Table 6.2). If sponsored by an overseas business, they also must demonstrate that they are genuinely and realistically committed to establishing a business activity in Australia or will be fulfilling contractual obligations for the overseas business. Visa extensions within Australia are possible, but the employer must remain a sponsor; the approved nomination must exist for the position; and the visa holder must apply for a new visa before his or her existing visa expires. Extensions have a processing time of up to six weeks.

Labour Agreements, negotiated among the DIMIA, Department of Employment and Workplace Relations, and employers or industry representatives, allow for the overseas recruitment of a specified number of workers for a defined set of vacancies and criteria in response to identified or emerging shortages. These agreements usually run for three years, and most are for temporary entry only. Entrants under these agreements receive priority processing, and there is no charge to the

TABLE 6.2   Application Fees and Charges, Australia

	PQBS	SBS	LA/RHQ	Service Seller
Sponsorship	$3,395	nil	n.a.	n.a.
Sponsorship renewal	$1,135	n.a.	n.a.	n.a.
Nomination	nil	$235 per nomination	nil	n.a.
Visa	160	160	$160	$160

n.a.: Not applicable.
Note: PQBS = Pre-qualified Business Sponsor; SBS = Standard Business Sponsor; LA/RHQ = Labour Agreement/Regional Headquarters Agreement.
Source: DIMIA (2002b).

employer, although a visa application fee is payable (see Table 6.2). Employers or industry associations are required to make commitments to the employment, education, training, and career opportunities of Australians as part of the agreement.

When employers or industry associations apply to DIMIA to establish a Labour Agreement, they must describe the company's or industry's background and structure; details of the skills of the persons to be recruited; efforts to recruit domestically; the employer's training record; and the special circumstances requiring an agreement. Once an agreement is in place, an employer seeks approval for a particular nomination, which DIMIA assesses to ensure that it is consistent with the agreed number of positions, terms and conditions of employment, and skills/qualifications covered by the agreement. Finally, the foreign worker applies for a visa, demonstrating that he or she has the necessary skills and qualifications and can satisfy any mandatory licensing registration or professional membership requirements under the agreement.

Overseas companies choosing to establish their regional headquarters in Australia are eligible for streamlined entry processing under RHQ Agreements. These agreements are normally valid for five years; provide for the transfer of key expatriate executive and specialist personnel of the company group; and receive higher-priority processing than applications under standard Labour Agreements. The Commonwealth minister for industry, science and resources determines which companies qualify for RHQ Agreements. After companies submit a proposal to establish an RHQ, they lodge a nomination form, and then the applicant applies for a visa.

The second category of temporary business residents is *Service Sellers*. This category, introduced for the GATS, allows representatives of overseas suppliers of services seeking to negotiate or enter into agreements for the supply of services to apply for a temporary business visa valid for up to six months. This category does not cover people actually supplying or directly selling services in Australia—they are covered by sponsored visas (if supplying services for an employer) or Independent Executive visas (if wishing to establish their own businesses).

Applicants must provide evidence that they are a representative of an overseas service supplier; details of their relevant skills and experience; evidence that the supplier is actively engaged in business; a statement describing the business activities of the supplier and its plans to expand its trade in Australia; and a statement or proposal with details of how the applicant proposes to represent the supplier in Australia. No sponsorship or nomination is required, but applicants must apply for a visa and pay the application fee (see Table 6.2). Members of a family unit may apply together, and applications may be made in Australia or overseas.

The third category of temporary business residents, *Independent Executives*, which covered people interested in starting a new business in Australia as owner or part owner or buying into an existing business, ceased on March 1, 2003. However, as of November 1, 2001, a two-year multiple entry visa allows existing Independent Executives to remain and continue their business activities as owner and principal, in recognition of the fact that they were legitimately on business and needed more time to be eligible to apply for permanent residence. Conditions for the new visa (457IE FAO) include that the applicant must have conducted a business in Australia for at least 15 months as a principal; maintain direct and continuous involvement in the management of the business and make decisions that affect its overall direction and performance; have a background relevant to and consistent with the business, with nothing adverse; have net assets of $250,000 (or a lesser approved amount) available to conduct the business; and have a need to be temporarily resident in Australia to conduct the business. The business itself must be of benefit to Australia. There is no sponsorship requirement.

Statistics on Entrants

In the last few years Australia has seen increases in every category of temporary entrant. In 2000–01, 3,847,240 temporary entry visas were granted, of which the vast majority were visitors. Of those, the vast majority were tourists, with business visitors accounting for only 7.4 percent of total visitors. Of the remaining categories of entrants, WHMs and overseas students dominated, but the numbers for business (long-stay) visas and other relevant categories were not insignificant (see Table 6.3). The number of temporary entry visas rose by 9.3 percent over 1999–2000, driven mainly by the 9.3 percent increase in the visitor (including business) visas issued (perhaps because of the Olympic Games).

Business Visitors (less than three months).   In 2000–01 a total of 260,957 business visitor visas were granted, 11.1 percent more than the 234,825 visas granted in 1999–2000. A breakdown by country of citizenship and number of business visitors from the top five countries appears in Table 6.4. A notable fact is that "other" is the largest category, reflecting the range of countries from which these entrants originate—a fact resulting perhaps from the wide range of countries from which the current Australian population is drawn. The countries of origin of business visitors also largely reflect Australia's trading relationships, with the top countries of origin being many of its major trading partners—the United States, China, United Kingdom, Japan—with the exception of the sixth largest entrant, India.

Temporary Business Residents (up to four years).   In 2000–01 a total of 40,493 temporary residence business visas were granted, an increase of 15.7 percent over 1999–2000 (see Table 6.5 for a breakdown by country of citizenship). Again, "other"

TABLE 6.3   Temporary Entry Visas Issued, Australia, 2000–01

Category	Number	Percent Share
VISITORS	3,540,506	92
Of which:		
Tourists	3,279,549	92.6
Business	260,957	7.4
OTHER		8
Of which:		
Students	146,577	48
Working Holiday Maker	76,576	25
Business (long stay)[a]	40,493	15
Economic		
Medical practitioners	3,438	
Educational	1,738	
Social/cultural	23,036	8
International relations	14,876	5
Total	3,847,240	100

a. Includes Independent Executives.
Source: DIMIA (2002a).

TABLE 6.4   Business Visitors by Country of Citizenship, Australia, 2000–01

Country	Percent Share
Other	29
United States	22
China	15
United Kingdom	7
Japan	7
India	5
Indonesia	4
Canada	3
France	3
South Africa	3
Thailand	2

Source: DIMIA (2002a).

TABLE 6.5   Business Temporary Residents by Country of Citizenship, Australia, 2000–01

Country of Origin	Percent Share
Other	33
United Kingdom	23
United States	8
India	8
South Africa	6
Japan	6
China	4
Ireland	4
Canada	3
Korea	3
France	2

Source: DIMIA (2002a).

TABLE 6.6   Business (Long-Stay) Independent Executive Visas by Country of Citizenship, Australia, 2000–01

Country of Origin	Percent Share
Other	29
United Kingdom	19
South Africa	13
China	9
Indonesia	9
Singapore	7
Taiwan, China	4
Zimbabwe	3
Fiji	3
Malaysia	2
Korea, Rep. of	2

Source: DIMIA (2002a).

is the largest group, followed by the United Kingdom and the United States. India and South Africa are the next largest entrants (although their percentages are considerably smaller), followed by China and Japan.

The country breakdown under the previous Independent Executive stream (Table 6.6) is slightly different perhaps reflecting the link between this scheme and subsequent applications for permanent migration. While the leading category

TABLE 6.7   Top Five Occupations Sponsored by Employers, Australia, 2000–01

Occupation	Percent Share
Computing professional	10.2
Applications and analyst programmer	6.2
General manager	4.8
Registered nurse	4.4
Accountant	3.9

Source: DIMIA (2002a).

is again "other," the major countries are United Kingdom, South Africa, China, and Indonesia, with many more developing countries represented.

In terms of occupations, figures for 2000–01 are only available for those entering under the employer-sponsored categories. The top five occupations sponsored by employers appear in Table 6.7. The leading categories reflect areas of shortages—notably IT and nursing—although more general business occupations such as general managers and accountants also are included. The percentage shares for the top five professions are relatively low, suggesting again a range of occupations among employer-sponsored entrants.

However, figures for 1999–2000 include a breakdown of temporary business residents by skill level. These figures indicate that temporary business residents are predominantly in the higher skill levels. It also includes figures for WHMs, illustrating the difficulty of categorizing this group for mode 4 purposes—for example, WHMs also are well represented at the higher and intermediate skill levels, although to a lesser extent (see Table 6.8).

WHMs are a significant group, with more than 76,500 visas granted in 2000–01, up by about 3 percent from 1999–2000. The main country of origin was overwhelmingly the United Kingdom, with about half of visas, followed by Ireland and Japan (see Table 6.9).

A breakdown of visas issued to other specified categories of entry of relevance to mode 4 appears in Table 6.10. The largest single category is entertainment visas, followed by occupational trainee and sports. Visiting academics and medical practitioners are the next largest groups, with numbers dropping to the next categories (educational, exchange, and retirement). Recall that these numbers do not reflect with any accuracy the actual numbers of mode 4 entrants. Although some categories (medical, educational) are very close to mode 4, other categories (sports, occupational trainee) may include some non–mode 4 activities or non-commercial activities falling outside the scope of the GATS.

**TABLE 6.8   Temporary Entrants with Right to Work
by Occupation. Australia, 1999–2000**

Occupation	WHM (number)	WHM (percent)	Temporary Business Entrant (number)	Temporary Business Entrant (percent)
Managers/admin.	2,214	8.3	17,100	37.7
Professionals	7,652	28.8	16,270	35.8
Associate professionals	2,548	9.6	6,788	15.0
Tradespersons	3,024	11.4	1,020	2.2
Advanced clerical and service	1,214	4.6	458	1.0
Intermediate clerical and service	6,677	25.1	2,310	5.1
Intermediate product and transport	536	2.0	150	0.3
Elementary clerical, sales, service	2,106	7.9	1,038	2.3
Laborers	607	2.3	262	0.6
Total work force	26,578	100.0	45,394	100.0
Not in work force	15,182		18,326	
Not in employment	12,598		350	
Not stated	25,546		29,872	
Total	79,904		93,942	

Source: Hugo (2002).

**TABLE 6.9   Working Holiday Makers by Country
of Citizenship, Australia, 2000–01**

Country	Number of Visas	Percent Share
United Kingdom	39,558	52
Ireland	11,426	15
Japan	9,200	12
Canada	5,498	7
Netherlands	5,111	7
Germany	3,744	5
Korea, Rep. of	1,823	2

Source: DIMIA (2002a).

TABLE 6.10   Numbers of Visas Issued for Other Relevant Categories of Entrants, Australia, 2000–01

Category	Number of Visas
Social/cultural	
Entertainment	8,850
Sports	6,407
Exchange	2,038
Media and film staff	506
Public lecturer	27
Domestic worker (overseas executive)	40
Education	
Occupational trainee	6,660
Visiting academic	3,546
Educational	1,738
Foreign government agency	387
Medical practitioner	3,438
NZ citizen family relationship	—
Retirement	2,061
Supported dependent	233

— not available.

Source: Adapted from DIMIA (2002a).

Of the 3,438 visas that were granted to medical practitioners in 2000–01 (1,780 principal applicants and 1,658 dependents), the majority came from the United Kingdom, although "other" was again a significant category at 24 percent. Two developing countries, South Africa and India, were the next largest recipients, followed (at some distance) by Ireland and the United States (see Table 6.11).

The United States: A Case Study

[The September 11, 2001, terrorist attacks on the United States had a substantial impact on both the arrival of temporary visitors to the United States and the administration or management of these arrivals. Although more than 32.8 million nonimmigrant admissions were counted during 2001, that number represents a decrease of almost 866,000 admissions (2.6 percent) since 2000. This decrease was the first since 1983–84. Preliminary data for 2002 indicate a further decrease of about 14 percent (INS 2003). Administrative and management functions that once resided in the Immigration and Naturalization Service (INS) now reside in the new Department of Homeland Security (DHS). Also, new classes of admission were established (including prior to September 11) with entries under these

TABLE 6.11 Medical Practitioner Visas by Country of Citizenship, Australia, 2000–01

Country of Origin	Percent Share
United Kingdom	28
Other	24
South Africa	16
India	11
Ireland	4
United States	4
Canada	3
Pakistan	3
Fiji	3
Nigeria	2
Malaysia	2

Source: DIMIA (2002a).

classes starting in 2001. To the widest extent possible, relevant changes affecting regulations governing admission and stay of nonimmigrants are reflected in the following section; however, information is still sparse in some areas.]

Notwithstanding recent events, the United States has an "open door" policy for most nonimmigrant classes of admission—that is, there is no set limit on the total number of temporary admissions each year. Of the more than 30 million nonimmigrants admitted to the United States each year, a large majority (76.7 percent) enter as visitors for pleasure (tourists), with the next highest class of admission, temporary visitors for business, accounting for 14.6 percent.[13]

The absence of a limit on the total number of temporary admissions does not mean that such admissions are not regulated. Areas such as the grounds for nonimmigrant admission, length and extension of stay, employment in the United States, accompaniment by family members, travel restrictions within the United States, and change in admission status are all governed by regulations. Moreover, the applicable regime varies with the class of admission and, sometimes, with the origin of the alien (e.g., visa exemptions). Indeed, conditions of temporary admission to the United States may vary considerably with the status of the entrant. For example, the admission regimes applicable to North American Free Trade Agreement (NAFTA) professional workers (TN visas) and temporary visitors for business (B1 visas) are quite flexible, with some formalities waived.

However, some classes of temporary admission are subject to numerical limitations: H1B (workers with "specialty occupations"), H1C (nurses going to work in health care shortage areas), and H2B (nonagricultural workers performing services unavailable in the United States). The annual caps for these categories are 195,000 (H1B), 500 (H1C), and 66,000 (H2B). But in reality the number of visas granted can exceed these numbers, because the cap does not apply, for example, to renewals. These limitations also are frequently revisited.

Generally, the nonimmigrant regime is tailored to help the United States respond to economic needs and labor shortages. It also attempts to minimize any negative impact on the domestic work force. Key features of the system include:

- Labor certification or consultation seeks to determine whether U.S. workers are available to undertake the employment sought by the applicant, and what would be the effect of the alien's employment on the wages and working conditions of U.S. workers similarly employed.
- The alien must have a certain level of education, skills, or recognition by the international community.
- The alien must be offered wages and working conditions similar to those of U.S. workers similarly employed.
- Specific regimes apply in sectors of particular importance—both economic and cultural—to the country, such as seasonal service activities, sports, entertainment, motion pictures, training, and cultural programs.

The system is generally flexible about the authorized length of stay. In most cases, nonimmigrants can stay until the completion of their project. Accordingly, renewals are often possible, with the exception of, for example, workers in international cultural exchange programs (Q1 visas). However, nonimmigrants must generally prove their intent to go back to their home country, and the overall period of stay (extensions included) is almost always limited.

The U.S. system also provides for the movement of families accompanying the nonimmigrants, but family members often, but not always, belong to another class of admission. Thus not only the flows of mode 4 workers but also related flows are measured. Family members include spouses and minor unmarried children. They may not engage in employment, but they may attend school or college. However, they can apply for a change of status in order to take a job or to receive education in the United States after they turn major.

Visa Categories of Most Relevance for Mode 4

The following list aims to present briefly the U.S. nonimmigrant classes of admission that, in the authors' view, are of most relevance for mode 4. It includes a breakdown of temporary entry, conditions of admission for each category, and possible mode 4 coverage. Most classes of admission appear to be a mixture of mode 4 and non–mode 4 activities, but, for the purpose of this study, each class of admission even partially made of service suppliers is included. Although it is sometimes unclear what may be considered a service for GATS purposes, temporary agricultural workers have been excluded, as have some categories of entrants whose activities would not seem to constitute a commercial supply of services (e.g., religious workers). In accordance with Article I.3 of the GATS, foreign government officials, representatives of foreign organizations, and North Atlantic Treaty Organization (NATO) officials also have been excluded.

In general, all categories that might include some activities of relevance for mode 4 have been included, but with the appropriate caveats. For example, although there is some debate over whether foreign employees of domestic firms are covered by mode 4, they have been included for the purposes of this study (petitions can be filed either by a U.S. company, for most classes of admission, or by a foreign business, for intracompany transferees). Similarly, no class of admission is excluded on the basis of the type of contract existing between the service provider and the service consumer or his or her employer (independent contractors, project-tied workers, employees, or others).

B1—Temporary Visitors for Business. *(This category appears to be a mix of mode 4 and non–mode 4 activities because it may include activities beyond services.)* This category includes aliens entering the United States to engage in commercial transactions that do not involve gainful employment in the country (i.e., they are engaged in international commerce on behalf of a foreign firm, are not employed in the U.S. labor market, and receive no salary from U.S. sources). Among the conditions attached to admission, the petitioners must show that they intend to leave the United States after they have conducted business activities; that they have sufficient financial means to ensure no need for employment while in the United States; and that they have a permissible temporary activity that gives them a reason for requesting entry to the United States. Visitors may not receive salary or payment of any kind in the United States. Visitors may be admitted for not more than one year and may be granted extensions in increments of not more than six months each.

A visa waiver program initiated in 1986 became permanent as of October 30, 2000. It permits certain nonimmigrants from qualified countries to enter the United States on a temporary basis without nonimmigrant visas. As of 2002, 29 countries were members of the program. No admission can exceed 90 days.

E1—Treaty Traders, E2—Treaty Investors. *(This category appears to be a mix of mode 4 and non–mode 4 activities because it includes nonservice activities.)* This category includes aliens entering the United States, under the provisions of a treaty of commerce and navigation between the United States and the foreign state of such alien, to carry on substantial trade or to direct the operations of an enterprise in which they have invested a substantial amount of capital. Several requirements apply. For example, the applicant must be employed in a supervisory, executive, or highly specialized skill capacity (ordinary skilled or unskilled workers do not qualify), and the investment must generate significantly more income than just that needed to provide a living to the investor and family (E2 visas), or it must have a significant economic impact in the United States. A treaty trader or investor may be admitted for an initial period of not more than two years and may reside in the United States as long as he or she continues to maintain his or her status with the enterprise (increments of not more than two years each).

H1B—Specialty Occupations.   *(This category appears to be a mix of mode 4 and non–mode 4 activities.)* This category includes workers with "specialty occupations" admitted on the basis of professional education, skills, or equivalent experience. Among the conditions attached to admission, the U.S. employer submitting a petition must offer the alien a position that is a skilled professional one (specialty occupation) related to the alien's professional background and must pay the alien a minimum prevailing wage (Labor Condition Application). The alien must be professionally qualified to fill the job duties (four-year university degree or equivalent experience).

H1B visas are for an initial period not exceeding three years, with extensions of another three years possible for an overall total of six years. Numerical limitations apply to H1B visas. The annual H1B cap was set at 195,000 for fiscal 2001–03. (Workers previously approved for H1B employment are exempt from the cap.) However, workers may have a second (or more) petition filed on their behalf in order to (a) extend the period allowed to work with their current employer, or (b) notify INS of changes in the conditions of employment, or (c) request concurrent H1B status with another employer.

H1C—Registered Nurses.   *(This category appears to fall under mode 4.)* This category includes registered nurses who are entering the United States to work temporarily in "health care shortage areas." It was established by the Nursing Relief for Disadvantaged Areas Act of 1999 and replaced the former H1A visa category.[14] Among the conditions attached to admission, the employer must be a hospital located in a health care shortage area; the employer must show that employment will not adversely affect the wages and working conditions of similarly employed nurses; and the employer must have taken timely and "significant steps" to recruit and retain U.S. citizen or eligible immigrant nurses. H1C visas allow a period of admission not to exceed three years and no extension is possible. Numerical limitations also apply (annual cap of 500).

H2B—Nonagricultural Workers Performing Services Unavailable in the United States. *(This category appears to be a mix of mode 4 and non–mode 4 activities because it includes activities beyond services such as manufacturing.)* This category includes temporary nonagricultural workers entering the United States to perform temporary services or labor if unemployed persons capable of performing the service or labor cannot be found in the United States. Among the conditions attached to admission, the U.S. employer must be offering a position that is temporary and based on unusual need (the contract must have a specific end date); the employer must obtain a temporary labor certification (employment will not adversely affect U.S. workers); and the employer must pay the worker the minimum prevailing wage.

H2B visas are granted for an initial period not to exceed one year. Extensions are possible for a total stay of three years maximum, but a beneficiary must then depart the United States for at least six months. Numerical limitations apply (annual cap of 66,000).

H3—Industrial Trainees. *(It is unclear whether this category is mode 2 consumption of training services because it includes both classroom and on-the-job training hours. It may fall partially under mode 4 if trainees are receiving remuneration in the host country.)* This category includes aliens coming temporarily to the United States as trainees, other than to receive graduate medical education or training. Among the conditions attached to admission, the U.S. employer must provide a detailed description of the training program and previous training or experience of the alien, and explain why the training is required and what will be the benefits for the employer and the alien (with a perspective of a career abroad).

I1—Representatives of Foreign Information Media. *(This category appears to fall under mode 4.)* This category includes aliens coming temporarily to the United States as bona fide representatives of foreign press, radio, film, or other foreign information media. Among the conditions attached to admission, the alien must be traveling to work on informational or educational material, and he or she must be able to demonstrate that he or she is an accredited media representative. Employees of U.S. media organizations are not eligible. Freelance media workers may qualify if they are working under contract on a product to be used abroad by an informational or cultural medium to disseminate information or news. Admission may be authorized for the time of employment.

J1—Exchange Visitors. *(This category appears to be a mix of mode 4 and non–mode 4 activities because exchange programs can be of all kinds and do not necessarily imply the provision of services or even work—for example, exchange students* *would fall under mode 2. It is unclear whether activities funded by the sponsoring organization in the form of a scholarship or other stipend would qualify as commercial for GATS purposes.)* This category includes aliens coming temporarily to the United States as participants in programs approved by the secretary of state for the purpose of teaching, instructing or lecturing, studying, observing, conducting research, consulting, demonstrating skills, or receiving training. Among the conditions attached to admission, the alien must show that he or she has an adequate educational background and English-speaking ability, and that he or she has the intent to leave the United States at the end of the program. A J1 visa may be continued in status for the duration of the exchange program, as long as the visitor maintains the program and does not engage in other work without authorization. After the completion of the program, the visitor must reside in his or her country of nationality or last residence for two years before becoming eligible to apply for an immigrant or temporary resident worker visa.

L1—Intracompany Transferees.   *(This category appears to be a mix of mode 4 and non–mode 4 activities because it includes activities beyond services.)* This category includes aliens, employed by an international firm or corporation, who seek to enter the United States temporarily in order to continue to work for the same employer, or a subsidiary or affiliate, in a capacity that is primarily managerial, executive (L1A), or involves specialized knowledge (L1B). Unlike in most other visa categories, the petition must be filed by a foreign business. Among the conditions attached to admission, the alien must show that he or she has worked for the foreign company continuously for at least one year out of the last three in a managerial or executive capacity, or in a job requiring specialized knowledge. The alien also must show that the host company is a branch, parent, affiliate, or subsidiary of the foreign company. For an established company, the visa may be issued for an initial period of up to three years. For a start-up business, the initial admission period is limited to one year. However, upon renewal, the alien working in a start-up can obtain a three-year admission. For established companies, two-year extensions can be granted, inside or outside the United States, for the maximum allowed time period. Executive and managerial L1 visas may be issued for a maximum of seven years, whereas a specialized knowledge employee L1 visa may be issued only for five years.

O1—Workers with Extraordinary Ability/Achievement.   *(This category appears to fall under mode 4.)* This category includes temporary workers with extraordinary ability or achievements in the arts, sciences, business, education, athletics, or the motion picture or television industry, who wish to enter the United States to perform for a U.S. employer temporary services related to an event or events.

Among the conditions attached to admission, the petitioner must prove that the alien is at the very top of his or her class; that the alien is entering the United States to participate in a specific event(s) requiring his or her expertise; that the alien is entering the United States to perform temporary services for a U.S. employer or the U.S. agent of an international employer; and that the petitioner has obtained an advisory opinion from an appropriate peer group and can provide extensive documentation to serve as compelling evidence of the beneficiary's qualifications. O1 visas are granted for an initial period not to exceed three years. Extensions can be granted in one-year increments until the project is finished (no time limit).

O2—Workers Accompanying and Assisting in Performance of O1 Workers. *(This category appears to fall under mode 4 because the workers are receiving remuneration in the host country for services supplied on a commercial basis.)* This category includes temporary workers entering the United States solely for the purpose of accompanying and assisting workers with extraordinary ability/achievement. Among the conditions attached to admission, the beneficiary must demonstrate that his or her skills are essential to the performance of the O1 (O2 visas are not available to domestic helpers and unskilled "artist assistants"); that, after labor consultation, the support services cannot be readily performed by a U.S. worker; and that he or she will leave the United States at the end of the authorized stay. O2 visas are granted for the period necessary to complete the event (not to exceed three years).

P1—Internationally Recognized Athletes or Entertainers. *(This category appears to be mostly mode 4 activities. However, unpaid participation in a competition such as by amateur athletes would fall outside the GATS.)* This category includes internationally recognized artists, entertainers, or athletes entering the United States to participate in a performance for an American employer or an international employer working through a U.S. agent. Among the conditions attached to the admission of athletes, the U.S. employer must consult with an appropriate labor organization and prove the athlete's international recognition in the sport. For entertainment groups, the U.S. petitioner must demonstrate that prior consultation with a labor organization was held, and that the group is internationally recognized and has been operating for at least one year. P1 visas are granted for an initial period not to exceed five years. Extensions can be granted until the project is finished (not to exceed 10 years overall).

P2—Artists or Entertainers in Reciprocal Exchange Programs. *(This category appears to fall under mode 4 [note existence of contract].)* This category includes artists and entertainers entering the United States to perform as part of a reciprocal exchange program with a U.S. organization. Conditions attached to admission include a formal reciprocal exchange program between the U.S. organization sponsoring the alien and the organization in the foreign country that will receive the U.S. artists or entertainers; labor consultation; a contract that includes conditions (e.g., of pay), a time frame, and a schedule of events; and proof of the performers' international credentials. P2 visas are granted for a period limited to the length of the project (not to exceed one year). Extensions are possible as long as the performance continues.

P3—Artists or Entertainers in Culturally Unique Programs.   *(Relationship to mode 4 is unclear because the sponsoring organization or program may not be for profit. This category appears to fall under mode 4 if the performer is receiving remuneration.)* This category includes artists or entertainers entering the United States solely to perform, teach, or coach in a program that is "culturally unique" (such as a traditional ethnic, cultural, musical, folk artistic, or theatrical performance or presentation). The conditions attached to admission include the objective to enhance the development or understanding of or to promote or facilitate the petitioner's art form; a consultation with an appropriate labor organization; a contract providing an itinerary and duration; and documentation that the performance is culturally unique and that the performer has achieved national or international recognition or acclaim. P3 visas are granted for an initial period not to exceed one year. Extensions can be granted as long as the performance continues.

Q1—Workers in International Cultural Exchange Programs.   *(This category appears to be a mix of mode 4 and non–mode 4 activities, because it may include nonservice activities.)* This category includes aliens entering the United States temporarily as participants in an international cultural exchange program approved by the attorney general for the purpose of providing practical training, employment, and the sharing of the history, culture, or traditions of their home country. Conditions for admission include the requirement that the exchange visitor be at least 18 years old and able to communicate effectively about the cultural attributes of his or her country. A designated sponsoring organization should file a petition and offer the alien wages and working conditions similar to those accorded U.S. workers. The visa is granted for the duration of the program or 15 months, whichever is shorter. After the first visa is granted, program participants may not join another international cultural exchange program until spending at least one year abroad.

TN—Professional Workers, North American Free Trade Agreement.   *(This category appears to be a mix of mode 4 and non–mode 4 activities because it includes nonservice activities.)* Entry is facilitated for visitors seeking classification as visitors for business, treaty traders or investors, intracompany transferees, or other businesspeople engaging in activities at a professional level. Such visitors are not required to obtain nonimmigrant visas, prior petitions, labor certifications, or prior approval, but they must satisfy the inspecting officer that they are seeking entry to engage in activities at a professional level and that they are so qualified (until 2004 requirements may vary between Mexican and Canadian citizens—for example, for labor certifications). Appendix 1603 D1 to Annex 1603 of the NAFTA lists professional occupations and professions eligible for temporary entry to the United States and the minimum requirements for qualification (diplomas) for each of them. Most of these occupations and professions belong to the services sector. The initial period of admission is not to exceed one year, although one-year increments are possible for as long as temporary employment exists.

Statistics on the Number and Origins of Nonimmigrants

The United States has a highly developed visa system consisting of many categories of immigrants and able to provide detailed information on the number, country of origin, and skill levels of persons entering the country on a temporary basis. However, traditional visa classifications do not include a mode 4 category as such. Most classes of admission include both mode 4 and non–mode 4 activities, and entrants falling under mode 4 can be found in various visa categories; the conditions of their admission vary with the type of services supplied or the skill levels. Only a few visa categories consist exclusively or mostly of mode 4 workers. (One example of such a category is the one for registered nurses). It is therefore impossible to determine precisely the number of admissions related to the supply of services. In most cases, the number of mode 4 workers will be less than the number of entrants in the classes identified as being of most relevance for mode 4.

Number of Entrants.   Table 6.12 lists the number of entrants in the classes of admission identified in this chapter as being of most relevance for mode 4. It reveals that for most visa categories the number of admissions to the United States has grown substantially over the last decade. Since 1995 (date of entry into force of the GATS) the fastest growing classes of admission, in relative terms, have been the "temporary non-agricultural workers performing services unavailable in the U.S. (H2B)," the "workers with specialty occupations (H1B)," and the "intracompany transferees (L1)." The number of admissions in other visa categories has increased even more rapidly (such as NAFTA professional workers), but these regimes were only recently installed, and no reliable comparison is yet possible.

In absolute terms, "temporary visitors for business" has been the fastest growing class of admission (+1.3 million entrants between 1995 and 1999) and represents

TABLE 6.12 Nonimmigrants Admitted by Class of Admission: Selected Categories and Fiscal Years, United States, Selected Years, 1985–2001

Class of Admission	1985	1990	1995	2000	2001
Temporary visitors for business (B1)	1,796,819	2,661,338	3,275,336	n.a.	n.a.
Visa waiver, business	n.a.	294,065	942,539	n.a.	n.a.
Treaty traders (E1)	65,406	78,658	53,557	51,241	51,443
Treaty investors (E2)	31,083	68,878	78,220	116,973	127,091
Registered nurses (H1A)	n.a.	n.a.	6,512	565	627
Registered nurses participating in the Nursing Relief for Disadvantaged Areas Act (H1C)	n.a.	n.a.	n.a.	n.a.	29
Specialty occupations (H1B)	47,322	100,446	117,574	355,605	384,191
Nonagricultural workers performing services unavailable in the United States (H2B)	n.a.	17,754	14,193	51,462	72,387
Industrial trainees (H3)	3,003	3,168	2,787	3,208	3,245
Workers with extraordinary ability/achievement (O1)	n.a.	n.a.	5,974	21,746	25,685
Workers accompanying and assisting in performance of O1 workers (O2)	n.a.	n.a.	1,813	3,627	3,834
Internationally recognized athletes or entertainers (P1)	n.a.	n.a.	22,397	40,920	42,430

TABLE 6.12 *(Continued)*

Class of Admission	1985	1990	1995	2000	2001
Artists or entertainers in reciprocal exchange programs (P2)	n.a.	n.a.	660	4,227	3,877
Artists or entertainers in culturally unique programs (P3)	n.a.	n.a.	5,315	11,230	9,484
Workers in international cultural exchange programs (Q1)	n.a.	n.a.	1,399	2,447	2,089
Representatives (and families) of foreign information media (I1)	16,753	20,252	24,220	33,918	34,488
Exchange visitors (J1)	110,942	174,247	201,095	304,225	339,848
Intracompany transferees (L1)	65,349	63,180	112,124	294,658	328,480
Professional workers, North American Free Trade Agreement (TN)	n.a.	n.a.	23,904	91,279	95,479

n.a. Not applicable.
Source: INS (2003).

the most important group of entrants (4,592,540 admissions in 1999). Half of these visitors benefited from the visa waiver program. "Specialty occupation" workers (H1B) are the second largest group of entrants, with 384,191 admissions in 2001. "Intracompany transferees" and "exchange visitors" count, respectively, 328,480 and 339,848 entrants in 2001.

Country of Origin of Entrants.   Table 6.13 shows the geographic origin of the nonimmigrants entering the United States in those classes identified as being of most relevance for mode 4. It reveals that, although temporary workers may come from any part of the world, the vast majority of entrants are from Europe, Asia, and North America. Europe is the first provider of temporary workers in seven visa categories—intracompany transferees, exchange visitors, workers in international cultural programs, artists or entertainers in culturally unique programs, workers with extraordinary ability/achievement (and those accompanying them), and industrial trainees. North America is the first provider of temporary workers in three visa categories—nonagricultural workers performing services unavailable in the United States, internationally recognized athletes or entertainers, and artists or entertainers in reciprocal exchange programs. Asia is the first provider of temporary workers in two visa categories—specialty occupations and registered nurses.

A Closer Look at Specialty Occupation Workers (H1B)

An even greater level of detail is available for "specialty occupation" workers (H1B). Because these workers are subject to an annual numerical limitation of entrants, the United States provides quarterly reports on H1B petitions. The United States also issues frequent reports on the characteristics of specialty occupation workers, which can be a useful source in determining the share of H1B entrants that might fall under mode 4. Because H1Bs represent the second largest nonimmigrant class of admission (more than 384,000 entrants in 2001) and their activities are essential to the U.S. economy (e.g., their role in computer-related occupations), more precise analysis of the mode 4 component of this group may provide useful insights into the size of mode 4 trade.

Characteristics of the "specialty occupations" category are revealed in Tables 6.14–6.16. Tables 6.14 and 6.15 demonstrate that a vast majority of the H1B petitioners are service suppliers. Eight out of the top 10 industries employing H1B beneficiaries are involved in trade in services: computer-related services, education, management/scientific and technical consulting, architecture/engineering, telecommunications, scientific research, accounting, and securities and commodity contracts intermediation and brokerage. Most H1B beneficiaries could therefore fall under mode 4 of the GATS.

TABLE 6.13 Geographic Origin of Nonimmigrants to the United States: Selected Categories of Most Relevance for Mode 4, 2001

	All Countries	Europe	Asia	Africa	Oceania	North America	Caribbean	Central America	South America
Registered nurses									
(H1A)	627	146	272	13	14	127	12	2	55
(H1C)	29	16	3	0	0	4	2	0	6
Specialty occupations (H1B)	384,191	111,382	178,411	8,573	9,499	37,554	3,693	2,982	38,251
Nonagricultural workers performing services unavailable in the United States (H2B)	72,387	3,411	1,893	809	1,916	62,673	10,503	4,723	1,483
Industrial trainees (H3)	3,245	1,218	1,076	95	56	294	50	45	502
Workers with extraordinary ability/achievement (O1)	25,685	14,981	3,504	422	1,579	2,464	311	163	2,686
Workers accompanying and assisting in performance of O1 workers (O2)	3,834	1,356	744	72	175	1,172	642	18	296
Internationally recognized athletes or entertainers (P1)	42,430	15,387	2,112	948	999	18,926	4,941	1,163	3,880
Artists or entertainers in reciprocal exchange programs (P2)	3,877	201	148	22	18	3,406	90	23	73

TABLE 6.13 *(Continued)*

	All Countries	Europe	Asia	Africa	Oceania	North America	Caribbean	Central America	South America
Artists or entertainers in culturally unique programs (P3)	9,484	3,095	2,682	548	63	1,971	1,618	47	1,053
Workers in international cultural exchange programs (Q1)	2,388	1,389	394	333	3	239	7	2	26
Exchange visitors (J1)	339,848	210,123	59,007	12,292	11,788	20,993	3,582	3,639	24,441
Intracorporate transferees (L1)	328,480	162,672	72,837	4,108	12,334	42,519	1,675	2,282	33,547

Source: INS (2003).

TABLE 6.14 Profile of H1B Beneficiaries by Top 10 Industries, United States, Fiscal 2001

Industry (NAICS Code)	Number of Beneficiaries	Median Age (years)	Master's Degree or Higher (percent)	Median Income	Leading Country of Birth (percent)
All industries	331,206	29	42	$55,000	India (49)
Computer systems design and related services (5415)	141,267	28	33	56,500	India (75)
Colleges, universities, and professional schools (6113)	15,372	34	93	36,999	China (24)
Management, scientific, and technical consulting services (5413)	12,721	28	41	55,000	India (54)
Architectural, engineering, and related services (5417)	12,148	30	42	50,000	India (26)
Telecommunications (5133)	9,638	29	48	69,000	India (39)
Scientific research and development services (5417)	6,929	32	81	55,291	China (24)
Semiconductor and other electronic component manufacturing (3344)	6,171	29	65	71,000	India (36)
Communications equipment manufacturing (3342)	4,383	29	58	68,000	India (36)
Accounting, tax preparation, bookkeeping, and payroll services (5412)	4,213	29	36	43,000	India (17)
Securities and commodity contracts intermediation and brokerage (5231)	3,676	28	45	75,000	India (21)

Note: Based on all beneficiaries with known level of income, education, or occupation. NAICS = North American Industry Classification System.

Source: INS (2003).

TABLE 6.15 All H1B Petitions Approved by U.S. Immigration and Naturalization Service, by Company Name, October 1999–February 2000

Rank	Company	Number	Rank	Company	Number
1	Motorola Inc.	618	30	Ernst Young LLP	137
2	Oracle Corp.	455	31	Agilent Technologies Inc.	136
3	Cisco Systems Inc.	398	32	Deloitte Touche LLP	130
4	Mastech	389	33	Birlasoft	128
5	Intel Corp.	367	34	Global Consultants	128
6	Microsoft Corp.	362	35	IBM	124
7	Rapidigm	357	36	R Systems Inc.	124
8	Syntel Inc.	337	37	Sprint United Mgt.	124
9	Wipro LTD	327	38	Wireless Facilities	124
10	Tata Consultancy Services	320	39	Cognizant Technology Solutions	123
11	PricewaterhouseCoopers LLP	272	40	Satyam Computer Services	123
12	People Com Consultants Inc.	261	41	Keane	114
13	Lucent Technologies	255	42	University of Washington	113
14	Infosys Technologies LTD	239	43	Analysts Intl. Corp.	110
15	Nortel Networks Inc.	234	44	Capital One Serv	109
16	Tekedge Corp.	219	45	Apar Infotech	108
17	Data Conversion	195	46	Modis Inc.	108
18	Tata Infotech	185	47	L&T Technology LTD	107
19	Cotelligent USA Inc.	183	48	Complete Business Solutions Inc.	105
20	Sun Microsystems Inc.	182	49	Techspan	101
21	Compuware Corp.	179	50	CMOS Soft Inc.	100
22	KPMG LLP	177	51	Renaissance Worldwide	99
23	Intelligroup	161	52	University of Pennsylvania	97
24	Hi Tech Consultants Inc.	157	53	Conexant Systems Inc.	96
25	Group Ipex Inc.	151	54	I2 Technologies Inc.	96
26	Ace Technologies Inc.	149	55	AT&T	93
27	Hewlett Packard Co.	149	56	Jean Martin	91
28	Everest Consulting GR	147	57	EMC	90
29	Bell Atlantic Network Services	141	58	Atlantic Duncans Intl.	87

TABLE 6.15 *(Continued)*

Rank	Company	Number	Rank	Company	Number
59	Merrill Lynch	87	81	Morgan Stanley Dean Witter	71
60	Unique Computing	86	82	Ericsson Inc.	70
61	Computer Intl.	85	83	Harvard University	70
62	Indotronix Intl.	85	84	Sabre Inc.	70
63	Nationwide Insurance	85	85	Yash Technologies Inc.	70
64	Interim Technology Consulting	84	86	Pyramid Consulting Inc.	69
65	Compaq Computer	80	87	MSX Intl. Inc.	68
66	GE	80	88	Softplus Inc.	67
67	MSI Majesco Software Inc.	80	89	Baylor College of Medicine	65
68	Data Core Systems	78	90	Microstrategy	65
69	IT Solutions Inc.	77	91	University of Minnesota	65
70	Allied Informatics Inc.	76	92	Universal Software	65
71	Ciber Inc.	75	93	Computer Horizons	64
72	Deloitte Consulting LLC	75	94	Ramco Systems	63
73	Goldman Sachs	75	95	Siebel Systems Inc.	63
74	Baton Rouge Intl.	74	96	Insight Solutions Inc.	62
75	Cyberthink	73	97	Synopsys Inc.	62
76	Stanford University	73	98	Texas Instruments Inc.	62
77	Cap Gemini America	72	99	Infosynergy	61
78	Infogain Corp.	72	100	Lason Systems Inc.	61
79	Ajilon Services	71	101	Vanguard GR	61
80	Allsoft Technologies Inc.	71	102	Yale University	61
	Subtotal for 102 companies listed	13,940			
	Subtotal for companies not listed	67,322			
	Grand total	81,262			

Note: Company name as listed on Form I-129, Petition for a Nonimmigrant Worker. Counts represent a minimum number of approvals. For some individual companies, multiple petitions were submitted with variations in the spelling or abbreviation of the name and were counted as petitions for different companies.

Source: INS (2000).

TABLE 6.16 Profile of H1B Beneficiaries by Top 10 Countries of Birth, United States, Fiscal 2001

Country of Birth	Number of Beneficiaries	Median Age (years)	Median Income	Bachelor's Degree or Higher (percent)	Master's Degree or Higher (percent)	Computer-Related Occupation
All countries	331,206	29	$55,000	98	42	58
India	161,561	28	55,000	99	35	85
China	27,331	32	57,500	100	81	44
Canada	12,726	33	70,000	94	37	30
Philippines	10,389	31	44,765	99	12	34
United Kingdom	9,682	33	70,000	91	33	24
Korea, Rep. of	6,468	33	48,000	98	57	21
Pakistan	6,313	29	52,440	99	40	59
Japan	5,902	30	39,520	97	34	12
Taiwan, China	5,808	30	50,000	99	72	33
Russia	4,589	31	55,000	99	65	52

Source: INS (2003).

As for the H1B petitions approved by country of birth (Table 6.16), nearly half were granted to persons born in India, which far exceeded China, the next leading country. India also is the leading country of birth of H1B beneficiaries in eight out of the top 10 employing industries (Table 6.14). H1B beneficiaries were, on average, 29 years old, and their median annual income was $55,000 in 2001.[15] Not surprising given the conditions of admission, the vast majority (98 percent) of the entrants have a university degree. Almost half of them have a post-graduate degree.

Disparities exist across countries of birth and occupations. For example, the median income of Canadian and UK H1B beneficiaries is $70,000, compared with $39,520 for Japanese beneficiaries. Across sectors, the median income varies from $36,999 (colleges, universities, and professional schools) to $75,000 (securities and commodity contracts intermediation and brokerage).

More than half of the H1B beneficiaries have computer-related occupations. This emphasizes the role of mode 4 in the supply of labor where shortages exist.

Conclusion

The Australian and U.S. case studies underline the increasing importance of temporary mobility in the globalized economy. In both countries, temporary entrants fill key skills shortages (e.g., IT, nursing), provide a range of cultural and educational services, and are essential parts of the conduct of globalized business (e.g., intracorporate transferees). Both the United States and Australia recognize the benefits from such temporary entry and have developed specialized and, in some instances, streamlined procedures. However, both countries also place important conditions on temporary entry, with the aim of protecting and promoting the employment of nationals. In both cases, foreign temporary workers are required to be paid at the same rates as nationals and work under the same conditions. Both countries also still largely limit mobility to the highly skilled and to certain defined areas of need.

These case studies also underline the difficulty of trying to identify those visa categories of most relevance to mode 4. Although temporary movement is distinguished from permanent, it is not always possible to know the sector in which the entrant is working (or even if it involves services and not manufacturing or agriculture), or indeed whether the activity would be considered commercial for the purposes of the GATS. As a consequence, it also is difficult to extract mode 4–relevant figures from general migration statistics. With the exception of some specific visas for certain professions (e.g., nurses and medical practitioners), many categories include mode 4 entrants with much larger aggregates.

These difficulties are perhaps not surprising given the fundamentally different purposes for which mode 4 and migration regimes were developed. However, if progress is to be made on mode 4 in the current GATS negotiations, a better mutual understanding of the requirements and constraints of both migration policy and mode 4 will be necessary. Achieving this understanding will require ongoing dialogue between trade and migration policy communities, a dialogue to which this chapter aims to contribute.

Notes

1. The views in this chapter represent the views of the authors and not the official position of either the Australian or U.S. government. Interpretations in this chapter about the relationships between visa categories and mode 4 are the sole responsibility of the authors. They do not bind Member states of the World Trade Organization in any way. Member states' obligations under mode 4 are governed by their specific commitments set out in GATS schedules.

2. The Services Sectoral Classification List, MTN.GNS.W/120 ("W/120"), sets out a list of 12 service sectors and about 160 subsectors, referenced to the United Nations Provisional Central Product Classification (Provisional CPC). Although its use was not obligatory, some WTO Members used W/120 in making their GATS commitments.

3. Accompanying family members can complicate the statistics from a mode 4 perspective, because they are generally included in the total number of entrants for that category of entrants.

4. The list of gazetted occupations is produced by the Department of Immigration and Multicultural and Indigenous Affairs and is available at its Web site (*www.immi.gov.au*).

5. These countries are: Canada; Denmark; Germany; Hong Kong, China; Ireland; Japan; Malta; Netherlands; Norway; Republic of Korea; Sweden; and United Kingdom.

6. Several classes and subclasses have been excluded because they do not seem to be relevant to mode 4: under social/cultural, (416) special program and (428) religious worker; under domestic worker, (426) domestic workers (diplomatic/consular); (432) expatriate class; and (425) family relationship class.

7. All dollar amounts in this section describing the Australian case study are Australian dollars.

8. They are Andorra; Austria; Belgium; Brunei Darussalam; Canada; Denmark; Finland; France; Germany; Greece; Hong Kong, China; Iceland; Ireland; Italy; Japan; Liechtenstein; Luxembourg; Malaysia; Malta; Monaco; Netherlands; Norway; Portugal; Republic of Korea; San Marino; Singapore; Spain; Sweden; Switzerland; United Kingdom; United States; and Vatican City.

9. They are Australia; Chile; China; Taiwan, China; Hong Kong, China; Indonesia; Malaysia; New Zealand; Philippines; and Republic of Korea. Brunei Darussalam, Peru, and Thailand have signed the operating framework, but they have yet to issue cards or grant pre-cleared entry to foreign cardholders.

10. Other sponsored categories such as the Employer Nomination Scheme and the Regional Sponsored Migration Scheme relate to permanent migration and are thus not included. Labour Agreements can cover permanent or temporary migration; only temporary migration is discussed in this section.

11. The groups listed in the Australian Standard Classification of Occupations include generalist and specialist managers; science, building, and engineering professionals and related associate professionals; business and information, health, education and social, arts, and miscellaneous professionals; business and administration, health and welfare, and other associate professionals; managing supervisors (sales and service); mechanical and fabrication

engineering, automotive, electrical and electronic, construction, and food tradespersons; skilled agricultural and horticultural workers; and other tradespersons and related workers. These categories are broken down into more detailed occupations. Positions not meeting the skill or salary threshold but for which there might be a shortage might be addressed under Labour Agreements.

12. This represents the average annual salary for all Australians on November 1, 2002, and is subject to change.

13. Percentage for fiscal 1999. More recent data for business and pleasure are not available separately because of the temporary expiration of the Visa Waiver Program from May through October 2000.

14. H1A entries subsequent to that represent readmissions of individuals who were previously admitted under this classification.

15. All dollar amounts in this section describing the U.S. case study are U.S. dollars.

References

Birrell, Bob, Ian R. Dobson, Virginia Rapson, and T. Fred Smith. 2001. "Skilled Labour: Gains and Losses." Australian Immigration Research. Centre for Population and Urban Research, Monash University, July.

DIMIA (Department of Immigration and Multicultural and Indigenous Affairs). 2002a. "Population Flows: Immigration Aspects, 2001 Edition"
<www.immi.gov.au/statistics/publications>.

———. 2002b. "Sponsoring a Temporary Overseas Employee to Australia." Publication 1154 <www.immi.gov.au>

———. 2003. "Charges—March 2003." Form 990I <www.immi.gov.au>.

Hugo, G. 2002. "Migration Policies Designed to Facilitate the Recruitment of Skilled Workers in Australia." In International Mobility of the Highly Skilled. Paris: Organisation for Economic Co-operation and Development.

INS (Immigration and Naturalization Service). 2000. "Leading Employers of Specialty Occupation Workers (H1B): October 1999–February 2000." Washington, D.C.

———. 2003. 2001 Statistical Yearbook of the Immigration and Naturalization Service. Washington, D.C.

Karsenty, G. 2000. "Assessing Trade in Services by Mode of Supply." In Pierre Sauvé and Robert Stern, eds., GATS 2000: New Directions in Services Trade Liberalization. Washington, D.C.: Brookings Institution.

WTO (World Trade Organization). 1998. "Presence of Natural Persons (Mode 4): Background Note by the Secretariat." Council for Trade in Services, S/C/W/75, December 8.

7

DRAFT MODEL SCHEDULE OF MODE 4: A PROPOSAL

Mark Hatcher*

This chapter presents a draft "model schedule" covering the temporary entry of natural persons under the General Agreement on Trade in Services (GATS). The model schedule is put forward as a basis to focus negotiations on mode 4 on a single document. It is divided into two parts. The first part deals with market access and national treatment commitments under Part III of the GATS. It is designed to supplement and improve the existing commitments World Trade Organization (WTO) Members have already undertaken in the Uruguay Round and in the extended negotiations that followed. As a model schedule it is not designed to be a "formula" of commitments that all Members are to assume. Rather, it is a specific proposal designed to generate improved commitments in this mode of supply, recognizing that Members may adopt different levels of obligations.

Existing obligations by nearly all WTO Members in the category of temporary entry of natural persons are structured to apply to all service sectors, and are therefore entered as "horizontal commitments" that apply to those sectors listed in their schedules of specific commitments. This structure follows the pattern of regulation in nearly all Members, where, with some exceptions, government measures governing the temporary entry of natural persons apply to all sectors. The model schedule described here follows the same structure, thus envisioning further entries in horizontal commitments pertaining to all sectors. However, it is recognized that it may be necessary for Members to schedule these commitments for a more limited set of service sectors, because they would entail a higher level of obligation. Nevertheless, the underlying presumption in the elements of the

---

*Mark Hatcher is head of public affairs, PricewaterhouseCoopers, United Kingdom.

model schedule is that the obligation is assumed for professional skill levels and that such a standard exists in virtually every service sector.

The second part of the model schedule, entitled "Best Practices," represents a set of proposed additional commitments under Article XVIII of the GATS. This part essentially encompasses domestic regulatory obligations that relate to the improvement of transparency of procedures. The objective of the second part would be for an acceptable number of Members to enter identical undertakings pursuant to Article XVIII, similar to the WTO "reference paper" obligations in basic telecommunications (WTO 1996). Some may question whether such regulatory obligations are nondiscriminatory because they pertain solely to foreign persons entering the country, not nationals. However, this issue of placement is a comparatively technical one, particularly at this early stage of the process. Of much greater importance is that these obligations are inscribed in the GATS schedules of commitments, and they are deliberately set apart from the obligations to Part I, because those willing to make such commitments would then have no discretion to take reservations from this particular set of obligations.

Finally, this proposed model schedule addresses exclusively the *temporary* entry of natural persons. As is clearly set forth in its Annex on Movement of Natural Persons Supplying Services under the Agreement, the GATS does not cover permanent residency or nationality.

Market Access and National Treatment

The commitments described in this section are intended for inscription in the horizontal commitments section of a Member's schedule and for application to two categories of persons entering countries on a temporary basis, as specified below.

Categories

1. *Short-term, intracorporate visits.* This category covers: (a) employees of a subsidiary or branch of a company or a partnership or its affiliate in another country who enter that country for short periods of stay, up to 365 days, to provide assistance and advice to its foreign office, or otherwise directly provide a service to a foreign client; and (b) employees of a company or partnership who are sent to its office in another country for training in business techniques or methods.
2. *Short-term visits to fulfill contracts.* This category covers persons who are employees of a foreign-based company or partnership and who travel to another country for short periods of stay, up to 365 days, in order to perform a

service pursuant to a contract between their employer and a foreign client located in a country where the employer does not have an affiliate office and where remuneration must be paid solely to the employer.

Conditions and Qualifications

Visas and work permits will be subject to the laws and regulations that apply to the temporary entry of natural persons in the host country, subject to the provisions specified below.

A special permit, entitled a "GATS Permit," can be obtained by nationals of one WTO Member from another WTO Member, when the applicant falls under the categories listed under category 1 above.

a. For employees falling under category 1 and category 2 above, the GATS permit will be extended strictly to personnel with requisite qualifications to fill a professional-level position, or a position that requires unique and specialized knowledge of the company or firm's technology or operations on the basis of technical training or extensive experience in working with the enterprise. Employees should be responsible either for management of operations or for provision of services at a level of complexity and specialty that require, at a minimum, a university degree or demonstrated experience.

b. Applicants seeking a GATS permit under both categories must fulfill certain specific requirements ordinarily imposed under existing procedures on intra-corporate transferees intending to work temporarily in the company's foreign office, such as the information necessary to support the application, proof of employment with current employer, and declaration of intention not to stay for a period of more than 12 months.

c. For persons falling under category 1, Members will authorize the GATS permit for a period of three years, allowing for multiple entry.

d. For categories 1 and 2, the provisions for renewal of the permit shall be based on the permit holder's continued status, as defined in (a) above, as an employee of the same company or partnership, and the absence of abuse of any of the conditions governing the use of the permit. GATS permit holders must seek renewal no later than one month from the date of expiration of the permit.

e. Wage parity or labor certification requirements (testing of the market), as well as economic needs tests, will not apply for category 1 holders of a GATS permit.

f. The GATS permit for both category 1 and category 2 persons will be issued without unreasonable delay and in any event no later than three weeks after the satisfactory presentation of documentation required by host country authorities. Where the GATS permit is denied, the applicant will have an opportunity to appeal the decision and obtain a determination within one month from the time he or she has lodged the appeal. GATS permit renewal procedures will follow the same conditions and maximum time frame for issuance or denial.

g. Category 2 permits are subject to the following conditions and are subject to renewal every three years:

  i. A copy of a contract or service made between the employer and a foreign client must accompany all applications between the permit holder's employer and the foreign client, demonstrating terms and conditions of the contract, as well as its monetary value.

  ii. The permit holder would be permitted to stay in the country where the contract is being performed for no longer than the duration of each contract, or 365 days, whichever is less. Remuneration provided under the contract must specify payment to the employer alone as a condition for issuing the GATS permit.

  iii. Contracts in excess of EUR50,000 (US$44,000) will be exempt from labor certification requirements, wage parity rules, and economic needs tests. Return visits (i.e., after-sales service) will be permitted under the contract and will not be subject to economic needs tests or labor certification requirements, provided they are covered under the terms and conditions of the contract and the contract exceeds EUR50,000 (US$44,000).

h. Applicants under categories 1 and 2 must submit information pertaining to level of education and qualifications (including professional accreditation when required in the home country), and submit proof of citizenship and wage statements showing the applicant has been an employee of his or her company for at least six months.

i. For services that require the GATS permit holder under categories 1 and 2 to be accredited in the host country in order to provide the service, any such limitations and conditions will be governed by specific commitments undertaken by the host country in the pertinent service sector.

j. Holders of GATS permits would not be authorized to change their status to another nonimmigrant visa category while using the GATS permit.

k. *Performance Bond.* For category 2 permit holders, the applicant company or partnership will post a performance bond with the local embassy of the GATS country to which its employee is seeking access in the amount of EUR250,000 (US$220,000).

l. *Fines and Penalties.* For category 1 permit holders, abuse of the GATS permit will result in requisite fines and a one-year program prohibition.

m. *Special Safeguards.* Notwithstanding (g) above, where a Member can establish that a pattern of practice among a number of companies of a Member has led to fraudulent use or misrepresentation of the GATS permit, recognition of the permit may be suspended by any WTO Member for a temporary period of time, not to exceed one year.

Best Practices

For all forms of temporary entry, Members will:

1. Make available in a consolidated text all measures—in particular, administrative measures—and any descriptive material accompanying such measures, that pertain to the temporary admission of natural persons (defined as entry, stay, and work authorization). Where possible, Members should provide this information electronically, on Web sites, or otherwise.
2. As part of the consolidated text, provide information on the materials or evidence required of an applicant seeking temporary admission into a Member's territory, as well as a description of the complete process for the application's submission, consideration, and approval.
3. Grant approval of applications for temporary admission within a defined period of time, and provide notice when any such deadlines cannot be achieved.
4. As part of the consolidated text, provide a full description of the manner in which any limitations to market access and national treatment for the temporary entry of natural persons are administered by Members' authorities.

Prior Comment

1. For new measures or alterations to existing measures that are being proposed by a Member, interested parties will be given a reasonable period of time to comment on any such proposed measures that would govern the temporary entry and stay of natural persons. Procedures will be followed that provide for public notice, on a timely basis, to any interested party that wishes to make comments, with a reasonable period of time allowed for the submission of views. Measures that would be subject to prior comment would include visa conditions and procedures to obtain them; changes or additions to worker categories covered by visa procedures; work permit conditions and economic needs tests; and any other proposed measure directly affecting the temporary entry and stay of natural persons. Provided: that the prior comment procedure can be waived when a measure is needed to address urgent problems of safety, health, environmental protection, and national security.
2. Except for the urgent circumstances in (1) above, Members will allow a reasonable interval between the publication of the measure in proposed form and its

subsequent entry into force in order to allow time for affected parties to become acquainted with it.

Economic Needs Tests

Members who place conditions on the temporary entry of natural persons on the basis of domestic economic needs will assume the following obligations with the objective of making this condition more transparent and predictable:

1. The economic needs test will be defined under a government measure.
2. Members will establish and make available the conditions for granting or denying temporary entry and stay on the basis of economic needs, providing quantitative and/or qualitative criteria for making determinations and specifying how the results of such tests are to be used in restricting entry of foreign service suppliers under mode 4.
3. Members will establish and make publicly available all procedures associated with the application of an economic needs test.
4. Members will establish time limits on the duration or review of the application for an economic needs test.

Review

Members will establish a contact point at authorized departments for both trade and immigration, allowing businesspeople to report on instances in which they have encountered special difficulties in the process of seeking temporary entry and stay in another country.

The Council for Trade in Services, or any body it so designates, shall periodically assess the effectiveness of the GATS permit system, as well as "best practices" undertakings, and consider possible adjustments on the basis of information drawn from regulators and users.

Reference

WTO (World Trade Organization). 1996. "Telecommunications Services: Reference Paper." Negotiating Group on Basic Communications. April 24 <*www.wto.org/english/ tratop_e/serv_e/telecom_e/tel23_e.htm*>.

8

MODE 4 AND THE SOFTWARE SERVICES SECTOR: AN INDIAN VIEW

Vaibhav Parikh*

L iberalization of trade in services under mode 4 of the General Agreement on Trade in Services (GATS) is of immense concern, especially to developing countries, which can capitalize on their labor-intensive services to increase and benefit from the international trade in services.

This chapter addresses, from the Indian viewpoint, the needs for liberalization in mode 4 in the computer and related service sectors, and particularly in the software sector, which is one of the most crucial and booming sectors of the Indian economy. The chapter outlines some of the issues and constraints that the software industry faces in the movement of natural persons and some of the policy reforms and initiatives that can be undertaken to mitigate these problems.

The Indian Software Services Sector

Before delving into the need for liberalization in the software sector, this chapter offers a bird's-eye view of the flourishing Indian software services sector.

- The Indian software services sector accounts for 16 percent of the country's overall exports, provides jobs to half a million people, and accounts for US$1.6 billion in investments.[1]
- The domestic software market in 2000–01 was $2.06 billion.
- Software exports amounted to $6.2 billion in 2000–01, and, of those, 62 percent went to the United States and 24 percent to Europe.

---

*Vaibhav Parikh is a member of Nishith Desai Associates, a research-based international law firm with offices in Mumbai, India, and Palo Alto, California.

- The *NASSCOM-McKinsey Report 2002* has predicted that by 2008 software exports from India will reach $50 billion and the domestic software market will expand to $27 billion (NASSCOM 2002).

These figures indicate the importance of the software sector to the Indian economy. However, even though the future of the Indian software sector seems bright, lack of proper implementation of the GATS provisions and inadequate liberalization in mode 4 may dampen the prospects of this sector.

Need for the Movement of Natural Persons

In their book *Blur: The Speed of Change in the Connected Economy*, Stan Davis and Christopher Meyers predict that in the future the distinction between products and services will become blurred, and there will be *productized services* and *servicized products* rather than stand-alone products or services (Davis and Meyers 1999). Today, with the advancement of technology, this prediction is becoming a reality.[2]

Although the GATS deals with trade in services and the General Agreement on Tariffs and Trade (GATT) regulates trade in goods, strong interdependence and a co-relationship exist between these two multilateral instruments. To ensure that the GATT is properly implemented, services under the GATS have to be progressively liberalized. The different modes of supply under the GATS also are co-related. For example, in the software sector in an offshore project for supplying software services

FIGURE 8.1 Coverage of the WTO Agreements

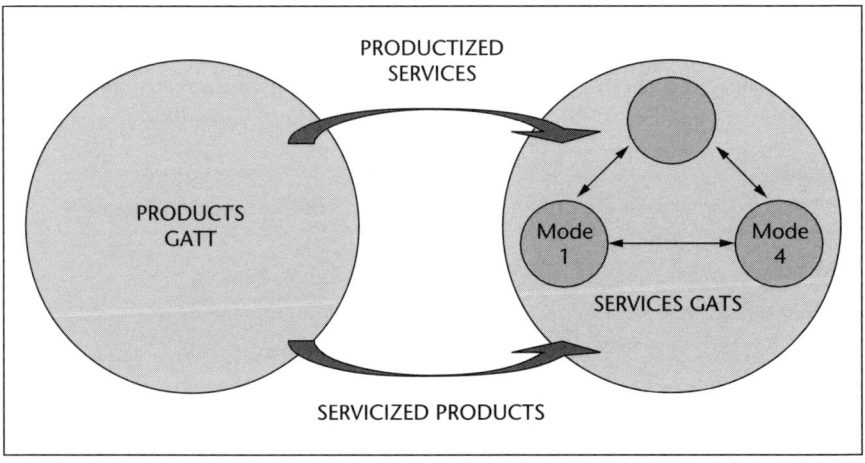

(mode 1), it may be necessary for some software professionals to be present onsite (mode 4) for various reasons, including (a) client comfort; (b) emergency or critical applications; (c) regular monitoring; and (d) maintenance of around-the-clock productivity (keeping in mind the time differences). If there is adequate liberalization under mode 1, but inadequate liberalization under mode 4, a situation may arise in which the liberalization under mode 1 is rendered ineffective.

Issues and Constraints Facing the Movement of Natural Persons

Several quantitative and qualitative constraints imposed on the movement of natural persons hinder the liberalization of services as envisaged by the GATS. Understandably, some of the constraints imposed by countries may be for reasons of national security, social obligations, cultural differences, and public policy.

Among the constraints, the most significant issues are: (a) immigration-related matters; (b) inadequate recognition of qualifications, training, and experience; and (c) differential treatment of foreign service providers. The rest of this section examines these issues in greater detail.

Immigration-Related Matters

Visa-related issues are the most critical barriers affecting Indian software professionals. Immigration regulations impose quantitative restrictions on the movement of natural persons, with the goal of creating a protected labor market. Without considering the needs of other countries, regulating countries change their regulations, depending on their economic and political situations. Moreover, immigration procedures are not sufficiently transparent. The list that follows considers some of the major issues in this context.

- *Prior adequate search in national markets.* The laws of some WTO Members mandate that employers carry out a thorough job search in the country before availing themselves of the services of foreign employees or service providers. Therefore, even though an Indian software professional may possess better qualifications or work experience than that available locally, if a local person is able to satisfy the needs of the employer, that person must be given preference over the Indian. A company that requires the services of a better-skilled professional may then be at a loss.
- *Wage parity requirement.* Under this national requirement, a foreign service provider must be paid wages equal to those paid to domestic service providers.

This requirement ultimately aims at providing a nondiscriminatory environment, but it often tends to erode the cost advantage of hiring software professionals from India. For example, if a software professional in the United States is paid $60,000, an Indian software professional may be willing to work in the United States for half or two-thirds of that amount. However, immigration regulations would prevent the employer from paying the lower wage for such labor-intensive services.

- *Differentiation in processing of visas.* Generally, in many countries the time required for processing visas for higher-level professionals is much less than that needed for processing visas for lower-level software professionals. It is believed that higher-level professionals can add more value to the host country's economy than lower-level professionals, which leads to discrimination in the treatment of the two categories.

- *Cumbersome and nontransparent immigration procedures.* Often, the lack of transparent immigration procedures makes it difficult and discouraging for software professionals to obtain visas in a short span of time. Applications for work visas may take several weeks or even months to process. Indeed, the long process of reviewing visa applications may render the purpose of a visit meaningless.

- *Quantitative limits.* Several countries also place quantitative limits on the number of visas they will issue for a certain category.[3] Not only can these quantitative restrictions serve as a cap on the economic expansion of the country itself, but they also can restrict cross-border trade in services. For example, in the United States quotas generally commence in October every year and normally are exhausted within a few months. Companies that then wish to send their software professionals overseas have to wait until the next October when the new quotas start. This situation sometimes causes companies difficulties.

- *Restrictions on flexibility.* Limitations that prevent visa holders from switching jobs or changing their status sometime restrict their flexibility. Although these limitations are in the interests of the regulating country, they can create many problems for software professionals, especially when those professionals have to move from one site to another.

- *Limited duration of stay.* The work permits issued by countries are limited in duration. Although these permits are extendable or renewable, the procedures for extending or renewing them are cumbersome, expensive, and stringent, which often discourages companies from hiring foreign nationals.

- *Economic needs tests (ENTs).* The widespread use of ENTs has emerged as one of the artificial barriers preventing the free movement of service providers. The discretionary nature of ENTs reduces the predictability of trade through mode 4 and actually nullifies the opportunity for market access.

Inadequate Recognition of Qualifications, Training,
and Experience

Inadequate recognition of qualifications, training, and experience restricts the opportunities for software professionals from India to provide services overseas. Several countries have certain restrictions on the issuance of visas based on the qualifications and experience of the applicant. However, even though the applicant may not satisfy the criteria, he or she may still qualify for the job. For example, at times the particular nature of the work may not require the qualifications or experience required to obtain a visa. Therefore, even if the software professional is competent enough to complete that work, he or she may not be granted the visa because of failing to meet the eligibility criteria. It also could happen that a software professional with lesser experience or qualifications in India may be capable of performing more complex work in another country. But because of the eligibility criteria, he or she may not be able to obtain the visa.

Differential Treatment of Foreign Service Providers

Trade in mode 4 also is restricted by policies that differentiate against foreign service providers. For example, in the United States foreign service providers have to pay social security and other taxes for which they do not get adequate tax credits in their home country in the absence of a treaty between the two countries. Furthermore, the service provider continues to pay taxes in his or her home country. This double taxation tends to erode the cost advantage of working in the United States.

Domestic service providers are often given a preference over foreigners in government procurements. Although this area is still not under the GATS, it should be included to facilitate freer movement under mode 4.

The nature of the government approval that foreign service providers must obtain to set up operations and even to remit monies to their home country is severe and often inflexible. The difficulties encountered discourage software professionals from rendering services abroad.

Besides the issues just described, problems related to commercial presence (mode 3)—including foreign investment restrictions, limitations on the nature of entities and the manner in which they can be set up, and conditions on staffing—could pose problems in fully realizing the potential of liberalizing mode 4.

Policy Reforms and Initiatives

India has already suggested to the World Trade Organization (WTO) that, to improve the liberalization in mode 4, Members take another look at and solidify the existing GATS commitments under mode 4 and also remove or curtail the other limitations they impose on the movement of natural persons. Some significant issues are summarized in this section.

Improving the Structure of GATS Commitments

WTO Members should improve their horizontal commitments in mode 4 by:

- Specifically including individual professionals
- Establishing clear eligibility criteria for entry
- Adopting uniformity in definitions of different classes
- Seeking further expansion to include mid- and lower-level professionals in the category of "other persons" or "specialists."

All industrial country Members should make specific and binding commitments in the computer and related service sectors. Moreover, any limitations must be clearly laid down in the schedule of commitments.

Removal of Existing Limitations

Visa Requirements.   These requirements could be relaxed through the following measures:

- Members should ensure that their visa application procedures are transparent.
- Members also should try to simplify visa application procedures.
- Less stringent norms should be imposed for the entry and stay of software professionals in the host country.
- Labor tests and conditions for software professionals should be waived or removed.
- Proper guidelines should be formulated for wage parity conditions to ensure that the cost-based advantage is not lost.
- Conditions should be imposed to prevent exploitation of foreign workers.
- Temporary visas must be de-linked from permanent visas, and separate criteria should be established for temporary visas. Often the immigration laws of countries permit temporary visa holders to convert to permanent status if they satisfy certain conditions. At the same time, these countries may not wish to encourage permanent migration into their territory. Because of this paradoxical situation, seekers of temporary visas may not be granted visas; host countries may feel that the intention of the visa seekers is to settle permanently in the country. Moreover, sometimes it may be necessary for software professionals to stay in the host country for a period longer than the one allotted in order

to complete their assignments. However, they may not be allowed to do so because they may then have an opportunity to convert their temporary status to a permanent one.

Occasionally, home countries also have worried about brain drain. One solution to this problem is to separate temporary migration from permanent migration by creating a special category of visas (like the GATS visa). Applicants must not be allowed to convert this special visa into a permanent one, and they also must be asked to return to their home country once the visa expires.

Clear Criteria for Economic Needs Tests.   Under Article XVI of the GATS, ENTs have often been used as a market access barrier under mode 4. Because there are no clear-cut guidelines for ENTs, Members must try to come together to establish the definitive criteria under which ENTs will be applied and to determine the impact of applying these tests on foreign service providers.

Furthermore, a consensus could be reached under which ENTs are not applied to software professionals or at least are minimally applied. Also the administrative and procedural formalities for application of ENTs must be transparent, and complete information should be available to the public at large.

Totalization Agreement.   Although this issue is particularly relevant to the United States, it also can be applied to other countries where foreign service providers have to pay taxes and make social security contributions in the host country.

As discussed earlier, foreign service providers have to contribute toward social security in the United States, but they do not receive adequate tax credits for such contributions from their home country in the absence of a totalization agreement. As a result, they end up paying double taxes. This double taxation can be avoided by concluding totalization agreements with the United States and other countries, if any.

Recognition of Qualifications and Experience of IT Professionals.   Members must try to establish certain criteria for the recognition of the qualifications and experience of information technology (IT) professionals. These criteria should be reflected in the sectoral and horizontal commitment in Members' schedules.

Members also could try to set up norms whereby work experience can be substituted for accredited educational qualifications. Such norms would be advantageous for the software industry, where skills are developed and polished on the job rather than only in educational institutions.

Conclusion

Because liberalization in mode 4 has not received as much coverage as the other three modes of supply under the GATS, it is essential that every effort be made to reduce trade barriers under this mode. Moreover, mode 4 liberalization has been enacted using a more horizontal approach. Specific sectoral commitments under this mode would be more effective, especially for skilled professionals and workers.

Future multilateral discussions in this area must focus on the implementation of the GATS at the domestic level. Unless Members independently modify or amend their local regulations to enforce their specific horizontal and sectoral commitments, discussions and negotiations will be endless and futile.

Members of the WTO also may wish to consider the possibility of a GATS visa for service professionals working temporarily overseas, on the basis of their horizontal and sectoral commitments. Although adoption of such a visa would require considerable deliberation and debate, it could ultimately streamline the movement of natural persons and also remove the scope for discretion and uncertainty.

Notes

1. All dollar amounts are current U.S. dollars.
2. The Microsoft.net platform is a move in this direction.
3. For example, the United States has a quota of 195,000 visas in the H1B category (for workers in specialty occupations).

References

Davis, Stan, and Christopher Meyers. 1999. *Blur: The Speed of Change in the Connected Economy.* New York: Warner Books.

NASSCOM (National Association of Software and Services Companies). 2002. *NASS-COM-McKinsey Report 2002.* Palo Alto, Calif.: NASSCOM.

9

INTERNATIONAL TRADE AND MIGRATION OF HEALTH CARE WORKERS: THAILAND'S EXPERIENCE

*Suwit Wibulpolprasert**

External Brain Drain in the Thai Health Sector

Industrial countries have occasionally opened their health care work force market in response to increasing domestic demand. In the 1960s the Vietnam War and initiation of the Medicaid and Medicare systems greatly increased the demand for health care workers in the United States. In response, the U.S. government temporarily opened its health care work force market, resulting in significant migration flows from developing countries.

Such migration is a great loss for poor countries, because medical doctors are usually among developing countries' best brains and their training is heavily government subsidized. In Thailand, all 11 of the 12 medical schools are public, and medical students contribute less than 5 percent of the cost of their training.

Thailand's Situation in the 1960s

In the 1960s Thailand lost more than 1,500 doctors, mainly to the United States. Between 1963 and 1965 more than one-third of new Thai medical graduates left for the United States (Table 9.1). Very few of these migrants returned home, resulting in a permanent loss.

This external brain drain was not related to any bilateral or multilateral trade agreement. It occurred mainly as a result of a market opening, a demand for continuing education, and an opportunity for career development and better living standards.

---

*Suwit Wibulpolprasert is deputy permanent secretary of the Ministry of Public Health, Thailand.

TABLE 9.1 Migration of Medical Doctors, Thailand, 1963–65

Year	Number of Emigrants	Total Graduates	Percent External Brain Drain
1963	56	233	24.03
1964	81	236	34.32
1965	140	276	51.72
Total	277	745	37.18

Source: Civil Service Commission, Thailand.

Government Response

In the late 1960s the Thai government introduced the following measures to mitigate the external brain drain:

- *Compulsory public work.* Medical students were required to sign contracts with public universities that committed them to serving the public for three years after graduation. In response to a breach of contract, a fine of US$12,000 would be levied.[1] At least two-thirds of the contracted new graduates were dispatched to hospitals in rural districts. Health facilities in the rural areas, particularly rural district hospitals, improved greatly in the early 1970s. In 2000 they covered more than 90 percent of all rural districts. They are well equipped, with modern facilities and trained staff.
- *Increased supply.* To increase the number of doctors, projects aimed at increasing the production of rural doctors—a system of rural recruitment and hometown placement—was initiated in 1974 (see Figures 9.1 and 9.2). As a result of these projects, up to 47 percent of new medical graduates belonged to this system. The system became less significant as the shortage of rural doctors began to be solved. However, because of the severe internal brain drain during the 1990s, the project has gained in importance since 1997.
- *In-country specialty training.* In 1971 the Thai Medical Council began to offer specialty training programs for medical doctors; 45 specialties are represented in Thailand, and more than 55 percent of Thai doctors are Thai board–certified specialists (Figure 9.3).
- *Increased allowance in addition to the basic salary.* A hardship allowance was introduced in 1972. Many more financial incentives were later added (Table 9.2).
- *Career development and social recognition.* The director of a rural district hospital is equivalent in status to the level of director of a division or a deputy director-general. In addition, annual awards are given to the best rural doctors.

FIGURE 9.1   Annual Output of Medical Doctors, Thailand, 1937–2020

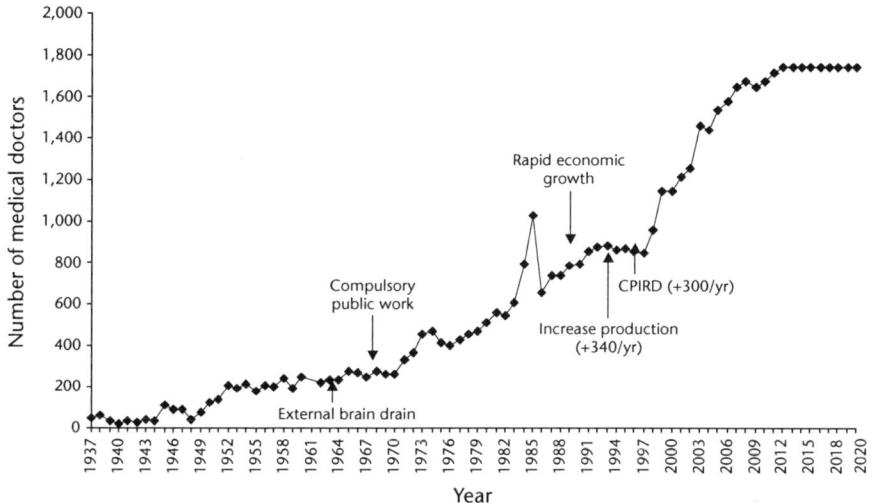

Note: CPIRD = Collaborative Project to Increase Production of Rural Doctors.
Source: Thai Medical Council.

FIGURE 9.2   Percentage of Rural Medical Students, Thailand, 1974–97

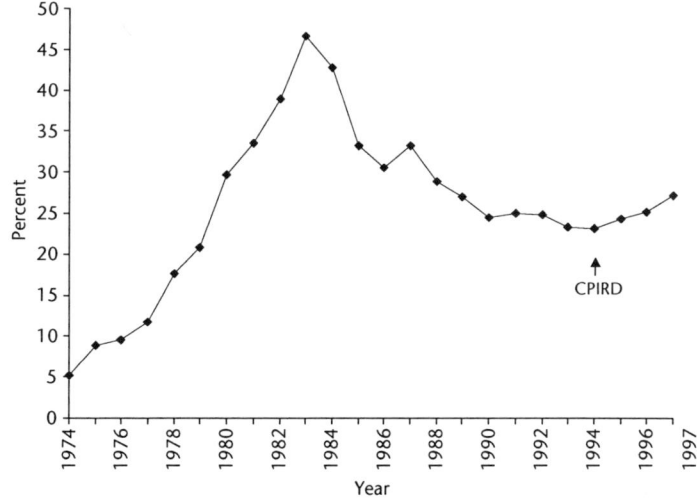

Note: CPIRD = Collaborative Project to Increase Production of Rural Doctors.
Source: Faculties of medicine of all universities.

FIGURE 9.3 Percentage of Medical Specialists and General Practitioners, Thailand, 1971–99

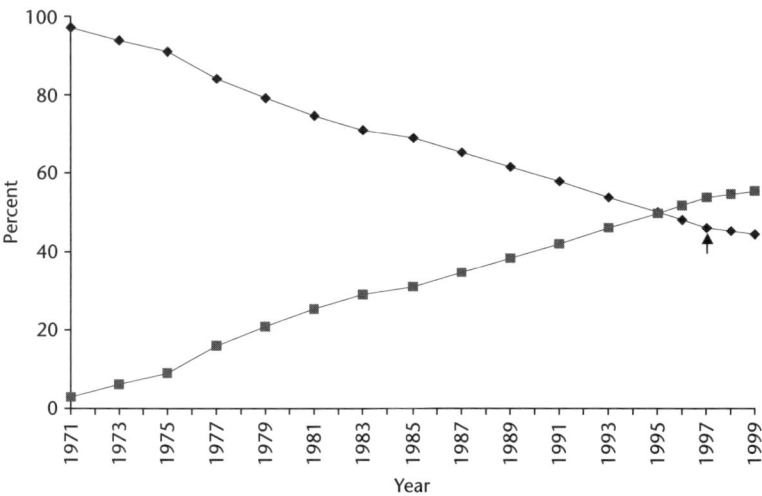

Source: Thai Medical Council.

TABLE 9.2 Monthly Remuneration of Medical Doctors Working in Rural Hospitals, Thailand, 2000 (U.S. Dollars)

	Monthly Remuneration
Salary (new graduates)	200
Nonprivate practice	250
On-call services	250–300
Special procedures	70–130
Special clinics	100–300
Hardship allowance	50–500
Total	920–1,680

Source: Thai Medical Council.

The Implications

Thailand's external brain drain has greatly diminished since the mid-1970s. It is not possible, however, to clearly attribute this outcome to the government measures introduced, because no systematic study of their effectiveness was ever undertaken. Other factors contributing to this result were the end of the Vietnam War and more restricted access to the United States for foreign health care workers during the same period, which greatly reduced the demand for doctors in the United States. Thailand's rapid economic growth during the late 1980s to mid-1990s and its increased ability to support the rapid growth of private hospitals were further factors in reducing external migration.

Internal Brain Drain

A big gap always exists between the density of health care workers in poor rural areas and their density in the richer urban areas. In 1979 the density of doctors in Bangkok was 21 times that in the northeastern region of Thailand, the country's poorest. The government measures just described greatly reduced this gap, bringing the figure down to 8.6 times by 1987 (Figure 9.4).

However, the mushrooming of private hospitals, as a result of the rapid economic growth during the late 1980s to mid-1990s, reversed this trend. The opening of the financial market in 1992 and the rapid influx of low-interest loans further enhanced the overgrowth of private hospitals (Figure 9.5), resulting in an over-supply of private hospital beds of almost 300 percent. This oversupply generated a severe internal brain drain, and the doctor density gap between Bangkok and the northeastern areas rose back up to 14 times by 1997 (Figure 9.4). In April 1997, a few months before the economic crisis, 21 rural district hospitals were being run without a single full-time medical doctor.

FIGURE 9.4   Distribution of Doctors, Thailand, 1977–2001

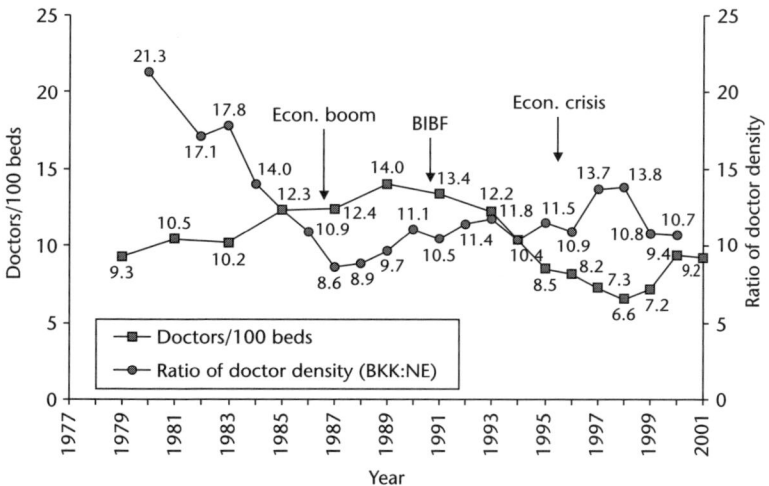

Note: BKK:NE = ratio of Bangkok to the northeastern rural areas; BIBF = Bangkok International Banking Facility.
Source: The author.

FIGURE 9.5 Private Doctors and Beds, Thailand, 1970–2000

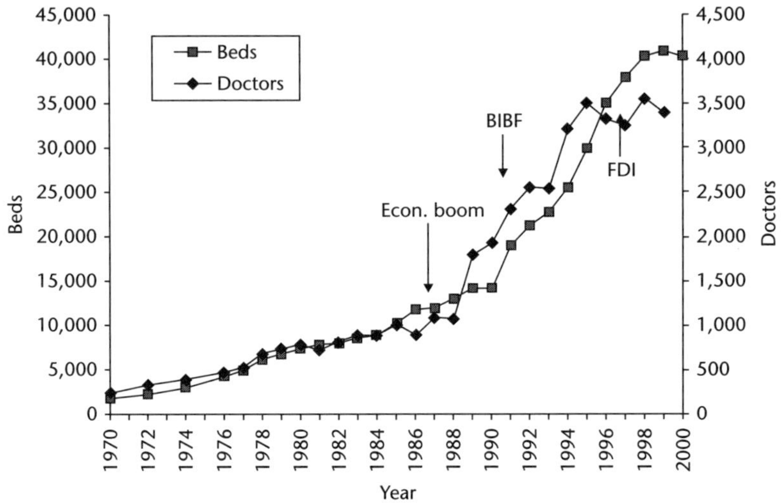

Note: BIBF = Bangkok International Banking Facility; FDI = foreign direct investment
Source: Thailand Health Profile, 1999–2000.

The economic crisis in 1997 resulted in the bankruptcy and downsizing of many private hospitals. As a consequence, the internal brain drain totally disappeared. The trend of doctor migration was reversed, and the gap between Bangkok and the northeastern areas went down again, to 10.7 times in 2000 (Figure 9.4).

Conclusion

As Thailand's experience shows, an external brain drain can occur independently of any bilateral or multilateral trade agreement. Unless a relevant market opening commitment is made under the General Agreement on Trade in Services (GATS), the level of access to a country's health care work force market is solely at the discretion of that country's government. If the host country's supply is sufficient, it can choose to close its doors completely to foreign practitioners. The external brain drain of the labor-exporting country will therefore be reduced.

If a GATS commitment on mode 4 is undertaken, however, once the market is opened it will be difficult to close it again. Thus if the industrial country Members of the World Trade Organization (WTO) decide to undertake commitments under mode 4 and permanently open their health care work force markets, the external brain drain in the countries supplying those markets may be continual and sustained.

Yet, apart from trade barriers, which may be removed under the GATS, other sociocultural barriers mitigate the brain drain. Knowledge of foreign languages is one such barrier; not very many Thai nurses leave the country, and one reason is their limited knowledge of English. Other barriers are the difficulties encountered obtaining entry visas, work permits, the license to practice, investment permits, and financing, including insurance. Two barriers that cannot be reduced by the GATS are sociocultural ones and effectiveness.

In addition to mode 4 commitments in the health-related sectors, commitments in other sectors and modes of supply can greatly influence the migration of health care workers. The internal brain drain in Thailand, which was related to the opening of the financial market, is one such example. Promotion of health tourism under mode 2 of the GATS could revitalize the bankrupt private hospitals and re-create the internal brain drain. Indeed, this is now the case in Thailand. Investment in private hospitals in other developing countries by Thai and foreign investors also may attract well-trained Thai doctors abroad. Therefore, multiple, integrated, holistic strategies, implemented seriously and concertedly, are needed to alleviate the problem of health care work force migration.

Note

1. All dollar amounts are current U.S. dollars.

10

BARRIERS TO THE TEMPORARY MIGRATION OF FILIPINO SERVICE PROVIDERS

Josephine J. Francisco[*]

The General Agreement on Trade in Services (GATS) offers opportunities for international migrants, because it provides a framework for negotiating the temporary stay of people in countries requiring their services. The challenge for the Philippines is to take advantage of the opportunities offered by this global trend. Meeting this challenge, however, depends on how the Philippines seeks to untangle the existing institutional barriers to liberalizing the movement of temporary migrants.

The first part of this chapter describes Philippine overseas employment, its economic contribution, and the composition of Filipino service providers. The second part describes the different barriers to the free movement of migrants, particularly Filipinos.

Trends in Overseas Temporary Migration

Labor migration is not a new phenomenon among Filipinos. During the first half of the last century, large numbers of Filipinos were working in Hawaii, Guam, and neighboring countries. With the inception of the overseas employment program under the 1974 Labor Code of the Philippines, Filipino labor migration began to serve as a temporary measure to ease the tight domestic labor market, stabilize the country's balance-of-payments position, and provide an alternative employment strategy for Filipinos.

---

[*]Josephine J. Francisco is president of NKY-Fil, the Philippines.

Deployment Level

From 1975 to 2000 the number of Filipinos working overseas increased from 36,035 to 841,438. From 1995 to 2000 overseas deployment continued to increase by 5.32 percent annually. However, after the financial crisis in 1997 overseas employment in 1999 and 2000 grew by less than 1 percent, compared with high of 14 percent in 1998.

Meanwhile, during the period 1995–2000, 198,134 sea-based workers were deployed overseas—a figure equivalent to 25 percent of the total land-based Filipino workers deployed overseas.

The Middle East continues to be a major destination of overseas Filipino workers (OFWs), accounting for 48 percent of the total land-based deployment (Figure 10.1). From 1995 to 2000, 44 percent of OFWs went to Asian countries.

Contribution to the Economy

Overseas employment provides work to job-seeking Filipinos and acts as a major generator of foreign exchange. Remittances of OFWs have grown rapidly, from a measly US$290.85 million in 1978 to an all-time high of $6.8 billion in 1999 (Figure 10.2).[1]

OFW remittances have been instrumental in helping the Philippine economy to offset foreign exchange outflows, and have been an especially saving grace during

FIGURE 10.1   Land-based Filipino Workers Overseas, by Region, 1995–2000

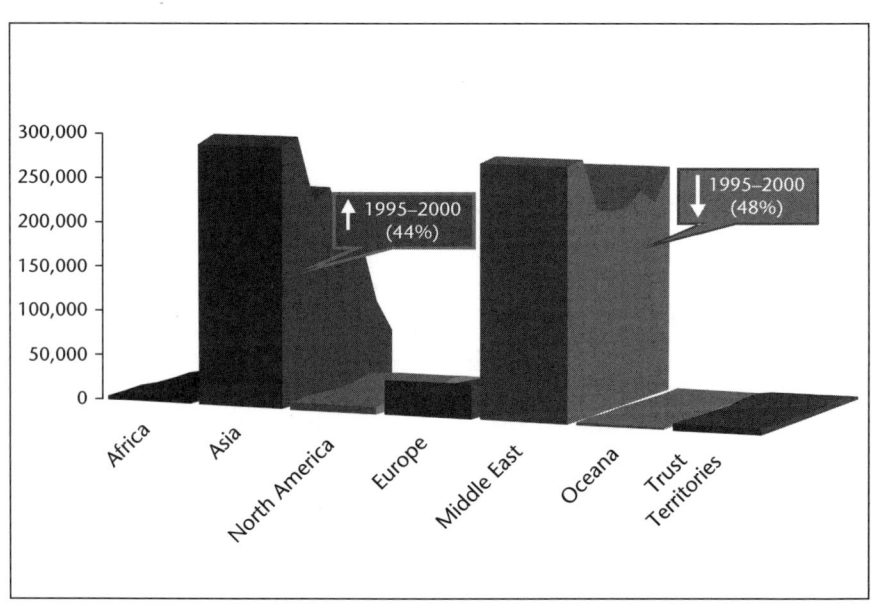

FIGURE 10.2 Contribution of Overseas Employment to GNP, 1990–2000 (percent)

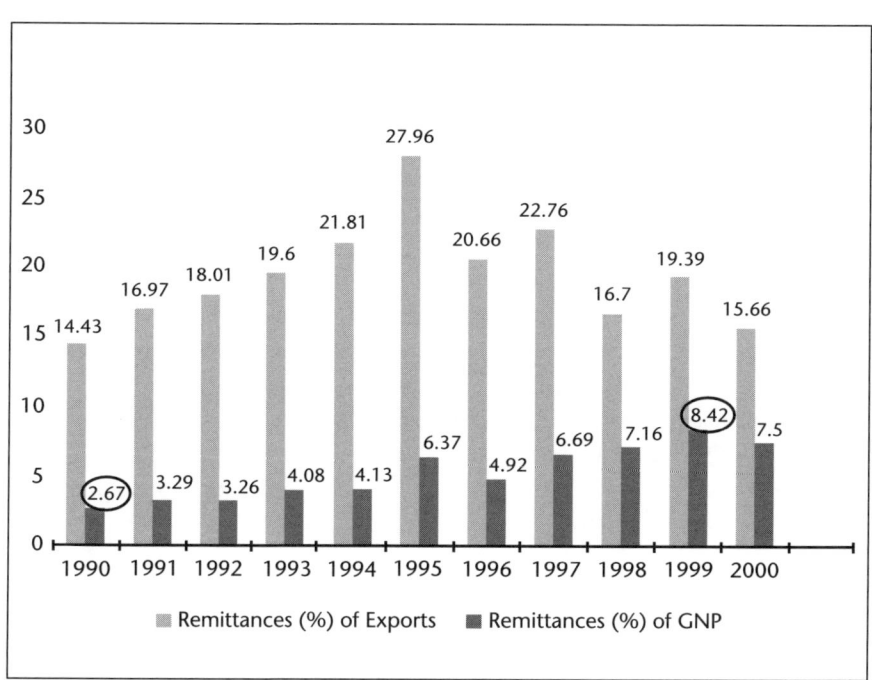

periods of negative growth in the gross domestic product (GDP), thereby helping to maintain a positive gross national product (GNP).

During the last decade, remittances, as a percentage of GNP, increased three-fold, from 2.67 percent in 1990 to 8.42 percent in 1999. In 1991 and 1998, when the country's GDP registered negative growth, the economy still managed positive, though slim, GNP growth because of the strong net factor income OFWs generated through their remittances.

Deployment of Service Providers

The 1990 United Nations Convention on the Protection of the Rights of All Migrant Workers defines an "*international service provider*" as someone who:

• has been sent by his/her employer to a foreign country in order to undertake a specific assignment or duty for a restricted and definite period of time; or

- engages in work that requires professional, commercial, technical, or other highly specialized skills for a restricted and definite period of time; or
- upon the request of his/her employer in the country of employment, engages in work that is transitory or brief for a restricted and definite period of time.

Based on these definitions, to be considered international service providers, temporary migrants must be engaged in consulting services, training activities, or supervisory functions. Thus seasonal and contract workers could not be considered service providers even if they are employed in labor-importing countries under temporary or short-term contracts to undertake predetermined, specific, project-tied jobs. "Overseas construction contracting" workers such as skilled engineers, managers or supervisors, and consultants are considered service providers. However, temporary migrants engaged in manufacturing activities are not service providers because they are involved in the production of goods.

The four major classifications of service providers are (1) intracorporate transferees; (2) individual service providers and specialists on specific assignments; (3) short-term or business visitors; and (4) diplomatic and international personnel.

Deployment Levels

Unfortunately, Philippine overseas employment statistics have not been categorized according to the definition and types of service providers just noted. Thus estimates of the number of Filipino service providers in this chapter are based on a tally of the data on the number of deployed, newly hired workers classified directly by the Philippine Overseas Employment Administration (POEA) as service workers, and those groups of workers more likely to be engaged as service providers, such as professional, technical, managerial, sales, and other skilled workers. The exclusion of other workers (i.e., clerical, production, and agricultural) from the estimate stems precisely from the definition of service providers just given.

The annual deployment overseas of newly hired, land-based workers classified directly as service workers was already ranging from 81,000 to 93,000 between 1995 and 2001. If the other groups of workers more likely to be working as service providers are added to these totals, the number of deployed Filipino service providers could easily range from 127,000 to 198,000.

Skills/Occupations, Destinations, and Length of Stay

Filipino workers are kind, loving, sacrificing, and loyal people, especially to their superiors. Thus Filipino workers are in great demand, especially in industrial countries.

Filipino service providers are spread around the world, but their skills and professions seem to determine their country of destination. Compared with other groups of workers, domestic helpers and related workers are spread a little more widely, although the bulk of those who left during the same period can be found in Hong Kong, China, and Saudi Arabia (Table 10.1).

Filipinos are natural entertainers. They love to entertain guests, and they are very artistic, cultured, and musically inclined. Thus there is an increasing demand for Filipino entertainers to perform in Japanese cities and the neighboring capitals of Southeast Asia. The United States seems to prefer workers in the field of information technology or accountants (Table 10.2).

Generally, Filipino service providers receive a two-year service employment contract in the Middle East, a six-month contract in Japan, and a one-year contract in Taiwan, China.

TABLE 10.1   Selected Top Skills Deployed, Philippines, 1995–2000

Skill	Destination	Number
Domestic helpers and related household workers	Hong Kong, China	136,339
	Saudi Arabia	54,522
	United Arab Emirates	27,692
	Taiwan, China	23,618
	Kuwait	20,454
	Malaysia	15,331
	Singapore	7,919
	Canada	6,133
	Italy	6,093
	Brunei	4,781
Choreographers and dancers	Japan	153,181
	Hong Kong, China	145
	Taiwan, China	16
Composers, musicians, and singers	Japan	53,989
	Malaysia	257
	Singapore	256
Electricians	Saudi Arabia	14,630
	Hong Kong, China	1,085
	Qatar	1,002
Waiters, bartenders, and related workers	United Arab Emirates	7,368
	Saudi Arabia	6,111
	Bahrain	1,179
	Kuwait	1,079

Source: Philippine Overseas Employment Administration.

TABLE 10.2   Selected Filipino Professionals Deployed, 1995–2000

Profession	Destination	Number
Nursing	Saudi Arabia	19,885
	United Kingdom	4,118
	Libya	1,488
	Singapore	1,241
Information technology	United States	2,730
(computer programmers and	Saudi Arabia	1,358
related workers, systems	Singapore	125
analysts)	Australia	102
	United Arab Emirates	57
Accounting	Saudi Arabia	988
	Northern Mariana Islands	211
	United States	180
	Papua New Guinea	129
	United Arab Emirates	129
Engineering	Saudi Arabia	7,945

Source: Philippine Overseas Employment Administration.

TABLE 10.3   Top 10 Seafarer Supplying Countries, as of 2000

Rank	Country	Officers	Ratings	Total
1	Philippines	50,000	180,000	230,000
2	Indonesia	15,500	68,000	83,500
3	China	34,197	47,820	82,017
4	Turkey	14,303	48,144	62,447
5	Russian Federation	21,680	34,000	55,680
6	India	11,700	43,000	54,700
7	Ukraine	14,000	23,000	37,000
8	Greece	17,000	15,500	32,500
9	Japan	18,813	12,200	31,013
10	U.S.-Great Lakes	13,204	17,667	30,871

Source: International Shipping Federation.

Deployment of Seafarers

The Philippines is considered the "ship manning capital" of the world; it accounts for 25 percent of the world's seaman population (Table 10.3). The demand for Filipino seafarers continues to grow, especially because the Philippines is included in the International Maritime Organization's list of Standards of Training, Certification, and Watchkeeping (STCW) compliant countries and because the Filipinos are considered the world's best seafarers; they are disciplined, organized, loyal, adaptable, English-proficient, and able to withstand the rigors of the sea.

Filipino seafarers on board ocean-going vessels are officers and ratings in deck, engine, and catering departments. They constitute a large pool of skilled temporary service providers on a per year contract.

Type of Movement

There is dearth of information on the type of movement made by Filipino service providers. Thus far, it seems that only Garnier (1996) has attempted to estimate the number of Filipino service providers abroad by type of movement. His estimates are: short-term Filipino service providers, 60,000; intracorporate transferees, 40,000; and long-term skilled migrants, 100,000.

Overall, based on the definition of service providers presented earlier in this chapter, there is no significant deployment of Filipinos as intracorporate transferees, individual service providers, or specialists and professionals. The bulk of deployment is temporary migrant workers under seasonal and contractual arrangements.

Barriers to the Mobility of Filipinos

The commitments made by Members of the World Trade Organization (WTO) under mode 4 are related to the entry and temporary stay of foreign nationals as service providers in their territory. Mode 4 presents opportunities for countries such as the Philippines. In addition, mode 4 is strongly linked to mode 3, because many services must rely on the applied knowledge, expertise, and technical skills of individuals.

Nevertheless, nearly all countries have restrictions in place that, in one way or another, impede or delay the movement of individuals. The GATS is aimed at dismantling these barriers, but, even though significant progress has been achieved so far under other modes, little progress has been made under mode 4.

The barriers to mobility under mode 4, which the Philippines finds difficult to overcome, fall into three categories: (1) the number and coverage of the current GATS commitments; (2) horizontal and sector-specific limitations on market access; and (3) limitations imposed through requirements and procedures.

Limited GATS Coverage

That developing country Members of the WTO such as the Philippines are seeking to liberalize commitments in mode 4 should come as no surprise because many of them are labor-surplus economies. Meanwhile, and also expected, industrial country Members are more cautious in their approach toward mode 4 while seeking to dismantle barriers in the other three modes.

So far, there is too much concentration on highly skilled labor and expertise in Members' commitments. The majority of entries concern executives, managers, and specialists, even though there is much to be desired in terms of entry commitments for less skilled labor. Such commitments are of particular interest to developing countries because they, like industrial countries, expect significant gains from the GATS. The holdoff stance of industrial countries toward less skilled labor is a double-edged sword that may inhibit the success of future GATS negotiations.

Commitments on intracorporate transferees are of limited interest to developing countries. Given their level of economic development, they are unable, because of lack of capital, to establish a commercial presence abroad. If mode 4 commitments continue to be tied to commercial presence, then what value is added to what has already been committed under mode 3?

A case in point is the construction and engineering services sector, which is labor-intensive and holds export potential. The commitments in this sector are very limited and confined largely to intracorporate transferees in skilled and highly skilled or managerial capacities. Few WTO Members have offered access for other categories, and where this has been done the emphasis has been on skills, as demonstrated clearly by the offers from Canada and the United States. Moreover, the access given is temporary and, in the case of the United States, subject to full state licensure and conditions about training and retention of U.S. workers.

In a sense, progress in mode 4 commitments could be seen as reactive to overall economic developments. The emphasis on associating high training and expertise with the mobility of persons may be related to the expansion of world trade and the growing role of intrafirm linkages. Commitments also reflect the proliferation of internal labor markets within multinational firms as well as limited institutional frameworks for facilitating the exchange of skills. Likewise, the increased numbers of specialized service providers or professionals such as doctors, therapists, and nurses, is a result of changing demographic patterns in certain developing countries. Thus, instead of proactively pursuing progressive liberalization under mode 4 for its own potential in increasing trade flows in services among and across industrial and developing countries, the current commitments are, in fact, only an extension of commitments in mode 3.

Quotas, Preemployment, and Wage Requirements

Horizontal and sectoral commitments on market access pose some entry restrictions. One is the numerical limit on what is allowed. A cursory look at sector-specific commitments would reveal restrictions, with a low number of quotas (ranging from 1 to 4) related to "ordinary staff," and with quotas also applied to senior staff.

Still tied to the intracorporate type of movement is the preemployment requirement, one of the most frequent restrictions. Many industrial countries require persons to be employed by the firm during the year immediately preceding the transfer, thereby effectively limiting the mobility of most temporary individual service providers.

Another effective form of barrier is the application of domestic minimum wage legislation, which at times is coupled with similar restrictions on work conditions, working hours, and social security benefits.

Recognition Requirements and Procedures

Licensing and qualifications systems pose an additional entry barrier. In many service sectors, certain requirements such as sufficient education, experience, and training are imposed in the public interest and must be met before entry can be allowed. These regulatory systems are being effectively carried out by government or by industrial or professional associations.

One of the problems associated with this requirement is the variety in the educational systems of WTO Members. For example, in the Philippines completion of education up to tertiary level takes 14 years; in other countries 15 or 16 years are required.

Variation in testing, certification, and licensing requirements, particularly for professionals and specialized skills workers, pose an additional restriction.

Because of these variations, the entry of foreign service providers becomes restricted. In many instances, they are given lower positions, salaries, or benefits, even if their actual qualifications or skills are comparable to those of local workers. Thus Filipino architects become draftsmen, engineers become technical staff, nurses become nursing aides, and dentists become dental assistants.

Administrative Barriers

Early negotiations in mode 4 have so far indicated the difficulty of devising a framework of rules to facilitate the mobility of workers. The vague terminologies and definitions used in schedules leave much room for administrative discretion, thus constituting another form of barrier. For example, there is no agreed-on definition of what constitutes "temporary" in the host country (some allot 90 days to business visitors; others allot two to five years to executives, and so forth). Without a uniform and standardized parameter for these terms, the numerous immigration officials at ports of entry and consular offices will offer various interpretations.

Interpretation problems mean that implementation of mode 4 commitments presents greater difficulties in practice than that for the other three modes. This may be the reason that progress in liberalization under this mode is significantly slower than that for the other modes.

Many WTO Members apply an economic needs test or labor market test to "open" categories of visa applicants, generally less skilled labor. The criteria for such tests should be more transparent to foreign service providers. Without an agreed-on set of parameters, this requirement might prove restrictive in certain instances and liberal in others.

Toward Greater Mobility

The GATS remains the most effective framework for pursuing liberalization of trade in services, and the WTO is the most appropriate forum. Indeed, the GATS is laying the foundation for future negotiations.

To overcome barriers, particularly those that limit the mobility of less skilled workers, the next round of services negotiations should seriously approach mode 4 with a proactive, developmental stance. The pattern of mode 4 commitments should gradually move its focus from highly trained and skilled service providers to those less skilled, and the linkage with commercial presence should be severed. The negligible impact in developing countries such as the Philippines of previous liberalization commitments under mode 4 should be an indication of the need to level the playing field if all Members are to benefit from the GATS.

Mutual recognition schemes, particularly those related to the testing, certification, and licensing of education, experience, and skills, would address bottlenecks in market access commitments. The limitations pertaining to wages, the regulations curtailing benefits under mandatory social insurance systems, and the administrative barriers across Members should now be addressed even outside of the GATS. Initiatives have been adopted by other regional cooperation forums, such as the Association of Southeast Asian Nations (ASEAN) and the Asia Pacific Economic Cooperation (APEC) forum, on qualification recognition, and the GATS can very well seek to collaborate in this undertaking to hasten the work.

Overseas deployment is an important contributor to the Philippine economy. Therefore, like other labor-surplus developing countries, the Philippines finds mode 4 of great interest. Facilitating trade in services through mode 4 presents a vast opportunity, particularly in an era in which information technology offers almost limitless forms of economic activities. A key element in expanding trade through mode 4 is negotiations to reduce barriers and facilitate greater and freer cross-border flows of service providers. Only when a proactive and developmental approach to negotiations is adopted will the GATS agreement achieve its goal of distributing opportunities to all.

Note

1. All dollar amounts are current U.S. dollars.

Reference

Garnier, P. 1996. "Service Providers: A Growing Dimension of Highly Skilled Migration in Asia." Paper presented at the Conference on the Dynamics of Labor Migration in Asia, Nihon University, Tokyo, March 6–8.

11

THE JAMAICAN EXPERIENCE WITH THE MOVEMENT OF NATURAL PERSONS IN THE PROVISION OF SERVICES

Enos A. Brown[*]

Developing countries are particularly concerned with the movement of natural persons under the General Agreement on Trade in Services (GATS), because they have a comparative advantage in the provision of labor-intensive services. The result of the initial phase of trade liberalization, which reduced tariffs and other entry barriers for goods, was that manufacturing and agricultural industries in many developing countries became globally uncompetitive. The production of goods then moved out of these countries, causing job losses and rising unemployment. In many instances, the labor component of production in these developing countries was price/productivity competitive when compared with that of their industrial counterparts. However, when the production moved out of these countries, no mechanism existed for the competitive labor factors to follow. This situation created a distortion in the global economy in which the free flow of goods, capital, and services across borders exists alongside restrictions on labor mobility. Many countries have questioned the long-term sustainability of such a development strategy.

The developing countries have a clear interest in ensuring that significant liberalization takes place in the movement of natural persons in the provision of services. This interest not only applies to the movement of professionals, but also, and probably more important, to semiskilled and unskilled workers, because of the comparative

---
[*]Enos A. Brown is with the HEART Trust/NTA, Jamaica.

advantage of the developing countries in the abundance of these workers as opposed to skilled professionals. In the absence of significant liberalization under mode 4, the value of the GATS to developing countries is significantly limited.

This chapter looks at the programs and activities that exist in the Jamaican context for providing services overseas through the movement of natural persons. The chapter closes with a review of Protocol II of the CARICOM (Caribbean Community) Single Market and Economy (CSME), which establishes a framework for the movement of labor within that region. These programs are not presented as an ideal or preferred example for the implementation of mode 4. Rather, they have various characteristics that can inform policymakers of potential issues to be considered as they move forward with the implementation of the GATS, particularly as it affects small developing countries.

Existing Formal Programs for Trade in Services

The genesis of modern Jamaican society is based on the movement of natural persons, most notably from Africa as part of the slave trade, but also from Europe, China, India, and the Middle East. This early labor migration was undertaken in response to the economic opportunities presented by the sugar plantations and the need to replace the indigenous labor force that had been destroyed in the wake of the Europeans' arrival. The cultural and ethnic melting pot that is Jamaica today is captured in the national motto "out of many, one people." This motto reflects the integration of people from various countries who have moved to Jamaica over the course of several centuries to participate in its economic activity, and, in this respect, Jamaica is similar to most modern societies that are multiethnic in structure.

With the decline of the sugar industry in the first half of the 1900s, Jamaica became, for the first time, a net exporter of labor as Jamaicans migrated to Britain in record numbers in search of economic opportunities. These migrants made significant contributions to the post–World War II redevelopment of their host country, particularly in the areas of transportation, construction, and health care. This increased migration continued throughout the second half of the twentieth century, with the destinations of choice being the United States and Canada in addition to the United Kingdom. These destinations were the obvious preference because of the similarities in culture based on an Anglo-centric focus.

In addition to the permanent migration of workers to industrial countries, Jamaica has entered into several bilateral agreements to provide workers to meet the temporary and seasonal demand for labor that could not be met by the host country counterpart in the exchange. The most established of these is the farm worker program with the United States and Canada. However, in more recent times the hospitality worker program with the United States and the schoolteacher work program with the United States and Britain have generated much activity, interest, and public debate.

Farm Worker Program

The farm worker agreements, aimed at meeting the seasonal demand for low-skilled laborers in the agricultural sectors of industrial countries, are Jamaica's oldest manifestation of the formal temporary movement of natural persons in the supply of services; they date back to the early 1900s. The program, in its various forms, has provided great economic value to both the home and host country. Jamaica, the home country, possesses a significantly greater abundance of low-skilled labor than can be absorbed in the local economy, whereas the host countries have a deficiency of human resources to meet the demand of the agricultural sector, particularly during the seasonal peak demand. This program, then, provides an ideal opportunity to expand the movement of natural persons, because both the home and host countries, and indeed the global economy, benefit from an arrangement that allows Jamaican surplus labor to be deployed in economic activity in a country where that particular kind of labor is in short supply.

Hospitality Worker Program

More recently, bilateral agreements have been reached for Jamaica to provide seasonal workers for the hospitality and tourism segments of industrial countries. The attraction of Jamaica is based on its well-developed local tourism industry, coupled with the proximity of Jamaica to the North American market and its English-speaking population. Like for farm work, these relatively low-paying jobs are not attractive to the host country labor force, which has other, more rewarding options. As a result, the enterprises in this sector are severely hard-pressed to meet the seasonal increase in demand for workers.

However, unlike in the farm worker program, Jamaica does not have an overabundance of trained hospitality workers. Faced with the recent growth in this form of service provision using Jamaican workers, the concerned local hospitality interests have seen their permanent employees resign in order to work temporarily in an industrial country. This short-term negative impact could be addressed through Jamaica's well-developed infrastructure for training hospitality workers. It could easily convert large numbers of unskilled persons into semiskilled persons to meet the demand of both the local and overseas industries. However, such an effort would require generally predictable growth in overseas demand and a policy framework that would make that demand accessible to increasing numbers of Jamaicans. Failing this, the increased training of hospitality workers would simply result in an oversupply of workers for the local market, further depressing the wages of this group of workers.

Schoolteacher Work Program

This program is the most recent example of the temporary movement of people to supply services overseas. It came into being out of the inability of the U.S. and the U.K. school districts to recruit sufficient numbers of primary and secondary schoolteachers for inner-city schools in and around New York City and London. Jamaican teachers were seen as an attractive substitute in the absence of a sufficient local labor source. This attraction is based not only on the English-speaking population, but also on the similarity between the education systems in the home and host countries, and the affordability of the teachers when their Jamaican salaries are compared with the cost of relocation and remuneration of teachers in the United States and the United Kingdom.

This program started out as a direct recruitment drive without the active involvement of the Jamaican government. The result was that in 2001 more than 500 teachers left their Jamaican classrooms to take up temporary assignments in the host countries. The loss of approximately 3 percent of the Jamaican teacher work force in such a short time period shocked the local education system, and that shock was compounded by the fact that the overseas recruiters were targeting the more experienced and qualified teachers. Jamaica does not have a competitive infrastructure for training teachers, a process that takes more than four years. If this level of recruitment is allowed to continue unabated, the result will be the desolation of the Jamaican education infrastructure. Quite simply, Jamaica is not currently in a position to satisfy the overseas market demand for this service. It was against this background that the Jamaican government intervened in this arrangement and is now seeking to control the outflow of teachers against the internal demand for this resource.

GATS Considerations

The above examples of the movement of natural persons highlight several significant considerations for the implementation of GATS mode 4:

- The movement of unskilled and semiskilled workers and the movement of persons with professional qualifications must be given equal consideration. Indeed, for many developing countries the former provides the greatest opportunity for economic participation in the global provision of services because of the comparative advantage they possess in this area.

- The movement of natural persons in the supply of services should not be tied to a commercial presence in the host country. Such a requirement would place developing countries at a significant disadvantage, because they lack the capital required to establish such a host country presence. At the same time, this precondition, though it would relate to multinational corporations, would not be relevant in a truly liberalized employment market.
- Home and host government control of the movement of persons in specific areas of services through the selection of persons and the service types being targeted should be reduced. Such an effort would require the removal of barriers to movement in the form of quotas and other bureaucratic prerequisites for service contracts such as work permit requirements and qualifications that are not indicative of the skills necessary to perform the work functions. These requirements serve only to suppress the cross-border mobility of workers and, consequently, the growth in this form of trade. Anything other than a significant reduction in government intervention in the cross-border trade in services will result in the continued inefficient utilization of labor on the global level and will not allow for the creation of increased numbers of service providers with the certainty that opportunities are available to absorb them locally and overseas.
- Economic needs tests in their current highly discretionary and arbitrary form should be removed, because they are a severe impediment to trade in services insofar as there is no predictability in their application and they nullify efforts to promote true global market efficiency.
- Some temporary provisions should be made to allow nations to prevent the short-term shock to the labor force of both home and host countries that can result from the rapid, uncontrolled outward or inward movement of service workers. One should be mindful of the complexities involved in developing and applying such safeguards, because they easily can discriminate against the very citizens they seek to protect. These provisions must be temporary, because the ultimate determinant of the efficient deployment of human resources should be market-driven.

Overview of Informal Initiatives Resulting in Trade in Services

During the last 50 years, increasing numbers of Jamaicans have migrated to the major cities of North America and the United Kingdom in search of economic opportunity. The majority of these migrants have been driven entirely by economic considerations, and as soon as their economic aspirations have been realized or they have completed their economically productive years overseas, they return to Jamaica to enjoy the fruits of their labor and their retirement years. If these people had the ability to temporarily participate in the labor force of their host country without having to take up permanent residence, it could be argued that this would be their preferred option. Today, of the 6.3 million persons who regard themselves as Jamaican, only 2.6 million reside in Jamaica—an indication of the economic migratory profile of the population. Jamaicans have historically been favorably viewed in host countries for employment in transportation, construction, and health care services.

The importance of trade in services to the Jamaican economy is reflected in the labor-related transfers from overseas. Jamaica is a large net recipient of remittances, which are the nation's third largest source of foreign currency.

Movement of Jamaican Professionals

In more recent times, permanent migration has been increasing among young professionals, primarily as a result of host country immigration laws that show preference to this category of worker, which includes computer programmers and accountants. The permanent migration of these people constitutes a brain drain on the local economy that further exacerbates initiatives to develop its competitiveness. In addition, such migration results in the need to import professional persons and services at costs that in many instances are above those found in the industrial world. This factor, together with that of the remaining local professionals demanding wages that are reflective of their scarcity, has caused a significantly higher differential in salary scales between professionals and semiskilled/unskilled workers than that found in industrial countries. This differential has contributed to the polarization of Jamaican society and the concurrent social tensions that are manifested in various forms of antisocial behavior, including crime and violence. Certainly, developing countries would prefer the temporary movement of its professionals as opposed to permanent migration. Temporary movement also would be in the interest of the host country's work force, because the associated displacement of domestic workers would be reduced.

Movement of Jamaican Nonprofessionals

Many other Jamaicans who do not have the professional qualifications to pursue the formal migration opportunities available resort to informal mechanisms to participate temporarily in the overseas labor market. They include using nonimmigrant, visitor status to engage in temporary employment. These people, mainly employed in home care and health care services, engage in employment contracts with host country nationals to provide these services for a period of typically up to six months, depending on the length of stay permitted by the visitor visa. These contracts are not reported through any formal procedure because of the illegal nature of the employment. In reality, a market condition exists within the host country in which the demand for these types of services is best met by lower-cost temporary workers from overseas. These workers have no desire to permanently migrate, provided the opportunity for ongoing temporary employment exists. In many respects, this situation represents the very market condition that mode 4 of the GATS seeks to address—that is, bringing an efficient service provider in the form of a natural person in contact with a demand for services in another Member's territory. It is therefore instructive to note that the people in this category face the greatest barriers to offering their services outside of their home country.

GATS Considerations

The examples just given serve to highlight the following considerations for the implementation of the GATS:

- The GATS should be implemented in a manner that allows clear differentiation between persons who are seeking permanent migration for reasons beyond economics and those who are seeking to access temporary work opportunities. This differentiation can be achieved only by a very liberal approach to mode 4, with the removal of the strict eligibility conditions required for the temporary movement of workers under existing immigration regulations.
- The current immigration policy of industrial countries that favors the permanent migration of professionals from developing countries should be replaced by provisions facilitating mode 4-type temporary movement.
- Consideration should be given to host nations' legitimate public policy concerns about controlling the free movement of service providers across their borders, including consumer protection, public interest, and security.
- Once a liberalized approach is in place, market conditions will determine the efficient allocation of human resources. For the protection of the vulnerable small developing country, the potential for the mass movement of scarce professional resources in the short term needs to be regulated until market equilibrium of supply and demand is achieved.

The CARICOM Initiative

Protocol II, Right of Establishment, Services and Capital, is considered the most important instrument in the creation of the CSME. The objectives of this protocol are as follows:

- To complete the creation of the CSME by adding to the free movement of goods the free movement of services, capital, and select categories of skilled workers and the right of CARICOM nationals to set up business in any CARICOM country

- To ensure national treatment and nondiscrimination of CARICOM nationals who wish to carry out business in member states
- To facilitate access of CARICOM nationals to resources within the single market
- To create more business and employment opportunities, and to open opportunities for trade in services.

Relevant to mode 4 of the GATS, the protocol allows the free movement within member territories of graduates from approved universities. On the basis of reciprocity, member states of the World Trade Organization (WTO) have extended the prescribed list of occupations. In 1998 Jamaica extended the list to include sports persons, artists, media professionals, and musicians who are certified by their national professional body.

This list of approved occupations is itself discriminatory against the vast majority of CARICOM nationals who are not university graduates, highly skilled professionals, or members of the other approved occupations.

Protocol II includes only professional occupations because of the perceived absence of a mechanism to recognize through a formal methodology the knowledge, skills, and attributes of all CARICOM nationals. However, CARICOM does recognize the need to ensure that its nationals at all skill and certification levels are efficiently deployed in economic activity.

This concern has resulted in the dialogue moving toward a regional strategy for technical and vocational education and training (TVET). The TVET system encompasses a much broader expanse of occupations, ranging from work force entry-level skills to mastery-level skills equivalent to university degrees. This system therefore provides the opportunity for significantly more CARICOM nationals to participate in and directly benefit from the liberalization in the provision of services than the approximately 4 percent who are the recipients of university degrees.

The regional TVET strategy is based on the establishment of a national training agency (authority) in each CARICOM territory. These agencies, such as my organization, the HEART Trust/National Training Agency (NTA), have the mandate to establish the standards for TVET delivery and certification within the context of an agreed-on regional framework. The framework is competency based and driven by industry needs. Emphasis is on accreditation, articulation, and certification.

The NTAs have as their primary responsibility the development and approval of training standards for occupational areas that are critical to regional economic activity. Thereafter, both the public and private providers of training, whether in the formal school system, community colleges, or vocational schools, are accredited to deliver these training programs on the basis of their ability to adhere to the standards.

Both nationally and regionally, a framework is being developed to enable the cross-institution and cross-territory articulation of training programs through an evaluation of equivalencies. This evaluation is facilitated by the modular manner in which the competency standards are being developed.

Finally, the national certification of an individual's competence is a valid and reliable indication that he or she can perform at the level stipulated in the TVET standards. Having received the national certification, any CARICOM national can thereafter apply for a CARICOM Vocational Qualification (CVQ), which is issued by the local training authority and is recognized throughout CARICOM.

This certification can be equated to an international driver's license, which in this case makes the CARICOM national eligible for employment in any job that requires that particular qualification in any CARICOM territory, without the need for a work permit or any other bureaucratic prerequisite for employment. Full implementation of the free movement of labor under Protocol II is scheduled for 2005.

Observations of the CARICOM Model Relevant to the GATS

The following observations of the CARICOM model have some merit when considering implementation of the GATS:

- Notwithstanding the relatively small size of CARICOM, the model emphasizes the need for nations to document and publish the standards required for employment in all occupational areas. Although it is not necessary for all nations to adopt the same standards—and obviously they will not because local needs and technologies vary—these standards will form the basis for the evaluation and articulation of qualifications between nations.
- If national occupational qualifications that are recognized by other territories are to be the vehicle for the free movement of labor, then a mechanism is required to achieve some level of harmonization in professional and occupational service standards between nations. The mutual recognition agreement model is ideal for achieving this harmonization and should be promoted as the basis for member countries recognizing the certification of foreign nationals so that they can engage in service activities within its territory.
- Occupational certification is a preferred approach over professional qualifications, because it opens up the possibility of including semiskilled and skilled workers in nonprofessional areas. In addition, this approach recognizes both on-the-job experience and the academic qualification. This approach provides

a vehicle through which the Jamaican agricultural, hospitality, home care, and health care workers can be nationally certified and eligible to offer their services in any market for which there is a demand and recognition of the Jamaican/CARICOM standard. This condition could be applied on a global basis if a similar approach is taken at that level.

Conclusion

Greater liberalization in mode 4 movement under the GATS is a necessary, yet insufficient, condition for the sustainable development of small developing nations. These countries have to be cognizant of the need to strengthen all the factors of production in their local economy if long-term development is to be achieved. They should place more emphasis on the competitive creation of human capital that is aligned with local and global labor needs. To support this, multilateral agencies should work increasingly with developing countries to improve and expand their education and training infrastructure.

As for the GATS, greater liberalization is in the interest of all nations, and not moving rapidly in this direction runs counter to the global economic rationale. The notion that only highly skilled persons should be afforded freedom of movement in providing services is equally irrational. Global market conditions should be allowed to determine the service, price, and location that are in demand, along with the skill level of the persons providing the service.

The issue of recognition of competence to provide a service across territories can be addressed through an approach that focuses on worker certification against documented performance standards. Such an approach (e.g., CARICOM regional TVET strategy) will not only facilitate worker certification at various skill levels, but also form a basis for the evaluation and recognition of worker certification by other nations.

Finally, mode 4 of the GATS provides a great opportunity for both industrial and developing nations that is not mutually exclusive. One only hopes that the discussions proceed in an enlightened manner, recognizing that the nations prosper with each other, not at the other's expense.

12

MODE 4 AND TRADE UNION CONCERNS

*Mike Waghorne**

Public Services International (PSI) is a global trade union federation with 601 affiliated unions in 146 countries, organizing some 20 million members. PSI works in conjunction with another nine global trade union[1] federations covering other sectors of the economy and with the International Confederation of Free Trade Unions and the Trade Union Advisory Committee at the Organisation for Economic Co-operation and Development (OECD). PSI also works closely with various nongovernmental organizations (NGOs) on a range of World Trade Organization (WTO) issues, especially on the General Agreement on Trade in Services (GATS) and on development issues. Some of the mode 4 issues under examination are too recent and fluid for PSI to have a settled policy on them. Therefore, this chapter reflects my views of what shape PSI policy may take. Eventually, however, that policy is open to a democratic discussion that may reach conclusions different from those outlined here.

This chapter focuses solely on one part of mode 4 of the GATS: how mode 4 could work better. However, this focus should not be taken as unqualified support for the full GATS agenda. Nor should the fact that PSI works with NGOs that are critical of many aspects of WTO and World Bank policies be taken to imply that the views expressed here reflect the views of all of those NGOs on this topic.

The Services of Interest

The global unions group covers workers in all sectors of industry and services. Potentially, then, the implications of mode 4 trade in all services covered by the GATS are of concern. The reality, however, is that many services are not yet typified by a large movement of persons to provide services on a temporary basis as

---

*Mike Waghorne is assistant general secretary, Public Services International.

envisioned under mode 4. The following services are the main concern of global union federations:

1. *Professional services.* These services are typically offered by people such as architects, engineers, planners, and information and communication technology (ICT) professionals. These professionals often are not unionized when they operate as independent contractors, unless they are employed by multinational enterprises (MNEs) and are engaged in a project or operation that needs outside professionals or consultants on a temporary or project basis. These service providers could be working in any sector of the economy, but they are most likely to be found, if at all, in the sectors organized by PSI or Union Network International (UNI). It is unclear whether anyone knows the full extent of this kind of work, especially because MNEs' projects vary so much in both extent and intensity.

2. *Health and education services.* These workers may offer their services on an individual contract basis, but it is more likely that they are employed by a public health or education service or some private service provider such as a nursing home or private university. Again, accurate figures for this sector are not readily available. Current research at the World Health Organization (WHO) indicates that the United Kingdom recruits about 10,000 nurses a year from abroad, but how many of these fit a GATS classification is very difficult to assess. The numbers, across all services of this nature and across all WTO member states, appear to be substantial. Some of this movement is under some form of government control/oversight by both home country governments (such as the Philippines, which has a good registration and placement system for Filipino workers going abroad) and host country governments (such as the United States or the United Kingdom), neither of which keep data in a GATS-useful manner. Often, however, these workers are placed either on a self-election or informal basis or through recruitment agencies, some of which, as elaborated later in this chapter, have every reason to keep very little useful data. Health and education service providers, most of whom are eligible to join trade unions, are covered by PSI or Education International (EI). The length of employment varies from country to country, depending on domestic laws governing temporary employment and training.

3. *Construction services.* The International Federation of Building and Wood Workers (IFBWW) has joined the World Bank in looking at the concerns of construction workers. These often highly mobile workers work on major Bank-funded public works projects such as ports, airports, dams, and highways. The majority are likely to be local workers, but a substantial number of these workers go from project to project around the world, and the IFBWW has been

working with the Bank to ensure that workers are not subjected to discriminatory employment conditions, are guaranteed good health and safety procedures, and have adequate accommodation and social provisions, most of which are covered by appropriate International Labour Organisation (ILO) conventions. Again, even if only those working for Bank-funded projects are counted, their number is likely to be considerable. Adding domestically supervised projects that use an international work force would increase this number substantially. Projects may be as short as a few months but can run into several years.

Union and NGO Concerns

For the first category—the more or less independent contractor professionals—the concerns are relatively slight for trade unions. And it is not because trade unions do not care. Indeed, they advise such service providers that, if eligible to join a union, they should do so because, if they encounter problems, having access to a body that understands local employment, labor, contracts, and social security policies could be useful. However, many of these workers make their own arrangements or are within an MNE that takes responsibility, well or not, for them. Therefore, trade unions' concerns about these workers are similar to those about other temporary workers, and they are largely along the lines of the concerns expressed by India in its WTO submission. The concerns include visas, the loss of money paid into social security/insurance schemes, and the potential for such workers to be used as an unemployment buffer—that is, to be wanted or not—as the labor market waxes and wanes. The criteria to be used for judging the economic necessity of the temporary work (economic needs tests) are another issue. Trade unions would be interested in solutions that address all of these issues. On the last element, that of economic needs tests, unions have every interest in encouraging governments to have employment and industry policy plans that can gauge the need for training, recruitment, infrastructure, and so forth.

To those concerns can be added several others for workers in the health and education services and in construction services. First, the social security/insurance and unemployment schemes issue is more important for workers in these categories, because they are often required by law to pay into such schemes and may lose all of their contributions on their return home. It is possible for arrangements to be made to ensure that these workers or their home economy recoups these payments. (Apparently such an arrangement has been made between France and both Mali and Tunisia.) For many of these workers this money is a substantial part of their income.

A second set of concerns involves employment and labor rights. Many of these workers are subject to discrimination and harassment of many forms and need to be protected by the existing domestic legislation. Where such legislation does not cover such workers, it should be amended to do so. These workers need to be able to join relevant trade unions and to receive the normal workers' rights applied in the host country. They must be paid the same wages as others doing the same work.

This concern does not imply that the comparative advantage that such workers gamble on to get work is lost. They often will not have qualifications and certification up to the domestic standard or their experience will be less relevant than that of local workers with longer domestic experience. Many will, therefore, still earn less than domestic workers, but where qualifications and experience are equal, pay, conditions, and career structures also must be equal. There are too many examples of fully qualified immigrant nurses being tricked into employment that exploits their skills but pays them less than their local counterparts and denies them rights supposedly guaranteed by law.

Third, the IFBWW tries to insist that the World Bank and host governments ensure that environmental and social values are respected on major projects. Not only should these values be respected anyway but for the immigrant workers concerned, failure to respect environmental and social concerns could make these project workers possible targets for protest and violence. It is not surprising that people who have been forcibly removed from their land and houses to make way for a dam will take it out on the people who are now living temporarily on that land and making good wages while they build the invasive project. Naturally, this is a matter of concern for many NGOs, including environmental groups.

Fourth are the various concerns related to development and the brain drain. Many of the workers engaged in this kind of temporary work are essentially using the experience to build up contacts in the host country so that, even if they have to return to their home country after the approved term of employment, later they will be invited back on a permanent basis. In some cases, of course, temporary workers manage, legally or not, to convert their temporary status into a permanent one. Where this happens on a large scale—for example, with nurses from the Philippines and South Africa—a developing country is essentially subsidizing or covering the full cost of nurse training that should be paid by an industrial country.

In some cases, noted especially in the work of the Commonwealth Secretariat on the issue of migration of health workers, the loss of even one or two key personnel can be the deciding factor in closing a whole national unit. For example, it is claimed that the loss of one anesthetist in one Caribbean country meant that the national intensive care unit had to be closed. Therefore, it is not just mass losses that count in terms of the development capacity of developing countries.

In both home and host countries, temporary movement has a direct relationship to the operations of the labor market. In many developing countries, the pull of the industrial world is so strong simply because the developing country employer, typically a government, is not paying enough to keep its own work force. This situation is sometimes the direct result of policies imposed by international financial institutions—policies that undermine the very services for the poor that these institutions claim to want to develop. If half the nurses from country X go elsewhere because they cannot exist on their wages, then no amount of exhortation to country X to ensure that its health services meet the needs of the poor is going to achieve the stated objective.

For industrial countries, the unwillingness of the employers in those countries, including governments, to pay decent wages to their own employees becomes a direct means of denying to developing countries the chance of ever satisfying the needs of their own people, as governments from the North steal all the output from training schools in the South in order to make up for the loss of those in the North who quit the health service for better pay and conditions in other sectors. The United Kingdom, for example, in addition to undermining its own Overseas Development Administration aid policies, also sends its "excess" patients to overworked but better health systems in the rest of Europe. Before some governments in the North start talking about trade in services, perhaps they should develop some decent public services of their own.

Finally, the role of recruitment agencies raises other concerns. Many are perfectly reputable and are under some form of government supervision. Some, however, operate in quite unacceptable ways. Examples abound of agencies illegally taking passports and return air tickets from temporary workers; illegally deducting so-called recruitment fees that have already been paid by employers; sponsoring dishonest advertising that tricks people into work that they would not have accepted had they been correctly informed; administering various forms of harassment or even violence against workers; and attempting to control workers' private social lives.

Some Solutions

To some extent, the solutions to the problems and concerns just outlined are self-evident.

First, immigration procedures, such as a GATS visa, should be explored.

Second, governments should sit down with business and unions to develop sectoral employment and industry policies that plan for the future. And here *policies* does not mean the old-fashioned policies of attempting to pick winners. It is a matter of knowing what is coming down the track, where one would like (or not like!) to be in five or ten years' time, and what one needs to do to deal with that.

Third, not surprisingly, global union federations such as PSI believe that all governments should ratify and respect the workers' rights contained in the 1998 ILO Declaration on Fundamental Principles and Rights at Work. PSI, again not surprisingly, believes that these rights should apply to all workers, including so-called GATS workers, and must include the right to belong to a trade union and to use grievance procedures. Such rights are especially important for women, who are among the most frequently and most grievously abused workers, already in marginal circumstances because of their immigrant status.

Fourth, for the health and education services, it is essential that governments, employers, and recruitment agencies commit themselves to commonly accepted ethical recruitment policies. The Commonwealth is doing good work on this. The International Council of Nurses (ICN) has a good international policy on the ethical recruitment of nurses, and, working with ICN, PSI is trying to extend this policy to the whole health sector. The U.K. government also recently adopted such a policy, although, as noted earlier, it has not addressed the wage issue that undermines the policy. Such policies must be binding on private agencies.

Finally, unions internationally do not have concerns about whether temporary employment becomes permanent employment, at least not in relation to the issues raised by mode 4 of the GATS.[2] Individual unions in some countries will have such concerns where this situation is exploited to undermine wages and conditions. Unions want to see the free movement of people, where the motivating factors are career development, information, technology and cultural exchange, and an enrichment of life. If the push and pull factors that turn many workers into unwilling migrants and undermine the effective operations of labor markets can be taken away, then all would gain.

Notes

1. Unless otherwise specified, "union" in the rest of this chapter means "trade union."
2. Some unions may have other (im)migration concerns in general, but these are not relevant to this chapter.

13

THE TEMPORARY INFLOW OF NATURAL PERSONS FOR THE SWISS IT MARKET

Pierre E. Page[*]

The TKS Group, trading as TKS-Teknosoft, a Swiss independent company, was founded in 1985 to promote, sell, and support the services and products of TATA Consultancy Services (TCS) from Mumbai, India, on a mutually exclusive basis, first in Switzerland and then in France. Thus some 18 years ago, when TKS introduced Switzerland to the resources of the Indian information technology (IT) industry and long before the General Agreement on Trade in Services (GATS) came into force, an acute need existed to transfer IT specialists temporarily to Switzerland and to obtain the relevant work authorizations. This chapter, in outlining TKS's early experience in Switzerland, will therefore concentrate on the "host country view." It is limited to the experience in the Swiss IT market and in no way reflects the official position of the Swiss government in the World Trade Organization (WTO) services negotiations.

Switzerland's Economy

Switzerland is economically a strong country, very much open to international trade. Overall, one Swiss franc out of two in the gross national product (GNP) is generated by exports. Deprived of raw materials, Switzerland had to develop after World War II an economic structure based on products with low raw material content and very high added value, such as watches and pharmaceuticals, and on services, such as tourism and finance. Indeed, Switzerland has become a service economy. At the end of 2001, services employed approximately three-quarters of the active population of 3,938,000 and generated two-thirds of GNP.

---

[*]Pierre E. Page is president of Teknosoft Ltd, Switzerland, and founder of the TKS Group.

Switzerland's population also has some striking characteristics. The country's percentage of foreign population is high by Western standards: 19.7 percent at the end of 2001, or 1,419,095 people. Of these foreigners, 75 percent benefited from a permanent work permit. Also, in line with the traditional compassion of the Swiss for those who are less gifted or less fortunate, Switzerland has absorbed 149,596 asylum seekers during the last five years, which represents the highest proportion absorbed by any European country. These facts should not be forgotten when dealing with issues such as the movement of natural persons.

Switzerland is not only one of the main exporters of services on a worldwide basis, but also a net exporter of services. For the years 1996–99 the total Swiss services trade surplus reached CHF25.8 billion. But at the same time, Switzerland has experienced a net outflow of about 400 scientists and researchers a year. These young, talented people were trained in Switzerland at great cost. As a result of these two factors, the GATS is of cardinal importance to Switzerland.

The Swiss IT Market

Like any other service economy, Switzerland is moving quickly toward an information society that relies increasingly on IT. The use of personal computers and of the Internet is very widespread; more than 60,000 workers are considered to be IT professionals; and more than half of the workplaces are equipped with computers.

The flip side is that, until 2000, Switzerland faced severe problems in its IT market, because estimates revealed a shortage of more than 10,000 IT specialists. At the peak of the "dot com bubble" it was generally agreed that Europe had a shortage of 200,000 IT staff; the figure for the United States was 800,000!

The Swiss Federal Institutes of Technology in Lausanne and Zurich and Swiss engineering schools turn out only some 600 graduates in informatics a year. Under such circumstances, it is clear that the temporary inflow of IT specialists is not only needed but welcome, although the demand for such staff has substantially eased since 2001.

Switzerland's GATS Commitments

The conditions for obtaining a work permit under Switzerland's GATS commitments are clear. Five key conditions must be met:

1. Annual work permit quotas (decided every year by the federal government) must not be exhausted.

2. An employment contract must be signed with the candidate.
3. Minimum salary and social security conditions in line with the living standard in Switzerland must be met.
4. The candidate must have a university degree.
5. A change of job, profession, or location (canton) is not permitted.

The agreement brings two immediate and direct benefits for the employee. First, the priority criteria for recruiting have been suppressed for Swiss nationals and for preferential recruiting areas; there is now a level playing field in this area. Second, if a work application is turned down by an administration, the candidate can appeal to a court instead of only to an administrative authority.

Getting a Work Permit

In view of the first condition for obtaining a work permit in Switzerland—that quotas not be exhausted—one needs to underline that this condition is not enforced for a work permit application under GATS rules, Switzerland being compliant with its GATS obligations. As for IT staff, my own estimate is that about 5,000 work permits are granted every year for such specialists in Switzerland.

Various types of work permits, with durations of from 4 to 48 months, are available so that the needs of the economy can be met in a pragmatic, if not optimal, way. It is up to the employer and the candidate employee to request the type of work permit that best fits their interests, whether a short one or a multiyear one.

Because of the implementation in June 2002 of the Switzerland–European Union bilateral agreements, various types of work permits with different durations became available in Switzerland in 2002. Indeed, proposals have been made to replace the nonrenewable 18-month work permit with a 12-month work permit that can be renewed for an additional 12 months. But whatever the changes, it is Switzerland's goal to comply with the GATS obligations it has undertaken.

When one applies for a work permit, it is important to bear in mind that Switzerland is a federal state. As a result, a work permit procedure always originates with the cantonal labor market authority, the cantonal authority recommending the granting of the requested work permit. The role of the cantonal alien police authority is only to check that the candidate has no criminal record.

All in all, depending on the canton where the work permit application is submitted and on the type of work permit, the procedure is completed within four to eight weeks, during which the candidate cannot be in Switzerland.

Possible Improvements

TKS's experience is that the work permit procedure is completed in most cases without glitches. However, there are three areas for improvement:

1. *Issuing residence authorization for family.* With the implementation of the Switzerland–European Union bilateral agreements, the limitations in issuing residence permits for family have been eased and can no longer be considered a serious issue in 2003.
2. *"Off-Switzerland" period requirements for getting a second work permit.* The regulations for getting a second work permit in Switzerland for an IT professional— for example, in the case of a multiyear IT project partially executed offshore—are amazingly complex because of different "off-Switzerland" period requirements. Simplification and shortening of the "off-Switzerland" period (currently up to one year) would be welcome.
3. *Duration of business visa.* A business visa is delivered basically for business promotion only. The duration of such a visa is routinely limited to 15 consecutive days with one single entry. Depending on the size of the project proposal being prepared (a multimillion-dollar proposal cannot be prepared in just 15 days!), a longer-duration business visa, on an exception basis, would be very useful.

Concluding Observations

TKS's experience is that the Swiss authorities tend to be accessible, competent, and cooperative (unfortunately, this is not necessarily the case in large European countries). Swiss regulations are genuinely consistent; they are known and applied equitably, and there are no hidden hurdles. If one complies with the law and adheres to the applicable procedure, Switzerland guarantees a level playing field, where no problem, provided it is within the boundaries of the law, regulations, and guidelines, is impossible to solve.

14

MODE 4: THROUGH A CANADIAN IMMIGRATION POLICY LENS

Paul Henry[*]

The temporary movement of natural persons in the General Agreement on Trade in Services (GATS) negotiations will benefit from negotiators achieving a better understanding of the different policy contexts or perspectives, particularly those of trade, immigration, and labor market development. Trade policy officials should not neglect the immigration and labor market perspectives when considering various temporary entry or mode 4 issues.[1] Similarly, immigration and labor policy officials need to pay more attention to trade policy perspectives.

These policy communities often adopt adversarial approaches or fail to see the advantages of working together. They need not, however, consider each other as antagonists in the endeavor to advance mode 4 liberalization. Negotiators representing Members of the World Trade Organization (WTO) should avoid adversarial relationships and zero-sum games, which can perpetuate misunderstandings, foster defensive positions, and lead to incompatible results. Through concerted action these policy communities can identify common interests, find ways to improve mode 4 liberalization, and produce complementary results serving various interests—trade, immigration, labor policy interests, as well as those of service suppliers and investors. Indeed, the immigration, labor, and trade policy contexts or perspectives can be depicted as intersecting circles (Figure 14.1).[2]

This chapter will focus briefly on the immigration context in order to provide a glimpse of immigration officials' perceptions, attitudes, and preoccupations. Some views may be purely Canadian, while others may be similar to the views of immigration or labor policy officials from other GATS Member countries. It also

---

[*]Paul Henry is trade policy analyst in the Economic Policy and Programs Division, Selection Branch, Citizenship and Immigration Canada (CIC).

FIGURE 14.1   The Intersection of Policy Contexts

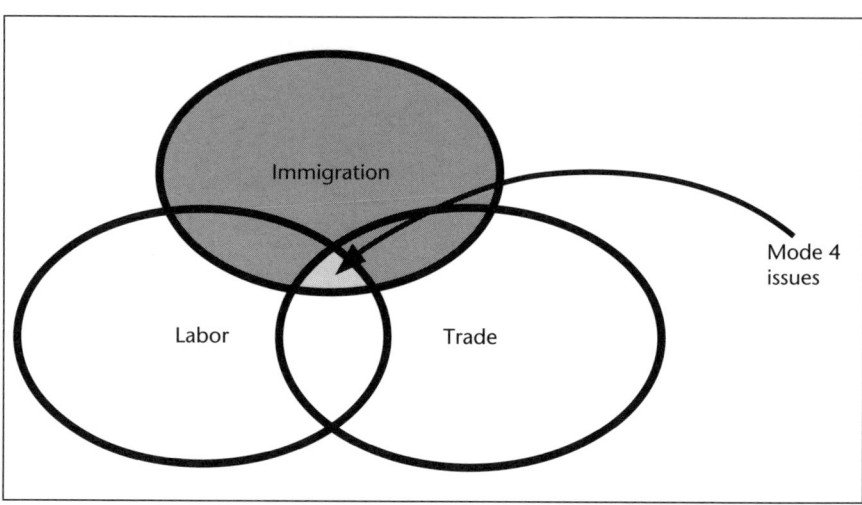

Source: The author.

is important to focus attention on the place where these policy contexts intersect (i.e., where mode 4 or temporary entry issues reside).

Role of Immigration and Labor Policy Officials

Before focusing on the immigration context, this chapter will consider the important role that immigration and labor officials can play in strengthening mode 4 liberalization. First, as mentioned earlier, they are key partners, not adversaries, of trade policy officials. They can provide a better appreciation of the horizontal mode 4 issues and regulatory regimes at the border.[3] They can help to explain the temporary entry laws and regulations of their countries and those regimes of other WTO Members. They also can explain why some horizontal commitments on mode 4 may not work well in practice because of related requirements or application procedures not mentioned in a schedule of specific commitments.[4]

Immigration officers in the field dealing with temporary entrants apply both general provisions (i.e., the existing national laws and regulations of general application, which often have various exceptions) and special rules, which are usually facilitative and may have resulted from the negotiation of international agreements, including trade agreements. These general and special provisions amount to a vast body of laws, regulations, administrative guidelines, interpretations, and field instructions. Immigration and labor policy officials can help to decipher that information. They can also help to clarify, and propose solutions for, the temporary entry problems cited by businesspeople.[5]

Immigration Perspective

A useful way to enter the immigration policy context is to look at the business lines of Citizenship and Immigration Canada (CIC):[6]

1. To maximize the benefits of international migration, which include the selection of economic immigrants, family reunification, and the admission of visitors (i.e., tourists, foreign students, and temporary workers).
2. To uphold Canada's humanitarian tradition, which involves refugee determination.
3. To promote the integration of newcomers, which involves settling in or adapting to Canadian society.
4. To manage access to Canada, which covers a range of border management, enforcement, and national security issues.

The first business line, maximizing the benefits of international migration, has two key aspects: permanent and temporary residency. A historical focus of so-called "settlement" or "immigrant-dependent" countries such as Canada is the selection of permanent immigrants leading to citizenship. The majority of time and resources is devoted to choosing permanent residents and helping them to adapt to Canadian society. In this context, temporary foreign worker issues are important, but not as high in priority as the others.

The fourth business line, managing access to Canada, also is an important preoccupation, particularly because of current international migration trends or events threatening national security. Border management, enforcement, and security issues are now very prominent. The smuggling and trafficking of people, for example, are increasing international problems, and enforcement officials find the deportation or removal of illegal immigrants difficult, especially when some countries refuse to cooperate in readmitting their nationals. Consequently, some enforcement officials have suggested that in international trade agreements commitments on greater temporary entry to Canada or similar countries be tied to commitments by certain countries to take back their nationals who have entered these countries illegally.[7]

Immigration and Trade Policy Contexts

The immigration and trade policy communities often misunderstand each other. One problem is that they do not speak the same language. Trade policy officials frequently do not know the rationale for immigration laws and regulations.

Immigration policy officials may not understand international trade or the negotiating process. A key reason for these difficulties is officials' different focuses or preoccupations.

Immigration policy has an inward focus; it is primarily concerned with the intake and settlement of permanent residents. Enforcement and security issues are high priorities—and even more so in the post–September 11 world. Furthermore, there is an emphasis on attracting foreign skilled workers for the economic viability of the country. Like in other industrial countries, Canada's aging population and low birthrates are factors in its skills shortages in the labor market. Permanent immigrants to Canada are expected to account for all net labor force growth by 2011 and all population growth by 2031. A Canadian government priority, therefore, is to find enough workers with the necessary education and skills to meet the needs of the economy. In this context, it becomes clear that immigration policy is responding to domestic needs or catalysts, and that a trend of more liberal immigration rules is discernible. Amid these preoccupations, international trade issues are low priorities. Nevertheless, immigration policy on temporary foreign workers does recognize a role for international trade agreements and other bilateral arrangements in furthering domestically defined economic objectives.

Similarly, trade policy must take into account domestically defined objectives with respect to temporary entry. Trade policy has both outward and inward focuses. Trade officials, whether concentrating on policy or business development, are concerned with barriers to exports and imports and the attraction or promotion of foreign direct investment. Temporary entry issues have assumed a higher profile, and more trade officials are focusing attention on mode 4 liberalization and business facilitation to advance domestically defined objectives.

CIC Views on International Trade Agreements

What are the views of CIC on international trade agreements? First, the CIC fully supports the Canadian government's international trade agenda. The mobility of businesspeople is similar to a basic infrastructure of the economy; it is a key means of promoting and conducting trade and investment. More trade and investment depend on businesspeople having unimpeded temporary access to markets. Furthermore, provisions in international trade agreements that liberalize temporary entry have benefited many businesspeople.[8]

The CIC has several concerns, however, about some practical effects of temporary entry provisions negotiated in international trade agreements. The first concern is the special rules on temporary entry created by these agreements. It is ironic that, in certain cases, those liberal rules have resulted in a burden for both immigration officers and businesspeople. For example, some businesspeople, instead of sailing smoothly through a port of entry, are pulled out of the queue and directed to a secondary inspection area where immigration officers must interview them to ensure they comply with the special rules of trade agreements.

It is important to understand this problem from the border management perspective. A port of entry is increasingly a place of heightened security, stretched resources, time pressures, and long lines of travelers, partly because of better transportation services, more trade or business activity, and outdated facilities. Immigration officers do not want to spend time screening business travelers who are considered to be low risk.[9] Furthermore, they worry about not having enough time to concentrate on high-risk individuals—a concern the post–September 11 security agenda has increased.

Consequently, key objectives now are to ensure not only that borders are secure, but also that trade and people flows are not hampered.[10] Since September 11, Canadian and U.S. border management officials have increased their cooperation. Besides strengthening security, they also are investigating ways to facilitate the temporary entry of legitimate businesspeople. This is the same objective that trade policy officials are pursuing in the mode 4 negotiations.

Another CIC concern is the lack of transparency of the horizontal mode 4 commitments. Opaque commitments can lead to implementation burdens at ports of entry for immigration officers and businesspeople. When the commitments or supplementary information is not clear, businesspeople will not understand the temporary entry rules well enough, and consequently they could face difficulties and delays at ports of entry.

Although CIC views of international trade agreements are positive, it does have a preference for the general provisions of Canada's immigration regime and the policymaking flexibility they allow. Canadian immigration and labor policy officials know the commitments in international trade agreements are permanent, and they favor the general provisions because of their flexibility. These officials prefer the general provisions because they can be used to respond to changes in the domestic labor market or economy, which is dynamic. Economic needs rise and fall; skills or labor shortages of today may not be the skills or labor shortages of tomorrow. The general provisions allow for temporary and managed policy responses to requests from domestic sectors that need foreign workers.[11]

Despite its preference for the general provisions and policy flexibility, Canada is willing to make legally binding horizontal commitments on mode 4 in exchange for specific benefits. Canada's record of temporary entry commitments in international trade agreements shows this. It recognizes that greater temporary entry for foreign businesspeople will provide various economic benefits to Canada, including advantages in outward and inward trade and investment.

Brief Answers to Some Key Questions

National regulators need to address some key questions. First, does Canada's domestic regime make a distinction between permanent and temporary immigration? Canada's immigration law and regulations treat permanent and temporary residency differently, and there are separate rules on each. Furthermore, the new Immigration and Refugee Protection Act (IRPA), implemented in June 2002, clarifies and strengthens this distinction.

Second, what changes can Canada make to facilitate mode 4? Canada's domestic regime on temporary entry is already very liberal, and the IRPA continues this trend. As well, Canada's horizontal mode 4 commitments set a standard for other WTO Members to emulate (e.g., no labor market tests or work permits for general business visitors, no labor market tests for three categories of intracorporate transferees, and no labor market tests for nine categories of independent professionals).

Third, what problems and solutions are associated with mode 4 facilitation? One problem is that some regulators and private sector stakeholders in WTO member countries are concerned about making binding commitments. This concern could be alleviated by more consultations in capitals among trade officials and negotiators, regulatory officials, and private sector stakeholders. In the end, it will be necessary to show that the benefits of greater temporary entry for foreign businesspeople (e.g., meeting certain skills shortages or allowing more competitive services) outweigh negative labor market or other effects.

A related problem is possible tradeoffs in the WTO negotiations. It is a challenge to evaluate a proposed exchange of benefits between service sectors. For example, how do trade negotiators in country A assess granting greater temporary entry to certain foreign businesspeople from country B in exchange for greater access for country A's service providers to a specific service sector in country B? Consequently, immigration and labor policy officials prefer reciprocal commitments or tradeoffs within mode 4 (e.g., a commitment on the employment of spouses or common-law partners in exchange for similar commitments from key trading partners). Such tradeoffs are likely to be more persuasive, because they are easier to evaluate and understand.

Finally, what steps might WTO Members take to strengthen mode 4 commitments? Several suggestions from a Canadian immigration perspective follow:

- WTO Members should be careful about adopting quick solutions such as some sort of GATS visa scheme. This proposal and others need to be considered thoroughly from all points of view, particularly from the immigration and labor policy perspectives.
- Based on the results of the previous round of GATS negotiations, member countries now have an opportunity in the new negotiations to improve their

horizontal mode 4 commitments. How could this be done? In these negotiations more WTO Members could make commitments that cover more categories of businesspeople, including visitors, intracorporate transferees, and independent professionals. They could reduce or eliminate key regulatory hurdles such as labor market tests or work permits. Commitments on independent professionals by more industrial countries, for example, should interest several developing countries and benefit their service providers.

- Members could improve the transparency of the horizontal mode 4 commitments by clarifying the commitments themselves and by producing better supplementary information. Businesspeople want to know what the existing rules are and that they are being applied fairly and consistently. In the new negotiations Members could work on organizing the transparency of mode 4 commitments—that is, negotiate improvements in the way all Members make or describe commitments. For example, commitments could be more explicit: details could be provided on economic needs tests or on when a labor market test or a work permit applies to certain categories of businesspeople. Members also could describe any additional conditions or requirements that apply to application processes for the categories of businesspeople covered by their commitments. Furthermore, supplementary information for businesspeople could be more user friendly. Immigration laws and regulations are not always barriers to trade and investment. What often helps is better information so that business travelers seeking temporary entry are well informed and better prepared.
- The trade, immigration, and labor policy communities in the capitals of WTO Members could increase their collaboration, and, to the extent possible, there should be a deeper discussion between these officials from developing and industrial countries.[12]

In conclusion, if WTO Members agreed, these suggestions on negotiating improvements to the substance and transparency of the horizontal mode 4 commitments could be objectives in the upcoming negotiations.

Summary

Negotiators and businesspeople should keep the following points in mind to enhance the GATS negotiations on mode 4 or temporary entry:

1. Trade, immigration, and labor policy officials are partners, not adversaries.
2. Immigration and labor officials can provide insight and contribute to progress on mode 4 issues.
3. Trade officials should engage their immigration and labor colleagues in productive discourse as much as possible.

4. The shared objective is more effective commitments on mode 4, which means commitments by more WTO Members that
    - facilitate temporary entry
    - avoid increased burdens for immigration officers and business travelers
    - cover more categories of businesspeople
    - reduce or eliminate labor market tests and work permits
    - produce clear information for businesspeople on the requirements and application processes.

In short, a better understanding of the policy contexts will lead to complementary results and stronger mode 4 commitments.

Notes

1. For a useful and comprehensive analysis of mode 4 issues, see OECD (2002a, 2002b).

2. Other contexts or circles could be added to this picture. For example, trade in goods and trade in services could be shown as separate circles and their related rules or issues would come into play (e.g., after-sales and after-lease services). If a customs policy context were included, duties or other customs rules affecting mode 4 would come into view (e.g., the issue of temporary, duty-free admission of goods, particularly professional equipment necessary for carrying out a business activity, trade, or profession). Such equipment is sometimes referred to as "tools of the trade."

3. It is sometimes useful to distinguish between immigration or labor measures that apply "at the border" on temporary entry and stay, and other regulatory measures (usually not immigration or labor) that apply "behind the border" to post-entry business activity (e.g., professional licensing and certification by national or subnational regulatory bodies).

4. A specific commitment that looks good on paper may not really facilitate temporary entry in practice. The schedules of specific commitments have been criticized as not being transparent enough. For example, some economic needs tests are not cited or other requirements that may impede temporary entry are buried in supplementary information or administrative guidelines and manuals.

5. Some problems are with the rules themselves, but many difficulties result from not knowing the rules well enough. Businesspeople are often too busy to understand the many and complex rules and procedures. In many instances, they would not have temporary entry problems if they were better informed and prepared before they travel. Better information is a responsibility of both regulatory officials and businesspeople.

6. The Web site for Citizenship and Immigration Canada (*www.cic.gc.ca/english/index.html*) has details on the department, its research and publications, and the rules, regulations, and application procedures for visitors, immigrants, refugees, and citizenship.

7. Some countries have negotiated bilateral readmission agreements or memorandums of understanding on returns, with enforcement provisions of varying clout.

8. It could not be otherwise. For example, under Canada's commitments in the GATS and the North American Free Trade Agreement (NAFTA), some businesspeople enjoy easier temporary entry because the usual requirements for a labor market test or a work permit have been waived, depending on the category of businessperson.

9. Canadian immigration officers at ports of entry are facilitative. If a businessperson does not qualify for temporary entry under, for example, the GATS or NAFTA, Canada's general

provisions may offer another way to enter. But helping a prospective temporary entrant in such a case also can use up precious time.

10. Government and business leaders from Canada and the United States have endorsed these objectives several times since September 11. For example, see the December 2001 Canada-U.S. Smart Border Declaration and action plan (*www.can-am.gc.ca/menu-e.asp?mid= 1&cat=10*) and the views of the Coalition for Secure and Trade Efficient Borders (*www.the-alliance.org/coalition/english/home.html*).

11. For further information, see, for example, "Working Temporarily in Canada" (*www.cic.gc.ca/english/visit/work_e.html*).

12. Several observers have pointed out that developing and industrial countries have many common mode 4 interests—see, for example, OECD (2002a).

References

OECD (Organisation for Economic Co-operation). 2002a. "Service Providers on the Move: A Closer Look at Labor Mobility and the GATS." TD/TC/WP(2001)26/FINAL. April 18 <*www.oecd.org*>.

————. 2002b. "Service Providers on the Move: The Economic Impact of Mode 4." TD/TC/WP(2002)12. March 6 <*www.oecd.org*>.

15

MODE 4: A GERMAN REGULATOR'S VIEW

Torsten Christen[*]

The exchange of information on national experiences with the temporary admission of service providers could be an important contribution to increasing the transparency of the regulations governing such admissions. This chapter outlines the basic features of German migration law that may be relevant to the General Agreement on Trade in Services (GATS). It focuses on the questions surrounding work permits and the temporary admission of workers to the German labor market.

Current German Regulations on the Admission of Third-Country Nationals

This section briefly describes German migration policy as a preface to a discussion of Germany's GATS commitments. To some extent, the German experience and the different approaches of German migration law may be exemplary for the experiences of other European countries.

In Germany the admission of third-country nationals—that is, from non–European Union (EU) countries—is regulated through the Aliens Act and various work permit ordinances. Several government agencies are responsible for the admission of foreign employees. The Aliens Office (*Ausländerbehörde*) is responsible for issuing residence permits, the Labor Offices (*Arbeitsämter*) for granting work permits.

Residence authorization does not fall within the scope of the GATS. As for work authorization, the admission of third-country nationals has been restricted since 1973. However, the approach will be more flexible in the future, especially toward the admittance of highly qualified employees. The granting of work authorizations is regulated by the *Social Code, Book III* (Act on Employment Promotion); the details are regulated by several ordinances.

---

[*]Torsten Christen is with the German Ministry of Labor, Germany.

The most important of these is the work permit ordinance. In accordance with this ordinance, German migration law differentiates between the temporary presence and the permanent presence of foreign nationals. The granting of a work permit (*Arbeitserlaubnis*) for a temporary presence is an act of discretion. The Labor Offices are required to consider the capacity of the labor market, a general consideration, and to determine whether domestic or EU workers are available for the job. Seventeen professions are exempted from the work permit requirement, such as truck drivers, specialized workers, artists, scientific researchers, students who work temporarily during the holidays, teachers, professors, and embassy and consulate personnel.

The permanent presence of foreign nationals is not within the scope of the GATS. Unlimited access to the German labor market (i.e., so-called work permission) is given only in certain specific cases. A third-country national has the legal right to obtain a work permit if he or she holds a residence authorization, has worked in Germany legally for five years and is covered by social insurance, or has been in Germany for six uninterrupted years.

"Privileged" foreigners fall into two categories: those who hold the Green Card for Information Technology (IT) Experts and those who are covered under agreements with Eastern European countries. In 2000 a new regulation was issued providing for the admission of up to 20,000 IT experts. This regulation represented a new approach to the employment of foreign workers in Germany, probably similar to that adopted by other European countries. It had in fact become clear that the continued implementation of the 1973 ban on recruitment in the IT sector would result in a competitive disadvantage if an urgent demand for IT experts could be filled only by foreign workers. Nearly 11,000 foreign employees were admitted under this new regulation. Admission is limited to foreigners with a university degree or a degree from a polytechnic university. Otherwise, if the applicant possesses outstanding specialist knowledge a work permit can be obtained, provided that an annual gross salary of at least EUR50,000 is guaranteed.

Germany also is committed to several bilateral agreements related to guest workers, contract workers, and seasonal workers concluded with several Central and Eastern European countries. *Guest workers* refers to employee exchanges of up to 18 months for the purposes of improving language skills. *Contract workers* are mostly construction workers. Work authorization is given for temporary employment if the salary paid is comparable to the salaries set out in German tariff treaties. The work permit is usually granted for two years. Finally, *seasonal workers* are employed mainly in the agricultural, hotel, and restaurant sectors. The number of seasonal workers increased to nearly 287,000 a year in 2001. The current legal regulations allow a maximum stay of three months a year.

Future German Regulations on the Admission of Third-Country Nationals

Although the new migration law (*Zuwanderungsgesetz*) is not yet in force, its essential features reflect Germany's desire to be more flexible on labor market needs. The new law is intended to regulate the admission of third-country nationals. Its main principles are:

- A "one-stop shopping" procedure that guarantees a quicker and more transparent admission process. The two-part approval procedure that was required for limited employment stays (work permission and residence permission) is replaced by an internal procedure of consent.
- From "migration stop" to "regulation," which represents a new approach toward labor migration.
- Privileged admission for highly qualified employees.

The details of the law will be covered in future ordinances, which will guarantee that the standards set out in the law are met.

GATS Implications

The GATS is explicitly mentioned in the German work permit ordinance, thereby providing a guarantee for the GATS commitments undertaken.

The European Communities and its member states their have made commitments that allow some foreign nationals to enter the EU temporarily for the purpose of providing given services. These commitments relate to three categories of service providers: intracorporate transferees, business visitors, and contract service providers.

For intracorporate transferees, commitments are limited to senior and specialized personnel, the latter defined as "persons possessing uncommon knowledge." Entry is permitted without compliance with an economic needs test, although all other requirements related to entry, stay, work, and social security measures continue to apply. Intracorporate transferees must have worked within the company for at least one year prior to transfer.

This commitment is reflected in the German work permit ordinance in the provision that managers do not need a work permit for a period of up to five years if they are employed at a top management level and if the employment is based on an intracorporate transferee program (§ 9:2).

For business visitors, the GATS commitment states that entry is permitted without compliance with an economic needs test, although all other requirements on entry, stay, work, and social security measures continue to apply. Access to the German labor market is not restricted.

Finally, for contract service providers GATS commitments specify that the length of the service contract must not exceed three months and must be obtained in one of a relatively limited list of activities. Examples of service sectors in which Germany has made commitments on contract service providers are legal services in the area of legal advice on home country law and public international law, with the exception of activities reserved to the *Rechtsanwalt* (attorneys); accounting services, with the exception of activities reserved to the *Wirtschaftsprüfer* (auditors); taxation advisory services; management consulting—managers and senior consultants working in management consulting services and in services related to management consulting; technical testing and analysis services; a limited range of services related to site investigation work; and tourism services—tour managers of travel agencies and tour operators service providers.

Future Developments and Suggestions

Mode 4 liberalization in Germany will be affected by several factors. First, Germany is experiencing high unemployment levels—about 4.1 million people are currently out of work. As a result, liberalization of the barriers to the temporary movement of natural persons in the provision of services under the GATS is likely to be a difficult objective. Second, it is predicted that significant labor migration from Central and Eastern European countries will accompany the enlargement of the EU. It is therefore important to Germany that potential new GATS commitments continue to not apply to measures affecting natural persons seeking access to the employment market.

As for the future, the communication tabled by the European Communities and their member states at the WTO on March 14, 2001, identifies some areas for reflection.

The first area is harmonization of the definitions and descriptions of the mode 4 categories. A discussion could begin on the opportunity to ensure that WTO Members agree on common terms and definitions for intracorporate transferees, executives, managers, specialists, and contract service providers. This harmonization effort could take into account, as far as relevant, the work already carried out by other international organizations. Common definitions could potentially form the basis of a model schedule.

The second area is the specification of labor market tests in future commitments in order to ensure effective application of mode 4 liberalization. In addition, the elaboration of a common code of practice for economic needs tests, with the objective of rendering them more specific and transparent, defining their application criteria, making them nondiscriminatory, and imposing a due process procedure, could be highly desirable.

The third area is the rights and obligations of service providers applying for entry. Building on GATS Article IV and with a view toward achieving greater transparency, Members should regulate appropriately and clearly the conditions under which service providers may temporarily enter and stay in the territory of Members, setting out providers' rights and obligations and ensuring that they have access to this information and that there are mechanisms in place to see that it is applied fairly. This approach could require, among others, provisions that facilitate the swift adoption of decisions on individual applications on the basis of objective and verifiable criteria and the development of clear, simple, and predictable application procedures. Such facilitation would be in the interest of both the enterprise delivering the service and the person concerned.

Finally, general policies on access to information would greatly enhance transparency. For example, national information points, such as Web sites, could be created and maintained. They could provide applicants with all the information they need on the admission of natural persons providing services, including how to contact the national authorities competent to receive applications for the relevant permits and applications.[1]

Note

1. For further information on residence authorization, see: *www.auswaertiges-amt.de/willkommen/einreisebestimmungen/index_html*; on work permits, see: *www.arbeitsamt.de*.

16

MODE 4: A U.S.
REGULATOR'S VIEW

*Howard R. Dobson**

The United States routinely admits many aliens into its territory on both a temporary and a permanent basis. [1] In 1998, 660,477 persons immigrated to the United States. A total of 30,174,627 persons were admitted for (temporary) nonimmigrant purposes that same year. Because data on the temporary entry of persons into the United States may include multiple entries by the same person during that time period, they should not be interpreted as the actual number of individual nonimmigrant persons who enter the United States in a single year.

For the General Agreement on Trade in Services (GATS), two sets of measures are important. Natural persons are admitted under the terms set out in Members' commitments on mode 4. However, these persons also are subject to the national laws of the admitting country.

Furthermore, admissions of a temporary nature are only a part of the admissions process that is administered at the national level under immigration law and regulations. Immigration regulators frequently view persons who are admitted temporarily into the United States as potential permanent residents, or immigrants.

Three government agencies have important responsibilities for immigration law in the United States. The Department of State issues visas for admission. The Immigration and Naturalization Service, an agency of the Department of Justice, manages the national border and enforces immigration and citizenship laws. The Department of Labor manages certain labor law and labor certification programs that cover migrants.

Temporary and Permanent Residence

Persons admitted temporarily into the United States are referred to as "nonimmigrants" and are subject to specific laws and regulations concerning their purpose

*Howard R. Dobson is an international economist, U.S. Department of Labor.

of entry and term of stay. For some nonimmigrant admissions, renewal of status may be given for additional periods of time, as necessary. Nonimmigrants are admitted with the understanding that they do not intend to establish permanent residence.

Persons requesting permanent residence are intending to stay in the United States as immigrants. These requests are usually made for reasons of family reunification, employment, refugee or asylee status, or for reasons of diversity.[2]

Although they are outside GATS mode 4, permanent residents and intending immigrants are an important area of national immigration law. Employers seeking permanent residence for aliens often view these persons as a permanent addition to the company's work force. Aliens often request permanent residence after they have been admitted into the United States on a temporary basis. An alien may independently elect to exercise rights that are available to the individual under national law.

Mode 4 Improvement and Changes

The United States seeks to maintain an open, transparent, predictable regime for the temporary admission of foreign nationals. U.S. measures are available to interested parties in publications and are posted on the Web.[3]

The U.S. Congress often changes the immigration law through enactment of new legislation. Members of Congress and officials in the executive branch of the U.S. government frequently consult with worker and business groups, as well as other interested parties, to ensure that laws and regulations are clear and provide appropriate treatment for aliens admitted into the United States.

For the GATS, U.S. trade legislation establishes advisory committees where members of the U.S. business community, representatives of organized labor, and other groups can provide advice on trade issues, including mode 4. Six policy committees are appointed by the U.S. trade representative. The Industry Committee has several subcommittees for important functions and economic sectors, such as trade in services.

The United States is reviewing proposals in several areas related to mode 4 of the GATS. One proposal calls for creation of a GATS visa that is intended to provide service firms and natural persons providing services with quick and ready access to the U.S. market. Proponents of this approach are hoping to create a model that can be used by all Members of the World Trade Organization (WTO) for the admission of service providers.

Evaluation of Proposed Changes to Mode 4

It is difficult to foresee the specific changes in immigration law that may result from negotiations under the GATS. However, several broad issues are relevant for consideration.

Temporary admission categories used in U.S. law that permit an alien to undertake economic activities will probably continue to be used in a general manner that does not specify service activities. The GATS does not contain an overall definition of services. Many activities undertaken by aliens in the United States may involve production of both goods and services.

An assessment is needed of whether extensive changes in U.S. law will be required. Some proposals that would clarify U.S. law may only require changes in regulations. Such an assessment might seek to answer the following questions.

What is the appropriate treatment for an alien under U.S. law? Is admission sought pursuant to a contract for employment with a U.S. employer? Is the alien seeking to provide services under an independent contract? Is this contract enforceable under U.S. law, or is it a contract for services under the laws of a foreign country?

What types of services does the alien seek to provide? Are the alien's services at a professional or highly specialized level? If so, how are these identified and defined? Is licensure required to perform this activity in the United States? Is the alien seeking to provide less specialized skills that are generally available in the domestic labor force?

What term of stay is useful for the alien in providing services? How should this term be defined in U.S. law? Should the alien find that the term granted for initial entry is inadequate for completion of the service contract, what measures should be developed for extension of stay, or change in nonimmigrant status, that would be useful and could not be construed as allowing permanent employment in the United States?

The General Agreement on Trade in Services

The GATS provides a framework for commitments on the movement of natural persons providing services and includes for this purpose the Annex on Movement of Natural Persons Supply Services under the Agreement. The annex gives some guidance on how the agreement should apply to the commitments undertaken. All Members recognize the need to make commitments on mode 4. Some of the language contained in the annex is clear, but ambiguities are found as well. It is presently unclear whether the language of this annex will be revised.

It is clear that countries may require a visa as a condition for admission. However, Members affected by these obligations frequently refer to the creation of "new visas," or individual requirements and administrative processes necessary to obtain a visa. This is ambiguous. Countries often require a visa for the admission of persons under the mode 4 commitments. A visa is a request to be admitted into the territory of a foreign country. This request encompasses considerations in the national law of the admitting country (e.g., national security and public health) that go beyond economic considerations. It may be useful to adopt the term *admission category* to describe the specific type of access the alien may seek and the individual considerations that pertain to the type of admission being requested.

The same annex states that the agreement does not apply to the employment market or employment on a permanent basis. Some people have argued that this wording may remove from coverage under the GATS foreign natural persons who are working for a domestic employer. Members should consider whether some additional clarification is needed in this area.

Finally, it may be useful to clarify the nature of the commitments undertaken in mode 4, and what types of information should be placed in country schedules. Commitments are based on the national law of the admitting country. How are these commitments best described? Should countries write into their schedules provisions that constitute requirements for natural persons providing services that are not strictly listed—for example, as market access limitations under Article XVI of the GATS? Should more information be made available for users? If so, in what form?

Notes

1. The publication "Developments in International Migration to the United States: 2001" and its 2002 update briefly describe immigration measures in the United States and their application (Kramer 2001, 2002).

2. A brief discussion of these considerations, as well as immigration statistics, can be found in Kramer (2001).

3. For further information on U.S. immigration laws and regulations, see the following Web sites: Department of State—basic information on visa issuance process: *travel.state.gov/visa_services.html*; recent data on visa processing: *travel.state.gov/visa_bulletin.html*. Department of Justice, Immigration and Naturalization Service—INS home page: *www.immigration.gov/graphics/index.htm*, immigration laws, regulations, and guides: *www.immigration.gov/graphics/lawsregs/index.htm* Department of Labor—Employment and Training Administration (ETA), hiring foreign workers: *www.dol.gov/dol/topic/hiring/foreign.htm*; online wage data library (prevailing wage calculation): *edc.dws.state.ut/owl.asp*.

References

Kramer, Roger G. 2001. "Developments in International Migration to the United States: 2001." WP #35. Immigration Policy and Research, U.S. Department of Labor, Washington, D.C.

———. 2002. "Developments in International Migration to the United States: 2002, A Midyear Report." WP #36. Immigration Policy and Research, U.S. Department of Labor, Washington, D.C.

17

MODE 4: A SOUTH AFRICAN REGULATOR'S VIEW

*Ivan Lambinon and
Mario G. R. Oriani-Ambrosini*[*]

Extension of the notion of international trade to include trade in services supplied by natural persons who cross international boundaries to deliver such services may bring about a profound revolution in municipal legislation regulating international migration.

In many countries, the interface between migration control and broader policymaking related to the international interest is somehow weak. Furthermore, the field of migration control is often charged with sensitive and difficult undertones that make it difficult to adjust policies to a serene assessment of national interest, the least of which is to assess national interest within a broader and long-term global perspective. For this reason, there is often a gap between the policy fluidity and modernity of the average field of legislative and policy efforts of many countries and their respective systems of migration control. Actually, many systems of migration control presently in force are the product of adjustments made to the original mold, often established in the first part of the twentieth century, and they are insensitive to a global dimension of trade that extends to the movement of people. They were formulated for a more parochial and slower age.

The South African experience may therefore be of particular interest. South Africa's new and complete reforms of its system of migration control could point toward a range of migration control techniques that may be more responsive to the needs and aspirations of the twenty-first century. Before its liberation in April 1994, South Africa, under the regime of apartheid, had operated with a system of migration control that was suited to a country in international isolation—that is,

[*]Ivan Lambinon is deputy director general and Mario G. R. Oriani-Ambrosini is ministerial advisor, Department of Home Affairs, Republic of South Africa.

the government emphasized security considerations and the ethnic composition of its population over any benefit associated with the international movement of people. Thus South Africa was faced with the need to start from scratch and had the unique opportunity to conceptualize a new system of migration control that could look toward the future. South Africa presents a mixture of characteristics. It is undoubtedly a developing country, but it has a higher level of prosperity relative to the rest of its continent, which makes it a target of migratory influxes. Therefore, it needs the management and control measures typical of industrial countries. Furthermore, South Africa finds itself operating under extreme budgetary restraints and social pressures that do not allow sufficient resources to be allocated to migration control. Thus any of its measures in this field must rely on minimum administrative capacity and must be aimed at maximum simplification, objectivity, and transparency to achieve maximum efficiency and effectiveness.

To combine these various elements, South Africa's minister of home affairs, Prince Mangosuthu Buthelezi, chose the hard option of developing a system of migration control that incorporates some unique innovations and reflects a visionary perspective of a more liberalized regime of the international movement of people. This chapter presents a few of such features as a contribution toward developing a process that may identify new techniques on migration control that may satisfy the concerns, habits, and—even—idiosyncrasies of the regulators, while fulfilling the obligations of the General Agreement on Trade in Services (GATS) and achieving its long-term objectives. Indeed, a new culture needs to be promoted within each line function of migration control of the Members of the World Trade Organization (WTO). Put differently, newer types of permits and techniques in migration control may be a better route to fulfilling the objectives of the GATS than creating artificial fast tracks and exceptions for certain sectors.

A New System of Migration Control

In many respects, the new system of migration control that the South African Parliament passed on May 8, 2002, will represent an advanced status of that "progressively higher level of liberalization" referred to in Article XIX of the GATS. In fact, South Africa realized that to capture its full potential for economic growth it must increase its available level of skills and reach a critical mass of skilled and productive people and consumers. Having crossed such an important policy threshold, the government had to formulate techniques to enable it to classify the skills needed and to determine the degree to which they were needed—that is, a "needs test" had to be devised. These tasks appear simple in theory, but in the practice of a government with limited resources they proved cumbersome and, to a certain extent, self-defeating.

In the classification of skills, the South African economy needs a range of skills, comprising not only those that are easy to classify, such as the customary liberal professions of medical doctor, accountant, engineer, and lawyer, but also those that are not so easy to classify such as the ability to operate complex machinery or to manage people. Needing both higher and lower level of skills, the government found it difficult to define their relevant thresholds and priorities. An added difficulty was that the government usually tends to assess skills through qualifications, but in today's labor market the link between skills and qualifications is often irreparably broken. Experts such as Web designers and computer technicians frequently do not have qualifications that can be reduced to a diploma or a degree, while many qualifications and job descriptions are no longer tied together, because, for example, engineers may act as business managers. In the end, only an employer has the capacity to determine whether a specific employee or service provider is suited, capable, and qualified to perform any given task.

A New Type of Work Permit

Accordingly, South Africa's new system of migration control, while contemplating different work permits, provides for a new type of work permit that is expected to become the one used mainly because of its simplicity. This work permit is subject to no quotas, numeric limitations, or skills classifications, nor to any fixed time frame. It is issued on the basis of two simple requirements. First, a certified public accountant must certify that the foreign employee will be remunerated at terms and conditions that, in terms of the applicable laws, collective bargaining agreements, and practices, are not inferior to those applicable to a South African national in the same or a similar workplace. The second requirement is that a simple licensing fee be paid on a quarterly basis into a fund established for the training of South African nationals. This mechanism embodies the needs test, because it assumes that if, at parity of labor conditions, someone is willing to pay a premium to employ a foreigner, then that foreigner has skills that are needed and may not be supplied by a national who would be cheaper to employ. This mechanism also maintains a connection between foreigners working in South Africa and the training of nationals.

Furthermore, this mechanism obviates the need to determine time limits for temporary work permits; as long as the employer is willing to pay the licensing fee, the employee will continue to be needed. The issuance of this type of work permit will require no evaluations and can be completed almost on site once all the information required for the application form has been provided. Naturally, in addition to the customary information satisfying security considerations such as police clearance and identity documentation, the application will require proof of whatever qualifications may be necessary to perform the intended job, together with the certification by a South African agency dedicated to this task that such qualifications are equivalent to those issued in South Africa.

The important feature of this new permit is that it does not rely on the need to distinguish between skilled and unskilled workers and to justify dividing them into groups or quotas. The tool of policy formulation available to the government to regulate migratory fluxes is that of the licensing fee, which can be lowered for those foreigners who, on an aggregate basis, are deemed to be most necessary to South Africa's economic growth. Thus the licensing fee may be extremely low for foreign surgeons who are needed and extremely high for foreign street sweepers, whom the South African labor market does not seem to require. As an individual guarantee, once a foreigner enters at a certain level, the licensing fee applicable to him or her cannot be raised for five years, which is the period required to qualify for permanent residence.

This system also does not require government to differentiate workers and service providers on the basis of their nationality or origin. The employers will make that determination. In this fashion, the fundamental objective of the GATS of most-favored-nation treatment will be respected. On another front, the Department of Home Affairs will have to carry out a new function—deterring and redressing xenophobia. Once the system grows into its full potential, it is envisaged that this function also will address potential xenophobic patterns developed by employers who, on the basis of prejudice, will give preference to foreigners from one country over equally qualified foreigners from other countries.

Corporate Permits

Another important feature of the South African reform of migration control is the corporate permit that will be issued to large corporations and not-for-profit organizations so they can employ a fixed number of foreigners. The corporate permit will enable such organizations to issue individual permits to foreigners directly from their human resources department and to pay an aggregate licensing fee to the government. By definition, the aggregate licensing fee will be lower than the total licensing fees the organization would have to pay if it were to employ the same number of foreigners on an individual basis through individual work permits.

Furthermore, the law enables the Department of Home Affairs to partially or entirely waive the licensing fee if an organization develops training programs for South Africans that are specifically designed to transfer skills from foreigners to South African nationals to reduce the organization's dependency on foreign labor. This is a freely negotiated process. It must be stressed that such an organization also has the opportunity to hire additional foreigners with ordinary work permits, in lieu of using a corporate permit or in addition to the number of foreigners it may hire under the corporate permit. Effectively, the corporate permit privatizes the issuance of work permits and enables a reliable and suitable organization to move the work permits allocated to it under the corporate permit from one foreigner to the other, thereby meeting its internal needs and enhancing labor market mobility. Government will supply the procedures, forms, and requirements that have to be verified and complied with in the issuance of such permits and will monitor and control their compliance, as it would do with one of its decentralized or satellite offices. If the corporate permit holder is found not to be in compliance, the privilege may be revoked.

These permits are expected to create a great deal of flexibility for providers of services and their employees. They complement the intercompany permits that enable the transfer of services from a company to its foreign subsidiary for up to three years and the investor permits that allow foreigners to establish businesses in South Africa. Intercompany permits will be subject to the usual methods of processing, which evaluate needs and justifications for the employment of the foreigner but do not include a labor market test—all of which may become less convenient than the procedure offered by the new type of permit. However, the investor permit also has been greatly simplified and the relevant procedures made objective so that no discretionary assessment is required. The elimination of stages of evaluation, interdepartmental consultation, and the review associated with the issuance of single permits is a better way to achieve the objective of the GATS than using a "model schedule" that creates fast tracks for special categories, or resorting to the GATS permits or visas. Undoubtedly, the notion of the GATS permits and visas is intellectually pleasing, but it is extremely difficult to introduce into the regulatory reality of migration control and at best may offer the opportunity for a few exceptions for high-level skills.

Adjusting to a New Mindset

South Africa's reform of migration control, which has been seven years in the making, has tried to register the latest requirements and trends emerging in the age of globalization. Effectively, it has tried to move all stages requiring evaluation, consultation, and discretion at the aggregate policy level so they would not be needed in the processing of the individual application. Furthermore, it has addressed the need to provide migration control with the highest degree of human rights protection. This is an unusual feature because throughout the world, even in highly developed and democratic countries such as the United States, the functions associated with migration control usually register the lowest level of human rights protection available in that country. For example, in South Africa warrants may be required for the deportation of foreigners, and each decision related to permits must comply with the full measure of available administrative justice, judicial review, transparency, and accountability. These are also significant elements of compliance with respect to Articles III, VI, XIX, and other provisions of the GATS.

Changing the Administrative Culture

Like many other countries, South Africa faces the challenge of having to change the administrative culture presently underpinning migration control. In discussions of mode 4 issues it becomes clear that many countries will need to face the challenge of a profound paradigm shift in their attitude toward the international migration of people and, perhaps, to question the continuing validity of long-standing classifications based on skills, qualifications, and differentiation between temporary and permanent residents. The reality of migration is that many of such elements are in a continuum, and even for the matter of residence the distinction between temporary and permanent does not survive the critique of the often observed phenomenon that temporary residence is a bridge to permanent residence. This transition might not be desirable, but it cannot be wished away and may need to be accommodated on a larger scale. For example, under South Africa's new system of migration control a foreigner may, after five years of temporary employment, graduate into permanent residence.

Enforcing Restrictions on Foreigners

By and large, South Africa also is about to make a profound paradigm shift from a mindset that wishes to control the admission of foreigners within its boundaries to a new approach that registers the fact that foreigners are part of its society in numbers and varieties that the government can no longer define or control up front. Therefore, the new policy will be less concerned with the presence of foreigners and much more concerned with enforcing the restrictions on their activities. The new system will shift administrative capacity and emphasis from the issuance of permits to the enforcement of the law in workplaces, educational institutions, and other places where foreigners may conduct unauthorized activities. If the government is to rely on the capacity of the market to regulate the number of foreigners who are really needed, then law enforcement becomes essential to prevent the creation of black labor markets and to ensure that the more liberal regime does not create an opportunity for vast situations of illegalities. It seems that worldwide the bulk of administrative resources available for migration control are more commonly employed in the processing of permits rather than in enforcing the law. A more liberalized regime will become viable and widely acceptable politically only if emphasis and resources are shifted toward law enforcement.

A New General Entry Permit

To simplify procedures, the many different permits that were typical of the South African tradition, and are common in most countries, had to be collapsed into one. In the modern world there is little practical value in and little administrative necessity for distinguishing between tourists and businesspeople and between them and those who come into the country for a short period of study or medical treatment. Therefore, a general entry permit has been designed. It is applicable for three months, renewable for another term of up to six months, and can be employed for tourism, business, studying, medical treatment, and any activity other than those for which a work permit is required. Work permits are usually required for subordinate employment only.

It must be noted that the definition of "work" for which work permits are obtained excludes work conducted for a foreign employer pursuant to a contract that only partially calls for activities in South Africa. The definition also excludes business and professional work mainly based outside South Africa but requiring activities within South Africa. Effectively, the exclusions cover the majority of the most significant aspects of trade in services. A work permit will not be required for these aspects; such work can be conducted with a general entry permit for a three-month term, renewable once. Therefore, the general entry permit seems to be a technique that greatly advances compliance with the provisions of the GATS and the fulfillment of its objectives.

Conclusion

As for the regulators, as long as they are satisfied that all the relevant security concerns have been addressed, such as police requirements, and that foreigners have sufficient means to support their activities in the country and earnestly intend to leave the country before permits expire, they are much less concerned about what the foreigners do in South Africa so long as they do not work. This new liberal system reflects the needs of the future and embodies the spirit and the mandatory provisions of the GATS. South Africa is moving into uncharted territory with the benefit of no memory from a past that is no longer applicable to the country's present and future challenges. There is no doubt that by doing so, it will discover error, shortcomings, and possibly even näiveté in its approach.

Minister Mangosuthu Buthelezi, however, has often indicated that he perceives the twenty-first century as a time to engage migration issues and formulate for them a new conceptuality and policy framework, almost on the same basis that the twentieth century struggled with developing concepts and the policy framework for human rights. We are all breaking new ground, and it is extremely exciting that perspectives are merging in a view of a globalized world. Therefore, it is proper and fitting that the trade perspective may force reform of migration control in all countries of the world. However, important difficulties do exist, because at present the language, concepts, and policy slant of trade and of migration control are profoundly different and cast in different molds and frames of reference. Perhaps migration control functions need to be pulled into the new perspective among resistance, suspicion, and rising political tensions.

Although migration control will need to adjust to international trade requirements, it might be necessary for, to a lesser degree, international trade requirements to adjust to migration control. For example, sectoral commitments will remain extraneous to many systems of migration control, and, with a few exceptions, horizontal policies will continue to characterize the practice of negotiations in this field. Moreover, sectoral commitments by themselves may not solve the problems encountered in trade in services. For example, work permits may be available, but the requirement that one must apply for them from outside the country and the prohibition against the adjustment of status may become effective barriers in obtaining a work permit.

Moreover, there may be exceptions for categories of sectors, but, as the world moves toward a more liberalized regime of international movement of productive people, such exceptions are bound to diminish if people rise to the challenge of changing systems of migration control so that those systems apply with equal transparency, efficiency, liberality, and expeditiousness to all productive people and service providers. There is a need for an interdisciplinary dialogue and cross-pollination within the framework of the understanding that mode 4 issues will set a foundation for a completely new mindset on the international movement of people.

INDEX

Note: f indicates figures and t indicates tables

Africa, 100, 107. *See also* South Africa
AFTA (ASEAN Free Trade Area), 104–105
Annex on Movement of Natural Persons Supplying Services under Agreement: allowance for discriminatory treatment, 41; categories of persons covered, 23; limitations in breadth of services covered, 97; negotiating history, 32–33; recommendations for changes, 229–230
ANZCERTA (Australia-New Zealand Closer Economic Relations), 100
APEC Business Travel Card, 124
ASEAN Free Trade Area (AFTA), 104–105
Asia Pacific Economic Cooperation (APEC), 106
athletic visas in U.S., 141
Australia: compensatory policies for trade liberalization, 88; labor mobility provisions in RTAs, 100; TMNP system (*see* Australia and TMNP)
Australia and TMNP: business consultation category, 119; business visitors, 123–124; criteria for visitors, 119; desired skills categories, 119; statistics on entrants, 129–134; system features, 117–118; temporary business residents (*see* temporary business residents in Australia); types of temporary entrants, 120–122
Australia-New Zealand Closer Economic Relations (ANZCERTA), 100

brain drain: Jamaican overseas employment, 194; quality gap between rural and urban areas in Thailand, 175–176

Canada: CIC views on trade agreements, 214–215; compensatory policies for trade liberalization, 88; immigration and trade policy contexts, 213–214; immigration policies considerations, 216; labor mobility provisions in RTAs, 101–102; negotiating proposal offered, 45; recommendations for mode 4, 216–217
Canada-Chile Free Trade Agreement, 101–102
CARICOM initiative (Caribbean Community), 11; labor mobility provisions in RTAs, 101; objectives of protocol, 197–198; relevancy to GATS, 199–200; TVET system, 198–199
Central European Free Trade Agreement (CEFTA), 106
Chile, 101–102
Citizenship and Immigration Canada (CIC), 214–215
Colombia, 103
commercial presence criteria, 39–40
commitments assessment in mode 4: categories of commitments to add, 158–159; establishment of a commercial presence, 39–40; impact on trade liberalization, 39; limitations in breadth of services covered, 37–38; limits, 8; patterns, 23–25; temporary entry consideration, 40;